Language Teaching and Testing
Selected Works of Renowned Applied Linguists

世界知名语言学家论丛（第一辑）

Series Editor: Rod Ellis

U0783574

Zoltán Dörnyei

语言学习动机

MOTIVATION IN LANGUAGE LEARNING

上海外语教育出版社
外教社 SHANGHAI FOREIGN LANGUAGE EDUCATION PRESS

图书在版编目（CIP）数据

语言学习动机／（英）德尔涅伊（Dörnyei, Z.）著.
—上海：上海外语教育出版社，2012（2021重印）
（世界知名语言学家论丛. 第一辑）
ISBN 978-7-5446-2810-5

Ⅰ.①语… Ⅱ.①德… Ⅲ.①语言学习－学习动机－文集－英文
Ⅳ.①**H09-53**

中国版本图书馆CIP数据核字（2012）第160506号

出版发行：上海外语教育出版社
（上海外国语大学内） 邮编：200083
电　　话：021-65425300（总机）
电子邮箱：bookinfo@sflep.com.cn
网　　址：http://www.sflep.com
责任编辑：蔡一鸣

印　　刷：江苏凤凰数码印务有限公司
开　　本：787×965　1/16　印张22.5　字数308千字
版　　次：2012年11月第1版　2021年1月第3次印刷

书　　号：ISBN 978-7-5446-2810-5 / H · 1364
定　　价：50.00 元

本版图书如有印装质量问题，可向本社调换

质量服务热线：4008-213-263　电子邮箱：editorial@sflep.com

世界知名语言学家论丛
第一辑

Editorial Advisors：杨惠中　庄智象
Series Editor: Rod Ellis

Contributors to the Series:

Charles Alderson

Gaby Kasper

Paul Nation

Peter Skehan

Rod Ellis

Zoltán Dörnyei

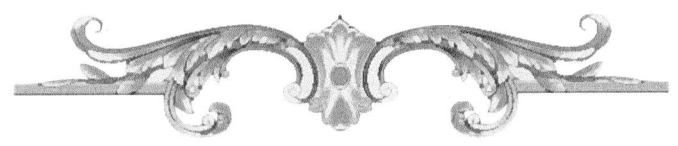

出 版 说 明

　　"世界知名语言学家论丛（第一辑）"由上海外语教育出版社约请国际知名学者、英语教育专家Rod Ellis教授担任主编。丛书作者均为国际应用语言学领域耳熟能详的权威专家。丛书中的每一本聚焦应用语言学领域的一个特定主题，收录一位在该研究领域最有建树和影响力的语言学家一生中最重要的经典文章，如：Rod Ellis:《语法学习与教学》；Paul Nation:《词汇学习与教学》；Charles Alderson:《语言测试》，等等。书中的每篇文章经由精心挑选，既有对某一领域理论主题的深入阐述，又探讨了对第二语言教学和测试颇具意义的话题；除了作者一生的代表性作品外，还有不少新作，体现了作者的思索过程和研究轨迹，也展示了应用语言学领域发展历程中理论和研究逐步完善的一个个精彩镜头。

　　相信本套丛书的出版定能为国内应用语言学研究提供一个新的平台，带来新的启示，进一步推动我国语言学研究的发展。

Preface

This book is a collection of articles for the series *Language Teaching and Testing — Selected Works of Renowned Applied Linguists*. This series collects articles written by a number of leading applied linguists. Each collection focuses on a specific area of research in applied linguistics — for example, on grammar learning and teaching, vocabulary language learning and teaching, language testing, and task-based language teaching. The aim of each book is to bring together older and more recent articles to show the development of the author's work over his/her lifetime. The articles are selected to address both theoretical issues relevant to a particular area of enquiry and also to discuss issues of significance to the teaching or testing of a second language (L2). As a whole, the series provides a survey of applied linguistics as this relates to language pedagogy and testing.

Each book begins with an autobiographical introduction by the author in which he/she locates the issues that have been important in his/her lifetime's work and how this work has evolved over time. The introduction also provides an outline of the author's professional career. The rest of the book consists of chapters based on articles published over the author's lifespan.

Each book, then, will contain articles that cover the author's career (over thirty years in some cases). Not surprisingly there are likely to be shifts (and possibly contradictions) in the author's positioning on the issues addressed, reflecting the changes in theory and research focus that have occurred in the specific area of enquiry over a period of time. Thus, the articles will not necessarily reflect a consistent theoretical perspective.

There is merit in this. Readers will be able to see how theory and research have developed. In other words, each book provides a snapshot of the kinds of developments that have occurred in the applied linguistic field under consideration.

This book brings together a collection of Zoltán Dörnyei's articles on motivation in language learning. Motivation is one of the two major determinants of L2 learning (the other being language aptitude). As Dörnyei (2005) noted 'it provides the primary impetus to initiate L2 learning and later the driving force to sustain the long and tedious learning process' (p. 65). Its central importance lies in the fact that 'all the other factors involved in SLA presuppose motivation to some extent'. Over the last 30 years no applied linguist has contributed more to our understanding of the role played by motivation in language learning than Zoltán Dörnyei. This book documents the evolution of his own thinking about motivation, from its origin in his own experience of teaching English as a foreign language in Hungary through to his ongoing work as a psycholinguist. Arguably no single researcher has contributed more to how motivation is currently conceptualized. And as a true applied linguist, he has never lost sight of what is the essential applied issue — how teachers can foster motivation in their students.

Rod Ellis
Auckland
October 2011.

Contents

Chapter 1 From English Language Teaching to Psycholinguistics: A Story of Three Decades 1

Chapter 2 Motivation and Motivating in the Foreign Language Classroom 13

Chapter 3 Psychological Processes in Cooperative Language Learning: Group Dynamics and Motivation 39

Chapter 4 Much More than Carrot and Stick 61

Chapter 5 New Themes and Approaches in Second Language Motivation Research 69

Chapter 6 Motivation in Action: Towards a Process-oriented Conceptualisation of Student Motivation 85

Chapter 7 The Motivational Basis of Language Learning Tasks 113

Chapter 8 Individual Differences in Second Language Acquisition 141

Chapter 9 Creating a Motivating Classroom Environment 173

Chapter 10 Researching Motivation: From Integrativeness to the Ideal L2 Self 193

Chapter 11 The L2 Motivational Self System 207

Chapter 12 Motivation and the Vision of Knowing a Second Language 249

Chapter 13 The Relationship between Language Aptitude and Language Learning Motivation: Individual Differences from a Dynamic Systems Perspective 259

Chapter 14　Motivation from a Complex Dynamic Systems Perspective
　　　　　　...... 287

Chapter 15　Conclusion: The Way Forward 301

References 305

Chapter 1

From English Language Teaching to Psycholinguistics: A Story of Three Decades

My story as an applied linguist starts at the beginning of the 1980s when as a hard-up university student of English and History of Art in Hungary, I realised that I could make very good money by teaching English as a foreign language in the evenings. At that time Hungary was still rather isolated from the western world, but people had already started to realise the significance of English as an international language. This created a growing demand for English instruction in an environment where the compulsory foreign language in the state school system was still Russian and where trained English teachers were scarce. In addition, a new education law had just allowed the opening of private language schools, and these schools were desperate to find English instructors. Thanks to this fortunate coincidence of language globalisation and favourable market conditions, even undergraduate English majors such as myself were offered lucrative teaching contracts that few of us could resist.

LANGUAGE TEACHING

When I walked into my first adult English language class, I soon found out that I was one of the youngest people in the room. The class was made up of a wide range of professionals, from company director to army officer, and therefore my only chance of establishing some authority for myself was by doing the job well. The school I worked for (the Budapest branch of the "International House Organisation") followed a communicative approach — I still remember the first coursebook I used: *Building Strategies* — and this suited me well in trying out a range of creative ideas. The particular period — the early 1980s — was literally the "Golden Age" of language teaching, with a variety of highly innovative materials appearing such as Alan Maley and Alan Duff's (1982) *Drama Techniques in Language Learning*, Carolyn Graham's (1978) *Jazz Chants*, Doug Case and Ken Wilson's (1979) *Off Stage* and Christine Frank and Mario Rinvolucri's (1983) *Grammar in Action*. I tried out as many of these as possible, and in retrospect I am amazed that all my "serious" adult students went along with, and even liked, these new approaches. This cemented the life-long conviction in me that teachers can get away with almost any language classroom task as long as they believe in it!

I kept teaching throughout the 1980s, and both my confidence and my repertoire of teaching techniques and strategies grew. So much so, that one day two friends (Margit Szesztay and Gábor Salamon) and I decided to write a language teaching coursebook. There must have been something infectious about our enthusiasm, because International House agreed to support us and publish the book. What emerged from our efforts was a self-study vocabulary-building coursebook, *Words on Your Own* (1986), which became a surprising hit in Hungary (and sold more copies than all my subsequent publications together) — I still meet people who remember "WOYO", as it was affectionately called by the learners. It was this success that set me off in my professional career: although I was also tempted to pursue my other university major, history of art, to become an art dealer, in the end I applied for a PhD grant to study applied linguistics and I was accepted: I was on track to becoming a scholar!

APPLIED LINGUISTICS

Why did I want to do a PhD? My main objective was not to prepare for a university job or to obtain the prestigious title of "Dr"; I was very much a language teacher at heart but a *frustrated* language teacher: I was aware of the almost unlimited creative possibilities within language teaching — particularly after I attended a teacher training course at the famous Pilgrims Language School in Canterbury (England), where my teachers included Penny Ur and Mario Rinvolucri — but I was far less successful in trying to figure out *why* certain things worked better than others. I also felt that the way forward in English teaching methodology was not through further increasing the entertainment value of language instruction but through making teaching more *principled*. But principled in what way? I instinctively knew that what would be needed to answer this question was a thorough knowledge of the psychology of second language learning, but this kind of scholarship did not seem to be available at that time: I had not come across it in my university studies, and neither did I find relevant coverage at the professional conferences that I managed to attend. Thus, my main purpose in deciding to do a PhD was the desire to understand the theory behind the practice that I was engaged in.

PHD STUDIES

When I initially decided to apply for a PhD in applied linguistics in 1985, I was told that there was no academic discipline called 'applied linguistics'. But surely, I pleaded, the theory of second language learning is an important theoretical question, worthy of scientific investigation. Yes it is, was the answer, but the relevant discipline to study it is not 'applied linguistics' but rather 'psycholinguistics'. This is how I ended up doing my PhD at the Department of Psychology, Eötvös University (Budapest, Hungary), even though my main research interest at that time had little to do with psycholinguistics. However, I never regretted this placement, which inevitably led to most of my subsequent work on SLA becoming influenced by psychological theories.

My supervisor was an eminent cognitive psycholinguist, Professor Csaba Pléh, who knew the international scene well as he had done research together with scholars like Brian MacWhinney. Yet, my very practical orientation and his much more theoretical interest in experimental psycholinguistics did not initially seem to have any obvious interface, so on our second academic advisory session he tentatively suggested that I look into the issue of language learning motivation, since he had recently attended an international conference where "a Canadian psychologist called Robert Gardner gave an interesting talk on the topic". I don't think he realised at that time the impact this suggestion would have on the rest of my career: I went away to write a literature review on L2 motivation and by the time I submitted my essay two months later, I was hooked. Motivation was the ideal research topic for me: it concerned the psychological core of the language learning enterprise, and it offered room for both theoretical investigations and practical work. My PhD dissertation, which I successfully defended in 1988, offered a broad survey of the field — including the related issue of group dynamics — as well as an empirical study of motivation (Dörnyei, 1990a, b) that utilised a questionnaire survey.

THE STUDY OF MOTIVATION

My initial research on motivation closely followed Gardner's approach, since this was the best available model at that time both in terms of its theoretical foundation and research methodology. Yet, over the next few years I became increasingly convinced that Gardner's (1985) socio-educational model did not do sufficient justice to two key aspects of motivation that I knew were important from my own teaching practice: classroom-specific (i.e. situated) motives such as the motivational role of the teacher or the syllabus and the temporal changes and fluctuation of motivation. In 1990 I was given an unexpected opportunity to address the first of these two areas when I received a scholarship to spend three months at Carlton University in Ottawa (Canada). It was only after I got there that I realised that one of my main "heroes" of L2 motivation research, Richard Clément, had his office literally round the corner, at the other university in the city, the University of Ottawa. I contacted him and his generous support opened up a new phase in my research development. Through Richard I also got to know Kim Noels, who was his PhD student at that time, and Peter MacIntyre, who was a post-doctoral research fellow in Ottawa having been Gardner's PhD student. Over the next several years, I often felt like being an "honorary" Canadian working with these excellent scholars. We first published a joint paper on a classroom-oriented study of motivation (Clément, Dörnyei & Noels, 1994) and then, in 1998, we wrote a conceptual paper to introduce the notion of "willingness to communicate" (WTC) in a second language (MacIntyre, Clément, Dörnyei & Noels, 1998).

The Clément et al. (1994) paper offered a considerable expansion of the scope of L2 motivation relative to Gardner's paradigm, and yet I felt that the boundaries could be pushed even further: I was getting ready for a serious reconsideration of what L2 motivation was about. This thinking gave birth to a paper in 1994 — "Motivation and motivating in the foreign language classroom" (see Chapter 2) — which then elicited responses both from Robert Gardner and Rebecca Oxford, adding up to what has often been referred to as the 'Modern Language Journal debate' (Dörnyei, 1994a, 1994b; Gardner and Tremblay, 1994a, 1994b; Oxford, 1994; Oxford and Shearin, 1994). Although I never questioned the validity of Gardner's social psychological approach, it became clear that my situated, educational interest was setting me on a course that deviated from its Canadian roots. Indeed, as the chapters in this book illustrate, over the next 15 years I explored a wide range of situated issues relevant to language learning motivation and I also outlined a "process-oriented" approach (see Chapter 6) that focused on temporal change. I will come back to these developments below when I address the dynamic nature of motivation, but before that I would like to describe three other areas of my professional work that I was engaged in parallel to my research on motivation: the study of (a) communicative competence and communication strategies; (b) group dynamics; and (c) research methodology.

COMMUNICATIVE COMPETENCE AND COMMUNICATION STRATEGIES

My interest in the communicative aspects of L2 proficiency grew directly out of my teaching practice. In the late 1980s I was involved in preparing learners for the oral part of the Hungarian State Language Examination, and when I was wondering how we could possibly prepare someone systematically for an unscripted oral interview, I started to design tasks that focused on the learners' 'strategic competence'. At that time I knew virtually nothing about communication strategies, and you can imagine how excited I became when I discovered in Rod Ellis's (1985) excellent early book on "Understanding Second Language Acquisition" that the study of communication strategies was a respected and developed research area in the field. I quickly 'jumped on the bandwagon', and wrote a number of papers on the topic (Dörnyei, 1995; Dörnyei & Scott, 1997; Dörnyei & Kormos, 1998; Dörnyei & Thurrell, 1991, 1994), which I still find fascinating although I haven't done any research on it for the past 15 years.

In 1992, I had the chance to spend eight months at UCLA as a Fulbright Scholar with Marianne Celce-Murcia as my host. This was an amazing period in my professional development, and besides becoming a personal mentor and friend, Marianne also made a huge impact on my thinking by adding a linguistic perspective to my primarily psychological approach. We started to work together on the issue of communicative competence (Celce-Murcia, Dörnyei & Thurrell, 1995) and how a more explicit description of the knowledge base that learners must possess in order to be able to communicate can help us to design a principled communicative approach (Celce-Murcia, Dörnyei & Thurrell, 1997, 1998); the mysterious third co-author "Thurrell" is my wife, Sarah — more on her in the next section on group dynamics. I recently returned to this line of research, when I was working on the "Instructed SLA" chapter of my book on "The Psychology of Second Language Acquisition" (2009c).

GROUP DYNAMICS

In 1987, I received a 'Soros Foundation' grant to spend six months at Oxford University doing research to complement my Hungarian PhD studies. This was the first time I had been able to spend time in a well-equipped library, which meant that I was often there till closing time. My friends thought this was rather weird, particularly Sarah, a young Modern Languages student, who thought I was a hopeless workaholic. I needed to show her otherwise and we got married in 1991... (I can honestly say that one of the most motivating methods of learning English as a second language is to marry a native speaker!) As well as getting to know Sarah, I spent my time in Oxford exploring the L2 literature widely, and it was as I was tracing down various leads and references that I came across the suggestion that student motivation can sometimes be influenced by the learner group — something every student knows who has worried about getting along with his/her new peers. Before long, I realised that groups did much more than just 'pull up' or 'pull down' learners in their studies; groups have a life of their own and — to my great surprise — this had been the subject of a whole subdiscipline within the social sciences called *group dynamics*. My next surprise came when I found out that this vigorous and, from an educational point of view, extremely relevant subdiscipline was virtually unknown in the L2 field.

My interest in group-based issues led me to write, with several colleagues, a number of shorter summaries (e.g. Dörnyei, 1997, 2007a; Dörnyei & Malderez, 1997, 1999) and two books (Dörnyei & Murphey,

2003; Ehrman & Dörnyei, 1998) on various theoretical and practical aspects of group psychology and group dynamics. Because groups significantly shape the learners' behaviour, I have come to see aspects of group dynamics (e.g. group norms, roles and cohesiveness) as the group-level equivalents of motivation (a view that is summarised in the paper reproduced in Chapter 9). I also think that for practising teachers group dynamics is possibly the *most useful* academic discipline, since it concerns such basic issues as classroom management, discipline and the conscious formation of learner communities that are keen, creative and active.

RESEARCH METHODOLOGY

Anybody who was studying language learning motivation in the 1980s had to master the main principles of quantitative research methodology, because the tradition set by Robert Gardner and his associates was rooted in quantitative social psychology. Therefore, as soon as I arrived in Oxford in 1987, I enrolled in an SPSS course and started to use statistics for my research. At that time, as I remember, only Version 2 of SPSS was available, which had no interactive features and required the user to write short programme files using the unique SPSS command language and syntax (I still often find it easier to type in commands than to use the various pull-down menus of the later versions). Survey research requires a lot of statistics and thus, before long, I found myself in the position of becoming an unofficial expert in quantitative research methodology.

My familiarity with research methodology was further strengthened when in the first edition of *Teaching and Researching Motivation* (Dörnyei, 2001c), the Editors, Christopher Candlin and David Hall, asked me to add a substantial research section. I surprised myself by how much I enjoyed writing the statistics guide and the directions for questionnaire design. So much so that soon afterwards I offered to write a short research monograph on questionnaire theory for a series edited by

Susan Gass (2003; second edition: 2010c). Two years later, my university department asked me to develop a distance learning programme teaching Research Methods in Applied Linguistics, and when I finished preparing the web-based material, I realised that it was already half of a book; once I had added the other half and the book was published (Dörnyei, 2007b), I "officially" became a research methodologist. This is, in fact, an ongoing interest of mine; one of my most recent papers (Dörnyei, in press) concerns the challenges of conducting research within the framework of dynamic systems theory.

COMPLEX DYNAMIC SYSTEMS

The latest phase of the story of my professional development has been shaped by a new theoretical perspective, the theory of complex dynamic systems. Chapters 13 and 14 offer an introduction to the new paradigm, but to summarise its essence in a nutshell, it represents a holistic approach that takes into account the combined and interactive operation of a number of different factors relevant to a specific situation rather than following the traditional practice of examining cause-effect relations between isolated variables. Although my shift to adopting a dynamic systems perspective for the study of individual differences was gradual, I can recall one particular trigger which made me rethink my views of learner characteristics. This happened when I read Nick Ellis and Diane Larsen-Freeman's (2006) position paper on 'Language emergence: Implications for applied linguistics', which introduced a special issue on language emergence in the journal *Applied Linguistics* (27/4). In this paper, the authors quoted the following description of motivation by Peter Skehan and myself (Dörnyei and Skehan, 2003, p. 617) as an example of an emergentist approach:

> During the lengthy process of mastering certain subject matters, motivation does not remain constant, but is associated with a dynamically changing and evolving mental process, characterized by constant (re)appraisal

and balancing of the various internal and external influences that the individual is exposed to. Indeed, even within the duration of a single course of instruction, most learners experience a fluctuation of their enthusiasm/commitment, sometimes on a day-to-day basis.

They then concluded that "Motivation is less a trait than fluid play, an ever-changing one that emerges from the processes of interaction of many agents, internal and external, in the ever-changing complex world of the learner" (Ellis & Larsen-Freeman, 2006, p. 563). This was an accurate summary of my thinking, and within the context of the special issue our conceptualization did indeed appear to be fully emergentist in nature. And yet, when I was originally developing my process-oriented approach to motivation (e.g. Dörnyei, 2000 — see Chapter 6; Dörnyei and Ottó, 1998), I had never for a moment considered the possibility that my views could be compatible with emergentism or dynamic systems theory. In retrospect, I can see that the process-oriented model I was proposing at that time had multiple parallel and interacting cause-effect relationships, accompanied by several circular feedback loops, and therefore it was only a matter of time before I had to accept that such a patchwork of interwoven cause-effect relationships would not do the complexity of the motivation system justice. There was clearly a need for a radical reformulation of L2 motivation and indeed of the nature of individual differences in second language acquisition in general. Having reviewed the potentials of the dynamic systems approach in some publications (particularly in Dörnyei, 2009c), I am now convinced that almost every facet of second language acquisition is best conceived within a dynamic systems framework; I am therefore committed to pursuing my research — including my research on L2 motivation — in a dynamic systems vein. I will return to this direction in the Conclusion of this book.

IN SUM

In the 1980s, I started out as a language teacher and then a teacher trainer, and although I have by and large become a full-time researcher since then, I hope that I am still a teacher at heart. I sincerely believe that the best foundation for any successful practice is a sound theoretical knowledge of the area, a principle that was famously expressed by the well-known social psychologist Kurt Lewin when he stated, "There is nothing more practical than a good theory." This is the recognition that led me to do a PhD over 25 years ago and this is what motivated me to conduct research throughout the next two decades. As I look back now, I feel fortunate that I got involved in researching psychological aspects of second language acquisition: language learning is ultimately a highly interpersonal enterprise, involving relationships between learners and teachers as well as native and non-native speakers; therefore, understanding the psychology of these relationships and of the agents involved in them is half the battle!

Chapter 2

Motivation and Motivating in the Foreign Language Classroom

Modern Language Journal, (1994), 78, pp. 273-284.

Motivation is one of the main determinants of second/foreign language (L2) learning achievement and, accordingly, the last three decades have seen a considerable amount of research that investigates the nature and role of motivation in the L2 learning process. Much of this research has been initiated and inspired by two Canadian psychologists, Robert Gardner and Wallace Lambert (see Gardner and Wallace, 1972), who, together with their colleagues and students, grounded motivation research in a social psychological framework (for recent summaries, see Gardner and Clément, 1990; Gardner and MacIntyre, 1993). Gardner and his associates also established scientific research procedures and introduced standardised assessment techniques and instruments, thus setting high research standards and bringing L2 motivation research to maturity.

Although Gardner's motivation construct did not go unchallenged over the years (see Au, 1988; Oller, 1981), it was not until the early 1990s that a marked shift in thought appeared in papers on L2 motivation as researchers tried to reopen the research agenda in order to shed new light on the subject (e.g. Brown, 1990; Crookes and Schmidt, 1991; Skehan, 1989, 1991). The main problem with Gardner's social psychological approach appeared to be, ironically, that it was too influential. In Crookes and Schmidt's words, it was "so dominant that alternative concepts have not been seriously considered" (p. 501). This resulted in an unbalanced picture, involving a conception that was, as Skehan put it, "limited compared to the range of possible influences that exist" (1989, p. 280). While acknowledging unanimously the fundamental importance of the Gardnerian social psychological model, researchers were also calling for a more pragmatic, education-centred approach to motivation research, which would be consistent with the perceptions of practising teachers and which would also be in line with the current results of mainstream educational psychological research.

It must be noted that Gardner's (1985a) motivation theory does include an educational dimension, and that the motivation test he and his associates developed, the Attitude/Motivation Test Battery (AMTB) (Gardner, 1985b), contains several items focusing on the learner's evaluation of the classroom learning situation. However, the main emphasis in Gardner's model — and the way it has been typically understood — is on general motivational components grounded in the social milieu rather than in the foreign language classroom. For example, the AMTB contains a section in which students' attitudes toward the language teacher and the course are tested. This may be appropriate for measurement purposes, but the data from this section do not provide a detailed enough description of the classroom dimension to be helpful in generating practical guidelines. As Gardner and MacIntyre (1993) recently stated concerning the learning situation-specific section of the AMTB, "attention is directed toward only two targets, largely because they are more generalisable across different studies" (p. 2). Finally, Gardner's motivation construct does not include details on cognitive aspects of motivation to learn, whereas this is the direction in which educational psychological research on motivation has been moving during the last fifteen years.

The purpose of this paper — following Crookes and Schmidt's and Skehan's initiative — is to help foster further understanding of L2 motivation from an educational perspective. A number of relevant motivational components (many of them largely unexploited in L2 research) will be described, and these will then be integrated into a multilevel L2 motivation construct. In addition, a set of practical guidelines on how to apply the research results to actual teaching will be formulated; I believe that the question of how to *motivate* students is an area on which L2 motivation research has not placed sufficient emphasis in the past.

Interestingly, a very recent paper by Oxford and Shearin (1994) sets out to pursue similar goals to those of the current author, by discussing motivational theories from different branches of psychology — general, industrial, educational, and cognitive developmental psychology — and by integrating them into an expanded theoretical framework that has practical instructional implications. This very comprehensive and insightful study, together with the works cited above and the author's current discussion, may provide a firmer basis for new directions of research in L2 motivation.

At the outset, I would like to acknowledge once again the seminal work of Robert Gardner and his colleagues. Gardner's theory has profoundly influenced my thinking on this subject, and I share Oxford and Shearin's assertion that:

> The current authors do not intend to overturn the ideas nor denigrate the major contributions of researchers such as Gardner, Lambert, Lalonde, and others, who powerfully brought motivational issues to the attention of the L2 field. We want to maintain the best

of the existing L2 learning motivation theory and push its parameters outward (1994, p. 13).

Indeed, there will be an attempt in this paper to integrate the social psychological constructs postulated by Gardner, Clément, and their associates into the proposed new framework of L2 motivation.

THE SOCIAL DIMENSION OF L2 MOTIVATION

One recurring question in recent papers has been how "social" a L2 motivation construct should be and what the relationship between social attitudes and motivation is. To start with, it must be realised that "attitudes" and "motivation" tend not to be used together in the psychological literature as they are considered to be key terms of different branches of psychology. "Attitude" is used in social psychology and sociology, where action is seen as the function of the social context and the interpersonal/ intergroup relational patterns. Motivational psychologists, on the other hand, have been looking for the *motors* of human behaviour in the *individual* rather than in the social being, focusing traditionally on concepts such as instinct, drive, arousal, need, and on personality traits like anxiety and need for achievement, and more recently on cognitive appraisals of success and failure, ability, self-esteem, etc. (Weiner, 1990, 1992).

L2 learning presents a unique situation due to the multifaceted nature and role of language. It is at the same time: (a) a *communication coding system* that can be taught as a school subject; (b) an *integral part of the individual's identity* involved in almost all mental activities; and (c) the most important *channel of social organisation* embedded in the culture of the community where it is used. Thus, L2 learning is more complex than simply mastering new information and knowledge; in addition to the environmental and cognitive factors normally associated with learning in current educational psychology, it involves various personality traits and social components. For this reason, an adequate L2 motivation construct is bound to be eclectic, bringing together factors from different psychological fields.

Coming from Canada, where language learning is a featured social issue — at the crux of the relationship between the Anglophone and Francophone communities — Gardner and Lambert were particularly sensitive to the social dimension of L2 motivation. The importance of this dimension is not restricted to Canada. If we consider that the vast majority of nations in the world are multicultural and most of these are multilingual, and that there are more bilinguals in the world than there are monolinguals (Gardner, 1985a), we cannot fail to appreciate the immense social relevance of language learning worldwide.

Integrativeness and instrumentality. Gardner's motivation construct has often been understood as the interplay of two components, integrative and instrumental motivations. The former is associated with a positive disposition toward the L2 group and the desire to interact with and even become similar to valued members of that community. The latter is related to the potential pragmatic gains of L2 proficiency, such as getting a better job or a higher salary. It must be noted, however, that Gardner's theory and test battery are more complex and reach beyond the instrumental/integrative dichotomy. As Gardner and MacIntyre state, "The important point is that motivation itself is dynamic. The old characterization of motivation in terms of integrative vs. instrumental orientations is too static and restricted" (1993, p. 4).

The popularity of the integrative-instrumental system is partly due to its simplicity and intuitively convincing character, but partly also to the fact that broadly defined "cultural-affective" and "pragmatic-instrumental" dimensions do usually emerge in empirical studies of motivation. However, in the last decade investigations have shown that these dimensions cannot be regarded as straightforward universals, but rather as broad tendencies — or subsystems — comprising context-specific clusters of loosely related components. As Gardner and MacIntyre concluded, it is simplistic not to recognise explicitly the fact that sociocultural context has an overriding effect on all aspects of the L2 learning process, including motivation.

Clément and Kruidenier found in their Canadian research that in addition to an *instrumental orientation*, three other distinct general orientations to learn a L2 emerged, namely *knowledge, friendship*, and *travel orientations*, which had traditionally been lumped together in integrativeness. Moreover, when L2 was a foreign rather than a second language (i.e. learners had no direct contact with the L2 community), a fourth, *sociocultural*, orientation was also identified.

Investigating young adult learners in a foreign language learning situation in Hungary, Dörnyei (1990b) identified three loosely related dimensions of a broadly conceived integrative motivational subsystem: 1) *interest in foreign languages, cultures and people* (which can be associated with Clément and Kruidenier's "sociocultural orientation"); 2) *desire to broaden one's view and avoid provincialism* (cf. Clément and Kruidenier's "knowledge orientation"); and 3) *desire for new stimuli and challenges* (sharing much in common with Clément and Kruidenier's "friendship" and "travel orientations"). A fourth dimension, the *desire to integrate into a new community* (cf. "travel orientation"), overlapped with the instrumental motivational subsystem.

Investigating secondary school pupils in the same context, Clément, Dörnyei, and Noels (1994) found that, in this population, *instrumental* and *knowledge orientations* clustered together, and they identified four other distinct orientations, *xenophilique* (similar to "friendship orientation"), *identification, sociocultural*, and *English media*. In another foreign language learning context, among American high school students learning Japanese, Oxford and Shearin also found that in addition to integrative and instrumental orientations, the learners had a number of other reasons for learning the language, ranging from "enjoying the elitism of taking a difficult language" to "having a private code that parents would not know" (1994, p. 12).

These studies confirm Skehan's (1991) argument that the most pressing difficulty motivation researchers face is that of "clarifying the orientation-context links that exist. There would seem to be a wider range of orientations here than was previously supposed, and there is considerable scope to investigate different contextual circumstances (outside Canada!) by varying the L1-L2 learning relationship in different ways" (p. 284). To put it simply, the exact nature of the social and pragmatic dimensions of L2 motivation is always dependent on *who* learns *what* languages *where*.

FURTHER COMPONENTS OF L2 MOTIVATION

Although the majority of past research has tended to focus on the social and pragmatic dimensions of L2 motivation, some studies have attempted to extend the Gardnerian construct by adding new components, such as intrinsic/extrinsic motivation (Brown, 1990, 1994), intellectual curiosity (Laine, 1981), attribution about past successes/ failures (Dörnyei, 1990b; Skehan, 1989), need for achievement (Dörnyei, 1990b), self-confidence (Clément, 1980; Clément and Kruidenier, 1985; Labrie and Clément, 1986), and classroom goal structures (Julkunen, 1991), as well as various motives related to learning situation-specific variables such as classroom events and tasks, classroom climate and group cohesion, course content and teaching materials, teacher feedback, and grades and rewards (Brown, 1981, 1990, 1994; Clément, Dörnyei and Noels, 1994; Crookes and Schmidt, 1991; Dörnyei, 1990a; Julkunen, 1989, 1991; Laine, 1981; Ramage, 1990; Skehan, 1989, 1998). In the following discussion, I will give an overview of these motivational areas and then outline a L2 motivation construct that attempts to integrate these components.

Intrinsic/extrinsic motivation and related theories. One of the most general and well-known distinctions in motivation theories is that between *intrinsic* and *extrinsic motivation*. Extrinsically motivated behaviours are the ones that the individual performs to receive some extrinsic reward (e.g. good grades) or to avoid punishment. With intrinsically motivated behaviours the rewards are internal (e.g. the joy of doing a particular activity or satisfying one's curiosity).

Deci and Ryan argue that intrinsic motivation is potentially a central motivator of the educational process:

> Intrinsic motivation is in evidence whenever students' natural curiosity and interest energise their learning. When the educational environment provides optimal challenges, rich sources of stimulation, and a context of autonomy, this motivational wellspring in learning is likely to flourish (1985, p. 245).

Extrinsic motivation has traditionally been seen as something that can undermine intrinsic motivation; several studies have confirmed that students will lose their natural intrinsic interest in an activity if they have to do it to meet some extrinsic requirement (as is often the case with compulsory readings at school). Brown (1990) points out that traditional school settings with their teacher domination, grades and tests, as well as "a host of institutional constraints that glorify content, product, correctness, competitiveness" tend to cultivate extrinsic motivation and "fail to bring the learner into a collaborative process of competence building" (p. 388).

Recent research on intrinsic/extrinsic motivation has shown that under certain circumstances — if they are sufficiently *self-determined* and *internalised* — extrinsic rewards can be combined with, or even lead to, intrinsic motivation. The *self-determination theory* was introduced by Deci and Ryan as an elaboration of the intrinsic/extrinsic construct. Self-determination (i.e. autonomy) is seen as a prerequisite for any behaviour to be intrinsically rewarding.

In the light of this theory, extrinsic motivation is no longer regarded as an antagonistic counterpart of intrinsic motivation but has been divided into four types along a continuum between self-determined and controlled forms of motivation (Deci, Vallerand, Pelletier and Ryan, 1991): *External regulation* refers to the least self-determined form of extrinsic motivation, involving actions for which the locus of initiation is external to the person, such as rewards or threats (e.g. teacher's praise or parental confrontation). *Introjected regulation* involves externally imposed rules that the student accepts as norms that pressure him or her to behave (e.g. "I must be at school on time," or "I should have prepared for class"). *Identified regulation* occurs when the person has come to identify with and accept the regulatory process seeing its usefulness. The most developmentally advanced form of extrinsic motivation is *integrated regulation*, which involves regulations that are fully assimilated with the individual's other values, needs and identities. Motives traditionally mentioned under instrumental motivation in the L2 literature typically fall under one of the last two categories — identified regulation or integrated regulation — depending on how important the learner considers the goal of L2 learning to be in terms of a valued personal outcome.

Proximal goal-setting. The theories presented above may suggest that extrinsic goals such as tests and exams should be avoided as much as possible since they are detrimental to intrinsic motivation. Bandura and Schunk (1981), however, point out that tests and exams can be powerful proximal motivators in long-lasting, continuous behaviours such as language learning; they function as proximal subgoals and markers of progress that provide immediate incentive, self-inducements, and feedback and that help mobilise and maintain effort. Proximal goal-setting also contributes to the enhancement of intrinsic interest through favourable, continued involvement in activities and through the satisfaction derived from subgoal attainment. Attainable subgoals can also serve as an important vehicle in the development of the students' self-confidence and efficacy — two concepts that will be analysed below.

Oxford and Shearin argue that in order to function as efficient motivators, goals should be specific, hard but achievable, accepted by the students, and accompanied by feedback about progress. As the authors conclude, "Goal setting can have exceptional importance in stimulating L2 learning motivation, and it is therefore shocking that so little time and energy are spent in the L2 classroom on goal setting" (1994, p. 19).

Cognitive components of motivation. Since the mid-1970s, a cognitive approach has set the direction of motivation research in educational psychology. Cognitive theories of motivation view motivation to be a function of a person's thoughts rather than of some instinct, need, drive, or state; information encoded and transformed into a belief is the source of action.

In his analysis of current theories of motivation, Weiner (1992) lists three major cognitive conceptual systems: *attribution theory, learned helplessness,* and *self-efficacy theory.* All three concern the individual's self-appraisal of what he or she *can* or *cannot* do, which will, in turn, affect how he or she strives for achievement in the future. The central theme in *attribution theory* is the study of how causal ascriptions of past failures and successes affect future goal expectancy. For example, failure that is ascribed to low ability or to the difficulty of a task decreases the expectation of future success more than failure that is ascribed to bad luck or to a lack of effort. In his exploratory study among Hungarian L2 learners, the current author (Dörnyei, 1990b) identified an independent "attributions about past failures" component to L2 motivation and argued that such attributions are particularly significant in foreign language learning contexts where "L2 learning failure" is a very common phenomenon.

Learned helplessness refers to a resigned, pessimistic, helpless state that develops when the person wants to succeed but feels that success is impossible or beyond him or her for some reason, that is, the probability of a desired goal does not appear to be increased by any action or effort. It is a feeling of "I simply can't do it," which, once established, is very difficult to reverse.

Self-efficacy refers to an individual's judgement of his or her ability to perform a specific action. Attributions of past accomplishments play an important role in developing self-efficacy, but people also appraise efficacy from observational experiences (e.g. by observing peers), as well as from persuasion, reinforcement, and evaluation by others, especially teachers or parents (e.g. "You can do it!" or "You are doing fine!") (Schunk, 1991). Once a strong sense of efficacy is developed, a failure may not have much impact. Oxford and Shearin emphasise that many students do not have an initial belief in their self-efficacy and "feel lost in the language class" (1994, p. 2); teachers therefore can and should help them develop a sense of self-efficacy by providing meaningful, achievable, and success-engendering language tasks.

Self-confidence. Self-confidence — the belief that one has the ability to produce results, accomplish goals or perform tasks competently — is an important dimension of self-concept. It appears to be akin to self-efficacy, but used in a more general sense. Self-confidence was first introduced in L2 literature by Clément (1980) to describe a secondary, mediating motivational process in multi-ethnic settings that affects a person's motivation to learn and use a L2. According to his conceptualisation, self-confidence includes two components, language use anxiety (the affective aspect) and self-evaluation of L2 proficiency (the cognitive aspect), and is determined by the frequency and quality of interethnic contact (cf. Clément, Kruidenier, 1985; Labrie and Clément, 1986).

Although self-confidence was originally conceptualised with regard to multi-ethnic settings, Clément, Dörnyei, and Noels (1994) showed that it is a major motivational subsystem in foreign language learning situations as well (i.e. where there is no direct contact with members of the L2 community). This is in line with the importance attached to self-efficacy in the educational psychological literature.

Need for achievement. A central element of classical achievement motivation theory, *need for achievement* is a relatively stable personality trait that is considered to affect a person's behaviour in every facet of life, including language learning. Individuals with a high need for achievement are interested in excellence for its own sake, tend to initiate achievement activities, work with heightened intensity at these tasks, and persist in the face of failure. Oxford and Shearin (1994) provide a detailed analysis on how need theories in general might be relevant to L2 motivation research, and in an earlier paper (Dörnyei, 1990b) I have argued that in institutional/academic contexts, where academic achievement situations are very salient, need for achievement will play a particularly important role.

MOTIVATIONAL COMPONENTS THAT ARE SPECIFIC TO LEARNING SITUATIONS

Since the end of the 1980s more importance has been attached in the L2 motivation literature to motives related to the learning situation (e.g. Brown, 1981, 1990, 1994; Clément, Dörnyei and Noels, 1994; Crookes and Schmidt, 1991; Dörnyei, 1990a; Julkunen, 1989, 1991; Skehan, 1989, 1991). In order to grasp the array of variables and processes involved at this level of L2 motivation, it appears useful to separate three sets of motivational components (motives and motivational conditions): 1) *course-specific motivational components* concerning the syllabus, the teaching materials, the teaching method and the learning tasks; 2) *teacher-specific motivational components* concerning the teacher's personality, teaching style, feedback, and relationship with the students; and 3) *group-specific motivational components* concerning the dynamics of the learning group.

Course-specific motivational components. Based on Keller's motivational system — which is particularly comprehensive and relevant to classroom learning — Crookes and Schmidt postulate four major motivational factors to describe L2 classroom motivation: *interest, relevance, expectancy,* and *satisfaction.* This framework appears to be particularly useful in describing course-specific motives.

The first category, *interest,* is related to intrinsic motivation and is centred around the individual's inherent curiosity and desire to know more about him or herself and his or her environment. *Relevance* refers to the extent to which the student feels that the instruction is connected to important personal needs, values, or goals. At a macro-level, this component coincides with instrumentality; at the level of the learning situation, it refers to the extent to which the classroom instruction and course content are seen to be conducive to achieving the goal, that is, to mastering the L2. *Expectancy* refers to the perceived likelihood of success and is related to the learner's self-confidence and self-efficacy at a general level; at the level of the learning situation, it concerns perceived task difficulty, the amount of effort required, the amount of available assistance and guidance, the teacher's presentation of the task, and familiarity with the task type. *Satisfaction* concerns the outcome of an activity, referring to the combination of extrinsic rewards such as praise or good marks and to intrinsic rewards such as enjoyment and pride. Attainable proximal subgoals (as discussed above) are related primarily to this component.

Teacher-specific motivational components. Perhaps the most important teacher-related motive has been identified in educational psychology as *affiliative drive* (Ausubel, Novak and Hanesian, 1978), which refers to students' need to do well in school in order to please the teacher (or other superordinate figures like parents) whom they like and appreciate. Although this desire for teacher approval is an extrinsic motive, it is often a precursor to intrinsic interest (Blumenfeld, 1992), as is attested by good teachers whose students become devoted to their subject.

A second teacher-related motivational component is the teacher's *authority type*, that is, whether he or she is autonomy supporting or controlling. Sharing responsibility with students, offering them options and choices, letting them have a say in establishing priorities, and involving them in the decision making enhance student self-determination and intrinsic motivation (Deci and Ryan, 1985; Deci, Vallerand, Pelletier and Ryan, 1991).

A third motivational aspect of the teacher is his or her role in direct and systematic *socialization of student motivation* (Brophy and Kher, 1986), that is, whether he or she actively develops and stimulates learners' motivation. There are three main channels for the socialisation process: 1) *Modelling*: teachers, in their position as group leaders, embody the "group conscience" and, as a consequence, student attitudes and orientations toward learning will be modelled after their teachers, both in terms of effort expenditure and orientations of interest in the subject; 2) *Task presentation*: efficient teachers call students' attention to the purpose of the activity they are going to do, its interest potential and practical value, and even the strategies that may be useful in achieving the task, thus raising students' interest and metacognitive awareness; 3) *Feedback*: this process carries a clear message about the teacher's priorities and is reflected in the students' motivation. There are two types of feedback: informational feedback, which comments on competence, and controlling feedback, which judges performance against external standards. Of the two, the former should be dominant. For example, praise — a type of informational feedback — should attribute success to effort and ability, implying that similar successes can be expected in the future. Praise should avoid, however, the inclusion of controlling feedback (e.g. the comparison of the students' success to the successes or failures of others) (Brophy and Good, 1986). Ames (1992) points out that social comparison, which is considered most detrimental to intrinsic motivation, is often imposed in a variety of ways in the classroom, including announcement of grades (sometimes only the highest and lowest), displays of selected papers and achievements, and ability grouping.

Group-specific motivational components. Classroom learning takes place within groups as organisational units; these units are powerful social entities with a "life of their own", so that group dynamics influence student affects and cognitions (for a review, see Forsyth, 1990; Shaw, 1981). In addition, group goals and the group's commitment to these goals do not necessarily coincide with those of the individual, but may reinforce or reduce them.

With respect to L2 motivation, four aspects of group dynamics are particularly relevant: 1) *goal-orientedness*; 2) *norm and reward system*; 3) *group cohesion*; and 4) *classroom goal structures.*

A *group goal* is best regarded as a composite of individual goals, that is, an "end state desired by a majority of the group members" (Shaw, 1981, p. 351). Groups are typically formed for a purpose, but the "official goal" may not be the only group goal and in extreme cases may not be a group goal at all. For example, the goal of a group of students may be to have fun rather than to learn. The extent to which the group is attuned to pursuing its goal (in our case, L2 learning) is referred to as *goal-orientedness.*

The group's *norm and reward system* is one of the most salient classroom factors that can affect student motivation. It concerns extrinsic motives that specify appropriate behaviours required for efficient learning. As has been discussed earlier, extrinsic regulations should be internalised as much as possible to foster intrinsic motivation. Rewards and punishment (typically expressed in grades) should give way to group norms, which are standards that the majority of group members agree to and which become part of the group's value system. In classes where, for example, doing home assignments and preparing for tests conscientiously have not become accepted group norms, bad grades and other punitive measures will not be efficient in getting students more engaged in their home studies. On the other hand, once a norm has been internalised and has become a self-evident precondition for the group to function, the group is likely to cope with deviations by putting pressure on members who violate it. This may happen through a range of group behaviours — from showing active support for teacher's efforts to have the norms observed, to expressing indirectly disagreement with and dislike for deviant members, and even to openly criticising them and putting them in "social quarantine".

Group cohesion is the "strength of the relationship linking the members to one another and to the group itself" (Forsyth, 1990, p. 10). In a meta-analysis, Evans and Dion (1991) found a consistent positive relationship between cohesion and group performance, and the findings of Clément,

Dörnyei, and Noels (1994) confirmed that perceived group cohesion is an important motivational component in a L2 learning context. This may be due to the fact that in a cohesive group members want to contribute to group success and that goal-oriented norms have a strong influence over the individual.

Classroom goal structures can be *competitive, cooperative,* or *individualistic.* In a competitive structure, students work against each other and only the best ones are rewarded. In a cooperative situation, students work in small groups in which each member shares responsibility for the outcome and is equally rewarded. In an individualistic structure, students work alone, and one's probability of achieving a goal or reward is neither diminished nor enhanced by a capable other. There is consistent evidence from pre-school to graduate school settings that, compared to competitive or individualistic learning experiences, the cooperative goal structure is more powerful in promoting intrinsic motivation (in that it leads to less anxiety, greater task involvement, and a more positive emotional tone), positive attitudes towards the subject area, and a caring, cohesive relationship with peers and with the teacher (Johnson and Johnson, 1991; McGroarty, 1993). Julkunen (1989) analysed the effects of these three goal structures on L2 motivation and his results supported the superiority of cooperative learning.

SUMMARY OF THE L2 MOTIVATION CONSTRUCT

The variety of relevant motivation types and components described above is in accordance with the earlier claim that L2 motivation is an eclectic, multifaceted construct. In order to integrate the various components, it appears necessary to introduce different levels of motivation, similarly but not in exactly the same way as was done by Crookes and Schmidt.

Based on the research literature presented above and the results of Clément, Dörnyei, and Noels' (1994) classroom study — in which a tripartite L2 motivation construct emerged comprising integrative motivation, self confidence and the appraisal of the teaching environment — we may conceptualise a general framework of L2 motivation. This framework consists of three levels: the *Language Level*, the *Learner Level*, and the *Learning Situation Level* (see Figure 2.1). The three levels coincide with the three basic constituents of the L2 learning process (the L2, the L2 learner, and the L2 learning environment), and also reflects the three different aspects of language mentioned earlier (the social dimension, the personal dimension, and the educational subject matter dimension).

Figure 2.1   Components of Foreign Language Learning Motivation

LANGUAGE LEVEL	Integrative Motivational Subsystem Instrumental Motivational Subsystem
LEARNER LEVEL	Need for Achievement Self-Confidence * Language Use Anxiety * Perceived L2 Competence * Causal Attributions * Self-Efficacy
LEARNING SITUATION LEVEL *Course-Specific Motivational Components*	Interest Relevance Expectancy Satisfaction
Teacher-Specific Motivational Components	Affiliative Drive Authority Type Direct Socialization of Motivation * Modelling * Task Presentation * Feedback
Group-Specific Motivational Components	Goal-orientedness Norm & Reward System Group Cohesion Classroom Goal Structure

The most general level of the construct is the *Language Level* where the focus is on orientations and motives related to various aspects of the L2, such as the culture it conveys, the community in which it is spoken, and the potential usefulness of proficiency in it. These general motives determine basic learning goals and explain language choice. In accordance with the Gardnerian approach, this general motivational dimension can be described by two broad motivational subsystems, an *integrative* and an *instrumental motivational subsystem*, which, as has been argued before, consist of loosely related, context-dependent motives. The integrative motivational subsystem is centred around the individual's L2-related affective predispositions, including social, cultural, and ethnolinguistic components, as well as a general interest in foreignness and foreign languages. The instrumental motivational subsystem consists of well-internalised extrinsic motives (identified and integrated regulation) centred around the individual's future career endeavours (cf. Dörnyei, 1990b).

The second level of the L2 motivation construct is the *Learner Level*, involving a complex of affects and cognitions that form fairly stable personality traits. We can identify two motivational components underlying the motivational processes at this level, *need for achievement* and *self-confidence*, the latter encompassing various aspects of language anxiety, perceived L2 competence, attributions about past experiences, and self-efficacy.

The third level of L2 motivation is the *Learning Situation Level*, made up of intrinsic and extrinsic motives and motivational conditions concerning three areas. 1) *Course-specific motivational components* are related to the syllabus, the teaching materials, the teaching method and the learning tasks. These are best described by the framework of four motivational conditions proposed by Crookes and Schmidt (1991): *interest, relevance, expectancy*, and *satisfaction*; 2) *Teacher-specific motivational components* include the *affiliative drive* to please the teacher, *authority type*, and *direct socialisation of student motivation* (modelling, task presentation, and feedback); 3) *Group-specific motivational components* are made up of four main components: *goal-orientedness, norm and reward system, group cohesion,* and *classroom goal structure.*

HOW TO MOTIVATE L2 LEARNERS

In this last section, a list of strategies to motivate language learners will be presented, drawing partly on the author's own experience and partly on findings in educational psychological research (for two excellent overviews, see Brophy, 1987; Keller, 1983). The reader is also referred to Oxford and Shearin's (1994) article mentioned above, which contains very useful practical instructional implications of the theories discussed, as well as to Brown's recent book (1994), which includes detailed discussion on how to capitalise on the students' intrinsic motivation in the second language classroom.

It must be emphasised that the following strategies are not rock-solid golden rules, but rather suggestions that may work with one teacher or group better than another and that might work today but not tomorrow as they lose their novelty. Nevertheless, such a list provides, in Brophy's (1987) words, "a 'starter set' of strategies to select from in planning motivational elements to include in instruction" (p. 48). The strategies will be organised according to the categories introduced in the proposed L2 construct above. As can be expected, most of the strategies will concern the *Learning Situation Level*. Motives belonging to the *Language* and *Learner Levels* tend to be more generalised and established and, therefore, do not lend themselves as easily to manipulations or modifications.

Language Level

1. *Include a sociocultural component in the L2 syllabus* by sharing positive L2-related experiences in class, showing films or TV recordings, playing relevant music, and inviting interesting native speaking guests.

2. *Develop learners' cross-cultural awareness systematically* by focusing

on cross-cultural similarities and not just differences, using analogies to make the strange familiar, and using "culture teaching" ideas and activities (such as the ones included, for example, in Celce-Murcia, Dörnyei and Thurrell, 1995; Valdes, 1990; Damen, 1987; Dörnyei and Thurrell, 1992, 1994; Robinson, 1998).

3. *Promote students' contact with L2 speakers* by arranging meetings with L2 speakers in your country, or if possible, organising school trips or exchange programs to the L2 community, or finding pen-friends for your students.

4. *Develop learners' instrumental motivation* by discussing the role L2 plays in the world and its potential usefulness both for themselves and their community.

Learner Level

5. *Develop students' self-confidence* by trusting them and projecting the belief that they will achieve their goal; regularly providing praise, encouragement, and reinforcement; making sure that students regularly experience success and a sense of achievement; helping remove uncertainties about their competence and self-efficacy by giving relevant positive examples and analogies of accomplishment; counterbalancing experiences of frustration by involving students in more favourable, "easier" activities; and using confidence-building tasks (for example, see Davies and Rinvolucri, 1990).

6. *Promote the students' self-efficacy with regard to achieving learning goals* by teaching students learning and communication strategies, as well as strategies for information processing and problem-solving, helping them to develop realistic expectations of what can be achieved in a given period, and telling them about your own difficulties in language learning.

7. *Promote favourable self-perceptions of competence in L2* by highlighting what students *can* do in the L2 rather than what they *can't* do, encouraging the view that mistakes are a part of learning, pointing out that there is more to communication than not making mistakes or always finding the

right word, and talking openly about your own shortcomings in L2 (if you are a non-native teacher) or in an L3.

8. *Decrease students' anxiety* by creating a supportive and accepting learning environment in the L2 classroom, avoiding hypercritical or punitive treatment, and applying special anxiety-reducing activities and techniques (for a summary, see Young, 1991).

9. *Promote motivation-enhancing attributions* by helping students recognise links between effort and outcome, and attribute past failures to controllable factors such as insufficient effort (if this has been the case), confusion about what to do, or the use of inappropriate strategies, rather than to lack of ability, as this may lead to learned helplessness.

10. *Encourage students to set attainable subgoals* for themselves that are proximal and specific (e.g. learning 200 new words every week). Ideally, these subgoals can be integrated into a personalised learning plan for each student.

Learning Situation Level: Course-specific motivational components

11. *Make the syllabus of the course relevant* by basing it on needs analysis, and involving the students in the actual planning of the course programme.

12. *Increase the attractiveness of the course content* by using authentic materials that are within students' grasp, and unusual and exotic supplementary materials, recordings, and visual aids.

13. *Discuss with the students the choice of teaching materials* for the course (both textbooks and supplementary materials), pointing out their strong and weak points (in terms of utility, attractiveness, and interest).

14. *Arouse and sustain curiosity and attention* by introducing unexpected, novel, unfamiliar, and even paradoxical events, not allowing lessons to settle into too regular a routine, periodically breaking the static character of the classes by changing the interaction pattern and the seating formation and by making students get up and move from time to time.

15. *Increase students' interest and involvement in the tasks* by designing

or selecting varied and challenging activities; adapting tasks to the students' interests; making sure that something about each activity is new or different, including game-like features, such as puzzles, problem-solving, avoiding traps, overcoming obstacles, elements of suspense, hidden information, etc.; including imaginative elements that will engage students' emotions, leaving activities open-ended and the actual conclusion uncertain, personalising tasks by encouraging students to engage in meaningful exchanges, such as sharing personal information; and making peer interaction (e.g. pairwork and groupwork) an important teaching component.

16. *Match difficulty of tasks with students' abilities* so that students can expect to succeed if they put in reasonable effort.

17. *Increase students' expectancy of task fulfilment* by familiarising students with the task type, sufficiently preparing them for coping with the task content, giving them detailed guidance about the procedures and strategies that the task requires, making the criteria for success (or grading) clear and "transparent", and offering students ongoing assistance.

18. *Facilitate students' satisfaction* by allowing students to create finished products that they can perform or display, encouraging them to be proud of themselves after accomplishing a task, taking stock from time to time of their general progress, making a wall chart of what the group has learned, and celebrating success.

Teacher-specific motivational components

19. *Try and be empathic, congruent, and accepting*; according to the principles of person-centred education, these are the three basic teacher characteristics that enhance learning (Schunk, 1991). *Empathy* refers to being sensitive to students' needs, feelings, and perspectives. *Congruence* refers to the ability to behave according to your true self, that is, to be real and authentic without hiding behind facades or roles. *Acceptance* refers to a non-judgmental positive regard, acknowledging each student as a complex human being with both virtues and faults.

20. *Adopt the role of a facilitator* rather than an authority figure or a "drill sergeant" (Young, 1991, p. 431), developing a warm rapport with the students.

21. *Promote learner autonomy* by allowing real choices about alternative ways to goal attainment, minimising external pressure and control (e.g. threats, punishments), sharing responsibility with the students for organising their time and effort and the learning process, inviting them to design and prepare activities themselves and promoting peer-teaching, including project work where students are in charge, and giving students positions of genuine authority.

22. *Model students' interest in L2 learning* by showing students that you value L2 learning as a meaningful experience that produces satisfaction and enriches your life, sharing your own personal interest in L2 and L2 learning with the students, and taking the students' learning process and achievement very seriously (since showing insufficient commitment yourself is the fastest way to undermine student motivation).

23. *Introduce tasks in such a way as to stimulate intrinsic motivation and help internalise extrinsic motivation* by presenting tasks as learning opportunities to be valued rather than imposed demands to be resisted, projecting intensity and enthusiasm, raising task interest by connecting the task with things that students already find interesting or hold in esteem, pointing out challenging or exotic aspects of the L2, calling attention to unexpected or paradoxical aspects of routine topics, and stating the purpose and utility of the task.

24. *Use motivating feedback* by making your feedback informational rather than controlling; giving positive competence feedback, pointing out the value of the accomplishment; and not overreacting to errors (for a summary of error correction without generating anxiety, see Young, 1991).

Group-specific motivational components

25. *Increase the group's goal-orientedness* by initiating discussions with students about the group goal(s), and asking them from time to time to

evaluate the extent to which they are approaching their goal.

26. *Promote the internalisation of classroom norms* by establishing the norms explicitly right from the start, explaining their importance and how they enhance learning, asking for the students' agreement, and even involving students in formulating norms.

27. *Help maintain internalised classroom norms* by observing them consistently yourself, and not letting any violations go unnoticed.

28. *Minimise the detrimental effect of evaluation on intrinsic motivation* by focusing on individual improvement and progress, avoiding any explicit or implicit comparison of students to each other, making evaluation private rather than public, not encouraging student competition, and making the final (end of term/year/course) grading the product of two-way negotiation with the students by asking them to express their opinion of their achievement in a personal interview.

29. *Promote the development of group cohesion and enhance intermember relations* by creating classroom situations in which students can get to know each other and share genuine personal information (feelings, fears, desires, etc.), organising outings and extracurricular activities, and including game-like intergroup competitions in the course.

30. *Use cooperative learning techniques* by frequently including groupwork in the classes in which the group's — rather than the individual's — achievement is evaluated (for L2 teaching-specific guidelines, see Kessler, 1992; Holt, 1993; McGroarty, 1993).

CONCLUSION

The intent of this paper was to make L2 motivation research more "education-friendly," that is, "congruent with the concept of motivation that teachers are convinced is critical for SL (second language) success" (Crookes and Schmidt, 1991, p. 502). Drawing on a long succession of research in second language acquisition, as well as on important findings in general and educational psychology, an attempt was made to outline a comprehensive motivational construct relevant to L2 classroom motivation. This construct comprises three broad levels, the *Language Level*, the *Learner Level*, and the *Learning Situation Level*; these levels correspond to the three basic constituents of the L2 learning process (L2, L2 learner, and L2 learning environment), and reflect the three different aspects of language (the social dimension, the personal dimension, and the educational subject matter dimension). Based on the components of this model, a number of practical motivational strategies were listed that may help language teachers gain a better understanding of what motivates their students in the L2 classroom.

Although the proposed division of levels of motivation appears to be parsimonious, and the construct integrates many lines of research, it is at this stage no more than a theoretical possibility since many of its components have been verified by very little or no empirical research in the L2 field. In fact, only the components at the Language Level and the self-confidence construct at the Learner Level have been analysed systematically, notably by Gardner, Clément, and their associates. There is clearly a need for much further research on L2 motivation; this paper is intended to be part of a discussion that will hopefully result in a more clearly defined and elaborate model of motivation in foreign language learning.

Chapter 3

Psychological Processes in Cooperative Language Learning: Group Dynamics and Motivation

Modern Language Journal, (1997), 81, pp. 482-493.

Cooperative learning (CL), the instructional use of small groups in order to achieve common learning goals via cooperation, has made an almost unprecedented impact in education during the last two decades. According to Johnson, Johnson, and Smith (1995), CL is one of the most thoroughly researched areas in educational psychology. As they assert,

> We know more about cooperative learning than we know about lecturing, age grouping, departmentalization, starting reading at age six, or the 50-minute period. We know more about cooperative learning than about almost any other aspect of education. (p. 4)

The explanation for this interest in CL is very simple: investigations have almost invariably indicated that CL is a highly effective classroom intervention, superior to most traditional forms of instruction in terms of producing learning gains and student achievement, higher order thinking, positive attitudes toward learning, increased motivation, better teacher-student and student-student relationships accompanied by more developed interpersonal skills and higher self-esteem on the part of the students. Furthermore, CL appears to be applicable "with some confidence at every grade level, in every subject area, and with any task" (Johnson, Johnson and Smith, 1995, p. 4).

Although there were attempts to introduce CL principles in language instruction over 15 years ago (Gunderson and Johnson, 1980), CL has only recently become an area of interest in the L2 field. By now a fairly solid body of literature has accumulated, including two edited volumes containing a rich selection of conceptual and research studies (Holt, 1993; Kessler, 1992), a number of journal articles (e.g., Bejarano, 1987; Chang and Smith, 1991; Jacob, Rottenberg, Patrick and Wheeler, 1996; Milleret, 1992; Szostek, 1994), as well as some practical language teaching materials specifically developed for the purpose of CL (e.g., Coelho, Winer and Olsen, 1989). In addition, in her well-known book on small group work, Cohen (1994) devotes a whole chapter to discussing the bilingual classroom, which includes foreign language classes.

An interesting question is why L2 researchers have only started to discover CL relatively recently. One reason is that small group work has been part of L2 methodology for a long time and, therefore, CL may have appeared to offer nothing startlingly new. However, typical group work activities associated with communicative language teaching are not equivalent to CL, because the small group format is not the essence of CL. While it is true that communicative groupwork (such as role-play or problem-solving tasks) is a prerequisite to CL and frequently embodies certain CL principles, small group activities in L2 classes often are not cooperative in nature, or they underutilise CL principles.

There are many ways of looking at cooperative language learning. The focus of this paper is not the analysis of how group interaction inherent to CL promotes the acquisition of the L2. For this, the reader is referred to the excellent summaries of the issue by McGroarty (1993) and Kagan and McGroarty (1993), and the seminal paper of Long and Porter (1985) that describes how the increased amount and variety of target language output and input in group work facilitates L2 development. Rather, I argue that by focusing on the psychological dimension of CL, we can find the key to its effectiveness in the affective domain. I highlight two interrelated psychological processes underlying CL which, I believe, contribute significantly to the outstanding learning potential of the method: (a) the unique group dynamics inherent to the CL process that generate a supportive learning environment characterised by strong cohesiveness among learners; and (b) the motivational basis of CL which underlies student achievement gains.

It is interesting to note that the approach I have taken in this paper bears a close resemblance to a framework recently set up by Slavin (1996), who identified three major theoretical perspectives to explain the achievement effects of CL: motivational, social cohesion, and cognitive. The first two perspectives are a direct match for the two psychological processes in this article. The cognitive perspective "holds that interactions among students will in themselves increase student achievement for reasons which have to do with mental processing of information rather than with motivations" (Slavin, 1996, p. 48). Thus the cognitive perspective is analogue to increased language learning through interaction, cited above.

The focal issue of this paper — the psychological processes forming the affective foundation of cooperative language learning — is relatively "subject-matter-free", which means that these processes are not so much dependent on the actual target of learning (i.e., the mastery of the L2) as on more basic components of the learning process such as the relationships and the interactions among learners and the psychological processes involved. Much of the research support for the arguments made here is drawn from first language (LI) contexts, without conclusive evidence that the results are directly transferrable to the L2 field. Although the increasing amount of knowledge about CL in L2 classrooms (see references above) has generally confirmed the validity of the claims made in non-language classrooms with regard to language learning, more focused research is needed to decide to what extent non-native speakers from different cultures and with different cultural expectations about student and teacher roles, group work, and interpersonal communication respond to CL in the same way as the (primarily North American and Israeli) first language users among whom the approach has been developed. It would also be interesting to see whether cooperative language learning works equally well with, for example, adults in evening language courses as with pupils in ordinary school contexts.

COOPERATIVE LEARNING IN A NUTSHELL

Cooperative learning has been defined in different ways and implies several related methods of organizing and conducting classroom instruction. However, three key components of CL make a learning approach "cooperative": First, learners spend most of the class time working in small groups of between 3 and 6 students. Second, the learning is structured so that group members are motivated to ensure that their peers have also mastered the material or achieved the instructional goal, and therefore an intensive process of cooperation is generated, involving various creative collaborative learning strategies. Third, evaluating and rewarding the group's achievement in a CL class becomes as important as, or more important than, evaluating and rewarding individual achievement.

A good way to understand the essence of CL is by contrasting it with *competitive* and *individualistic* classroom structures. In the former, only the best students are rewarded so that students are forced to work against each other in an attempt to outdo their classmates. This situation encourages the survival of the fittest. Competitive learning can be characterised by a negative interdependence among students. The learners' goals are "so linked that there is a negative correlation among their goal attainments"

(Deutsch, 1962, p. 276). In an individualistic classroom structure, by contrast, there is no interdependence. Students are required to work independently and the probability of achieving a goal or reward is neither diminished nor enhanced by the presence of a capable other. The cooperative classroom, on the other hand, is characterised by a positive interdependence of the students. As Johnson, Johnson and Smith (1995) summarise, positive interdependence occurs "when one perceives that one is linked with others in a way so that one cannot succeed unless they do (and vice versa) and/or one must coordinate one's efforts with the efforts of others to complete a task" (p. 31). In other words, positive interdependence is the belief that students "sink or swim together" (p. 31).

Positive interdependence results in *promotive interaction*, which can be defined as "individuals encouraging and facilitating each other's efforts to achieve and complete tasks, and produce in order to reach the group's goals" (Johnson, Johnson and Smith, 1995, p. 20). Students are divided into small groups and learning takes place in these basic social units through peer teaching, joint problem-solving, brainstorming, and varied interpersonal communication, as well as through individual study monitored by peers. Thus, in a cooperative learning situation, as the name indicates, everything is centred around the process of cooperation, that is, giving and receiving ideas and clarification, providing task-related help and assistance, exchanging needed resources (e.g., information or materials), and providing constructive feedback (Johnson, Johnson and Smith, 1995; Sharan, 1995).

The key question is, how can positive interdependence be achieved? That is, how can learners be "motivated" to cooperate? Olsen and Kagan (1992) list five principal ways to accomplish CL structures:

1. *Structuring the goal*: Groups work towards a single team product (e.g., joint performance).

2. *Structuring the rewards*: In addition to individual scores or grades, some sort of team score is also calculated and joint rewards or grades are given for the group's overall production.

3. *Structuring student roles*: Assigning different roles to every group member so that everybody has a specific responsibility (e.g., "explainer," "summariser," or "note- taker").

4. *Structuring materials*: Either limiting resources so that they must be shared (e.g., one answer sheet for the whole group) or giving out resources (e.g., worksheets, information sheets) which need to be fitted together (i.e., the jigsaw procedure).

5. *Structuring rules*: Setting rules that emphasise the shared nature of responsibility for the group product (e.g., no one can proceed to some new project or material before every other group member has completed the previous assignment).

Besides positive interdependence, Johnson and Johnson (1995) mention three other conditions necessary for the effectiveness of CL: individual accountability, mastery of social skills, and regular group processing. They argue that CL works best when the group rewards for learning are combined with individual accountability in order to ensure that participants perform their share of the work. In these CL formats, students are individually quizzed and receive recognition based on the sum of all team members' scores.

Social skills may need to be taught; simply placing students in a learning group and expecting them to cooperate effectively may not be successful. As Johnson and Johnson state, "We are not born instinctively knowing how to interact effectively with others. Interpersonal and group skills do not magically appear when they are needed" (1995, p. 122). This is particularly true in ethno-linguistically heterogeneous L2 classrooms, where the cultural dissimilarity among the students is a further source of divergence in the skills necessary for high quality cooperation, such as leadership, decision making, trust building, communication, and conflict-management skills. (For classroom recommendations on how to teach these skills to students by open modelling and controlled practice, see Cohen, 1994; Ehrman and Dörnyei, 1998).

Finally, according to Johnson and Johnson (1995), effective group work is influenced by whether groups regularly reflect on how they are functioning, what has been conducive to completing the tasks, and how they should continue or change — thus engaging in group processing. Such processing enhances group maintenance, facilitates acquisition and practice of social skills, reminds members of the group norms, and gives members feedback on their participation.

GROUP DYNAMICS AND COOPERATIVE LEARNING

CL has been rooted in a social psychological approach to the study of small groups. Its innovation and strength lies almost entirely in the conscious and systematic exploitation of the principles of group dynamics to enhance student learning outcomes. In this section, a group-dynamics-based analysis of CL is applied in order to see how the necessary conditions of interaction and cooperation develop.[1]

Group dynamics concerns the analysis of the behaviour of small groups, generally about 4 to 20 members (for more detailed overviews of the principles of group dynamics from a L2 perspective, see Dörnyei and Malderez, 1997; Ehrman and Dörnyei, 1998).[2] The educational applicability of group dynamics rests on three factors:

1. Most organised learning occurs in some kind of group (e.g., classes, seminars, workshops, discussion groups).

2. Group characteristics and group processes significantly contribute to success or failure in the classroom and directly affect the quality and quantity of learning within the group.

---

[1] In this chapter I will follow the use of the term "group dynamics" as established in social psychology, and include the entire language class under "group". Therefore, "group dynamics" in this paper does not only concern small group work within the class but also whole classroom dynamics.

[2] Group dynamics is a relatively young field in the social sciences, overlapping with disciplines such as social, industrial, organisational and clinical psychology, psychiatry, anthropology, sociology, and social work, since all these fields involve groups as focal points around which human relationships are organised.

3. Theoretical and practical knowledge about group dynamics might assist teachers to create learning environments where learning is a rewarding and efficient experience. An awareness of the principles of group dynamics can also help teachers to make classroom events less threatening, develop more efficient classroom management, and develop creative, well balanced, and cohesive groups.

Group cohesiveness and instructed language learning

One concept central to the explanation of many group-related phenomena is group cohesiveness, or "the strength of relationship linking the members to one another and to the group itself" (Forsyth, 1990, p. 10). It is an index of the level of group development, directly related to within-group cooperation and to both the quality and quantity of group interaction (see Bar-Tal and Bar-Tal, 1986; Greene, 1989; Shaw, 1981). Three recent meta-analyses of past studies addressing the relationship between group cohesiveness and group performance found a significant positive relationship between the two variables, indicating that cohesive groups, on average , tend to be more productive than non-cohesive groups (Evans and Dion, 1991; Gully, Devine, and Whitney, 1995; Mullen and Copper, 1994).

The cohesiveness-performance effect can be particularly strong in language classes in which the learners' communicative skills are developed primarily through participatory experience in real world language tasks. In these contexts, communication is unfolded and enlivened in positive relationships, and the warm, cohesive group climate significantly enhances peer interaction. Indeed, Levine and Moreland's (1990) review of the literature confirms that members of a cohesive group are more likely than others to participate actively in conversations and engage in self-disclosure or collaborative narration, which are student behaviours necessary for efficient communicative task involvement. In addition to promoting interaction, cohesiveness also mediates the effects of CL on achievement because "students will help one another because they care about one another and want one another to succeed" (Slavin, 1996, p. 46).

The development of group cohesiveness

In view of the arguments above, group cohesiveness is one of the most important attributes of the successful communicative language class. It is therefore particularly critical for language teachers to understand how it evolves among learners.

Group cohesiveness develops gradually throughout the existence of the group. The amount of time spent together and the shared group history are key factors that tend to develop stronger intermember ties. By far the most crucial ways of consciously fostering cohesiveness is to help students learn about each other by sharing genuine personal information. Acceptance of another person does not occur without getting to know that person well; enemy images and a lack of tolerance often stem from insufficient information about the other party.

In addition to getting to know one another, more concrete factors can also enhance affiliation (see Dörnyei and Malderez, 1997; Ehrman and Dörnyei, 1998; Johnson and Johnson, 1995; Levine and Moreland, 1990; Shaw, 1981; Turner, 1984; for practical group-building tasks for the L2 classroom, see Hadfield, 1992):

1. *Proximity*, or physical closeness (e.g., sitting next to each other), which is a necessary condition for the formation of relationships.

2. *Contact* in situations where individuals can meet and communicate (e.g., cafeterias and other relaxation areas, outings and other extracurricular activities, as well as in class opportunities).

3. *Interaction* in which the behaviour of each person influences the others' (e.g., group activities, project work).

4. *Cooperation* between members for common goals (e.g., to accomplish group tasks).

5. *The rewarding nature of group experience* for the individual; rewards may involve the enjoyment of the activities, approval of the goals, success

in goal attainment, and personal instrumental benefits.

6. *Successful completion of whole group tasks* and a sense of group achievement.

7. *Joint hardship* that group members have experienced (e.g., carrying out some difficult task together).

8. *Intergroup competition* (e.g., games in which groups compete); this has been found to bring together members of small groups.

9. *Common threat*, which can invoke, for example, the feeling of fellowship before a difficult exam.

10. *Group legends*, which are an efficient way of "pumping up group pride" (Mullen and Copper, 1994, p. 224); these may involve building up a kind of group mythology, giving the group a name, and inventing characteristics for the group.

11. *Investing in the group* to create cohesiveness.

12. *Public commitment to the group* to strengthen a sense of belonging.

13. *Defining the group against another*, that is, emphasizing the distinction between "us" and "them," a powerful but potentially dangerous aspect of cohesiveness.

Group cohesiveness is also fostered by leadership and teaching styles. The way leaders live out their role and encourage a feeling of warmth and acceptance can also enhance group cohesiveness. Kellerman (1981) argues that a prerequisite for any group with a high level of cohesiveness is a leader whose presence is continuously and strongly felt: "highly cohesive groups are those in which the leader symbolises group concerns and identity and is personally visible to the membership" (p. 16). Indeed, one of the surest ways of undermining the cohesiveness of a group is for the leader to be absent, either physically or psychologically (the latter idea referring to insufficient care for the group and its goals).

In addition, an efficient group leader's task is not so much to lead the group but rather to facilitate it, that is, to create the right conditions for development, in particular a safe and accepting climate, and to enable the group to do away with any emerging obstacles. Seen from this perspective, the traditional autocratic teaching style, whereby the teacher makes virtually all the decisions, dictating policy and actions, never discussing the schedule or asking for input from the members, is an obstacle to group development because it does not allow for the group to structure itself organically, or for the members to share increasing responsibility. The instructor who aims to be conscious of group dynamics should adopt a more "democratic" teaching style and be "prepared to step aside to give the learner a meaningful role" (McDonell, 1992, p. 169), only intervening when necessary. As Ehrman and Dörnyei (1998) summarise, democratic leaders invoke the group members in decision making about their own functioning, share with them the long-term goals and steps to be taken to achieve these, and take part in the activities themselves. That is, they consciously distribute influence and promote learner autonomy: Students are given positions and tasks of genuine authority, are invited to design and prepare activities themselves, and are encouraged to take part in project work and peer teaching.

Cohesiveness and the CL process

Nearly all reports on CL projects highlight the improved interrelations among students and between the students and the teacher. Researchers assert that CL is particularly effective in creating cohesive groups (see Johnson and Johnson, 1995). This increased group cohesiveness can be explained by three main reasons.

First, CL methodology consciously recognises the importance of team building, emphasizing the necessity of spending initial time training CL skills such as building trust, providing leadership, and managing conflicts. CL also contains regular self-evaluation, which ensures that any potential intermember tensions are properly processed.

Second, the emerging cohesiveness in CL classrooms is also the function of the special dynamics of the CL process, which organically includes several of the cohesiveness-promoting factors listed above. The small group format and the positive interdependence among students provide proximity, contact, and interaction. Promotive interaction through coordination and communication requires understanding each participant's needs, interests, and abilities, and results in knowing each other on a personal level, "rather than as complexes of performances (what persons do)" (Johnson and Johnson, 1995, p. 104). Although there is usually no joint hardship or common threat, CL formats often include intergroup competition. Because of the supportive environment and a lack of face-threatening competition, group experience for learners is typically rewarding. Because the CL process centres on the successful completion of group tasks, student satisfaction is further enhanced. Furthermore, as Johnson and Johnson argue, promotive interaction includes the public commitment to accomplish the group goals as well as considerable investment of time and energy toward this, which results in a growing attachment to the task and the group.

Third, students in cooperatively structured classes are in control of organizing their own learning, that is, there is considerable learner autonomy. The dominant small group format simply excludes the teacher from the primary student communication networks and considerably decentralises the decision-making process in the classroom, providing learners with an opportunity for self-regulation (Sharan and Shaulov, 1990). Learner autonomy is also ensured by the teacher's democratic teaching style, mentioned earlier.

In sum, based on the numerous factors promoting cohesiveness listed above, we may conclude that the dynamics of the CL process support the main conditions for organic group development and the emergence of a mature, well-balanced internal class structure, characterised by strong student cohesiveness. This cohesiveness is a strong mediator of CL processes on learning outcomes because it is a necessary requirement for communicative task involvement, and, as discussed below, it also fosters students' motivation to learn.

THE MOTIVATIONAL BASIS OF STUDENT ACHIEVEMENT IN COOPERATIVE LEARNING

The superior task performance and learning achievement repeatedly observed with students in cooperatively structured classrooms (for reviews, see Cohen, 1994; Johnson and Johnson, 1995) would not occur without a powerful motivational basis energizing the CL process. Cooperative goal structure and the learning format that characterise CL generate a special motivational system, which is largely responsible for the efficiency of CL.

Dörnyei (1994a) argues that the motivational complex underlying instructed L2 learning is a multi-dimensional construct comprising at least three fairly independent levels: (a) the language level (concerning ethnolinguistic, cultural-affective, intellectual, and pragmatic values and attitudes attached to the target language and its speakers); (b) the learner level (concerning various fairly stable personality traits that the learner has developed in the past); and (c) the learning situation level (concerning situation-specific motives rooted in various aspects of language learning in a classroom setting) (see Table 3.1). The most important impact of the CL process on learner motivation occurs at the learning situation level, but continuous exposure might influence motivational processes at the learner level as well.

Table 3.1   Components of Foreign Language Learning Motivation

LANGUAGE LEVEL	Integrative Motivational Subsystem
	Instrumental Motivational Subsystem
LEARNER LEVEL	Need for Achievement
	Self-Confidence*
	- Language Use Anxiety*
	- Perceived L2 Competence
	- Causal Attributions*
	- Self-Efficacy*

(continued)

LEARNING SITUATION LEVEL

Course-Specific Motivational *Components*	Interest*
	Relevance
	Expectancy*
	Satisfaction*
Teacher-Specific Motivational *Components*	Affiliative Drive
	Authority Type*
	Direct Socialization of Motivation
	- Modelling
	- Task Presentation
	- Feedback
Group-Specific Motivational *Components*	Goal-orientedness*
	Norm & Reward System*
	Group Cohesion*
	Classroom Goal Structure*

Note: Adapted from Dörnyei, 1994, p. 280.
*Components assumed to be affected by the CL-generated motivational system.

Motivational components at the learning situation level: Group-specific motives

Swezey, Meltzer, and Salas (1994) point out that most theories of motivation attempt to explain motivational processes at the individual level, even though action conducted within groups might show motivational characteristics that stem from the group as a social unit rather than from the individual members. Because in educational contexts this claim appears to be particularly valid, Dörnyei's (1994a) model of L2 motivation includes a set of group-specific motivational components related to four aspects of group dynamics: classroom goal structures, group cohesion, goal-orientedness, and the norm and reward system. Let us examine how these group properties affect motivation in cooperative classrooms.

Classroom Goal Structure. The classroom goal structure in CL is centred around positive interdependence and the resulting process of cooperation. L2 studies investigating the motivational role of cooperativeness confirm the positive effect found in L1 classrooms. In her conceptual analysis, Ushioda (1996b) concludes that collaborative learning in itself can create the appropriate psychological conditions for intrinsic motivation. Julkunen's (1989) investigation of the effects of competitive, individualistic, and cooperative goal structures on L2 motivation supports the superiority of CL. Julkunen and Borzova's (1996) results indicate that students tend to prefer CL situations to individualistic and competitive ones, and the researchers also found a significant positive relationship between cooperative goal structures and various aspects of L2 learning motivation.

Group Cohesiveness. The fact that group cohesiveness has a positive impact on further motivation to learn was made explicit by Deutsch (1962) in his initial theory of cooperation, which stated that promotively-oriented groups would show more achievement pressure. In a summary of research on the effect of cohesiveness on learner dispositions and behaviours, Johnson and Johnson (1995) verified this assumption. Furthermore, in their study of classroom motivation to learn a L2, Clément, Dörnyei, and Noels (1994) confirmed that group cohesiveness is indeed an important component of L2 motivation. This might be due to a sense of obligation and moral responsibility to the group. The group's goal-oriented norms have a strong influence on the individual. In cohesive groups, the likelihood of "social loafing" and "free-riding" (i.e., doing very little actual work while still reaping the benefits of the team's performance) decreases. In addition, positive relations make the learning process more enjoyable, thus promoting intrinsic motivation.

Goal-Orientedness. The extent to which the group is attuned to pursuing its goal (in our case, L2 learning) is referred to as "goal-orientedness." In school contexts the "official group goal" (mastering the L2) may not be a goal at all. Furthermore, members may not show the same degree of commitment to the group goal. However, due to the positive interdependence among students in CL, we can expect individual and group goals to converge more than in other educational contexts. This has been supported by Nichols and Miller (1994), who found that students in CL classes were more goal-oriented than students participating in traditional instruction.

Norm and Reward System. One aspect of positive interdependence is the fact that rewards are contingent upon group performance. As a result, because the whole group benefits from a member's high academic achievement, we do not find the common peer pressure against doing academic work in cooperatively structured classrooms. The "norm of mediocrity," which exists in many educational contexts, results in learners suffering social consequences for academic success, which is reflected in labelling hard-working students "teacher's pet," "nerd," or "brain" (Daniels, 1994, p. 1011). In contrast, Daniels found that the norm system of CL results in learners gaining social approval for academic excellence and helping each other to achieve this. This type of norm system exerts a powerful influence on group members' attitudes, values, and actions. Students in cooperatively structured classrooms are motivated to excel by their need for social approval and by the wish to avoid negative sanctions for not doing their fair share in working towards group success (Ames and Ames, 1984; Johnson and Johnson, 1995).

Teacher-specific motives

The primary teacher-specific motive in CL concerns the teacher's authority type. As described before, CL is typically accompanied by a democratic leadership style that fosters learner autonomy. Research shows that although controlling classroom contexts may result in higher short-term productivity, autonomy-supporting classroom contexts lead to a higher level of long-term, intrinsic motivation (see, for example. Ames, 1992; Deci, 1992; Klein, Erchul and Pridemore, 1994; Swezey, Meltzer and Salas, 1994; Sharan and Shaulov, 1990). Indeed, many researchers share Paris and Turner's (1994) assertion that "The essence of motivated action is the ability to choose among alternative courses of action, or at least, to choose to expend varying degrees of effort for a particular purpose" (p. 222).

The claim that autonomy is at the core of the motivation to learn is also central to Deci and Ryan's (1985) influential "self-determination" theory. According to Deci and Ryan, the need for autonomy is an innate human need, referring to the desire to be self-initiating and self-regulating of one's actions. Therefore self-determination, that is, engaging in an activity "with a full sense of wanting, choosing, and personal endorsement" (Deci, 1992, p. 44), is a prerequisite for any behaviour to be intrinsically rewarding. CL provides a learning environment that fully supports self-determination on the part of the students. The following summary of the educational relevance of self-determination by Deci, Vallerand, Pelletier, and Ryan (1991) applies almost literally to CL:

> The specific supports for self-determination we suggest include offering choice, minimizing controls, acknowledging feelings and making available information that is needed for decision making and for performing the target task. With a general attitude of valuing children's autonomy and by providing the type of autonomy support just mentioned, we stand the greatest chance of bringing about the types of educational contexts that facilitate conceptual understanding, flexible problem solving, personal adjustment, and social responsibility. (p. 342)

Learner autonomy has been shown to exert a significant positive impact on motivation in L2 contexts as well. In her extensive discussion of learner autonomy and L2 motivation. Ushioda (1996b) concludes that autonomy and motivation go hand in hand: "Autonomous language learners are by definition motivated learners" (p. 2). In another recent study, Dickinson (1995) also makes the initial assumption that an active, independent attitude to learning and personal involvement in decision making leads to increased L2 motivation. Dickinson's review of relevant motivational studies confirms this view:

> It has been shown that there is substantial evidence from cognitive motivational studies that learning success and enhanced motivation

is conditional on learners taking responsibility for their own learning, being able to control their own learning and perceiving that their learning successes and failures are to be attributed to their own efforts and strategies rather than to factors outside their control. Each of these conditions is a characteristics of learner autonomy as it is described in applied linguistics. (pp. 173-74)

Course-specific motives

The CL process has been found to increase three of the four components associated with course-specific motivation in Dörnyei's (1994a) construct: intrinsic interest, expectancy, and satisfaction. The increased student interest in the learning process stems from several sources, many of which have been discussed earlier: more varied and dynamic tasks, greater task involvement, the pleasure of working in a cohesive group, the self-determined nature of learning, and the informational feedback received from the peers. The expectancy of successful task fulfilment is enhanced by the group serving as a "resource pool that is greater in any given area than the resources possessed by any single member" (Douglas, 1983, p. 189) — that is, students know that they can count on their peers when in trouble. The satisfaction that students experience after they complete a task successfully is increased by the shared experience and the joint celebration. This has been confirmed by van Oostrum and Rabbie's (1995) experiment, in which cooperative groups reported higher satisfaction about their obtained results and performance than learners in competitively structured classes. In addition, Szostek (1994) has found in an L2 context that a great deal of the satisfaction group members feel comes from the success of coaching, teaching, drilling, and helping each other to learn.

Motivational processes at the Learner Level: Self-confidence

Almost every report on the outcomes of CL highlights some kind of improvement in the learners' self-esteem, self-efficacy, and confidence, often as the result of changes in the learners' attributional system or a decrease in the language anxiety they experience. Following Clément (1980; Clément and Kruidenier, 1985; Labrie and Clément, 1986; Clément, Dörnyei and Noels, 1994) these factors have been subsumed under a broad motivational process, linguistic self-confidence, in Dörnyei's (1994a) model.

According to Covington's self-worth theory of achievement motivation (Covington and Roberts, 1994), the highest human priority is the need for self-acceptance and therefore "in reality, the dynamics of school achievement largely reflect attempts to aggrandise and protect self-perceptions of ability" (p. 161). A primary feature of CL is that it avoids any social comparison of individuals and thus students do not equate their worth with the ability to achieve competitively. Rather, as Ames and Ames (1984) argue, the student's willingness to put forth effort serves as a primary criterion in the evaluation of behaviour. The absence of the detrimental effects of social comparison, accompanied by the increased peer acceptance and support that exists in cohesive groups, is expected to result in higher perception of ability, self-worth, and academic self-esteem (i.e., self-efficacy) in CL groups than in traditional classes. This was demonstrated by Johnson, Johnson, and Taylor's (1993) and Nichols and Miller's (1994) empirical studies.

Enhanced self-confidence in cooperatively structured classrooms is also a function of the attributional focus of such environments. The guiding principle in the attribution theory of motivation is that people search for understanding, asking "why" questions to explain their past successes and failures. These explanations, in turn, play a central role in the determination of future achievement. Failure that is ascribed to stable and uncontrollable factors such as low ability decreases the expectation of future success more than failure that is ascribed to controllable factors such as effort (Weiner, 1979). Ames and Ames (1984) argue that whereas in a competitive classroom structure the focus is on ability, in a cooperative setting the attributional focus is on effort and intent. This enhances achievement behaviour through the learners' increased self-confidence.

A final reason for increased self-confidence is the fact that cooperation typically generates less anxiety and stress than other learning formats (Deci and Ryan, 1985). This is partly caused by the positive emotional tone that characterises CL and partly by the increased level of self-determination. In addition, Johnson, Johnson, and Smith (1995) point out that cooperation also produces more effective coping strategies to deal with anxiety than does competition.

A summary of motivation in cooperative language learning

The overview of the motivational basis of cooperative language learning presented above helps us understand the consistently favourable affective impact of CL on L2-related attitudes and motivation. This positive influence was the central theme of the first L2 study on CL (Gunderson and Johnson, 1980), in which the authors concluded:

> Perhaps the most basic instructional objective in a foreign language class is to send students away with at least as favourable attitude toward learning the language as they had when they first arrived in the classroom. Certainly, students who finish one foreign language course should wish to take the second. While competitive and individualistic learning do have their place, the use of cooperative learning groups is an important teaching strategy for promoting positive attitudes toward learning a foreign language. (p. 43)

As argued earlier, the consistency of improved student attitudes and motivation observed in CL contexts suggests that the CL process generates a specific motivational system that energises learning. In Table 3.1 the components activated by this system are marked with an asterisk. The unmarked components are not necessarily irrelevant, but they are not assumed to be enhanced by CL in particular; for example, learners in a CL class may or may not be instrumentally motivated. The number of different motivational aspects which CL significantly affects explains the remarkable results obtained in a major study on the role of motivation in CL by Sharan and Shaulov (1990), who found that more than half of the variance in achievement in three academic subjects was caused by the "motivation to learn" factor. Such a substantial impact is very rare in motivation studies in general and is due to the fact that the motivational system promoted within cooperative situations (a) mediates between achievement and several significant independent variables related to the unique social structure of the CL classroom, and (b) considerably enhances the learners' achievement-related self-concept. Thus, we may conclude that from a motivational point of view CL is undoubtedly one of the most efficient instructional methods.

CONCLUSION

As stated earlier, the strength of CL lies in the small group learning format accompanied by positive interdependence among the learners, resulting in intensive interaction and a process of cooperation. CL, in fact, can be seen as the learning process which best maximises the beneficial effects of peer collaboration. By emphasizing the students' active participation in constructing their own knowledge, CL signifies a major departure from traditional educational contexts where "instruction is still largely viewed as a vast delivery service whose task is to deliver a completed manufactured product to the consumer" (Sharan and Shaulov, 1990, p. 196). Indeed, CL can also be viewed as an instructional approach that fully realises the principles of an emerging student-centred teaching paradigm (Johnson, Johnson, and Smith, 1995).

This article examined the psychological foundations of the success of cooperatively structured learning. Two interrelated processes, the group dynamics of CL classes and the motivational system generated by peer collaboration, were discussed. It was argued that CL tends to produce a group structure (including peer relationships and learning norms) and a motivational basis that provide excellent conditions for L2 learning. In a

CL class we would see motivated students engaged in varied interactions while working intensively towards completing group tasks — features that are considered crucial for efficient communicative L2 classes. Indeed, Coelho (1992) draws attention to the striking similarities between cooperative group skills emphasised by CL and L2 functions emphasised by communicative language teaching and argues that CL can provide the foundation for communicative language curriculum design.

Finally, I emphasise that although the discussion in this article focused entirely on cooperatively structured learning, the processes described are not restricted to CL but are also characteristic of any student collaboration, group work, or team work in general, as CL is only viewed as the learning format which maximises student collaboration. Therefore, an understanding of the "deep structure" of CL can help us understand some of the fundamental processes and concepts underlying modern language teaching methodology.

Chapter 4

Much More than Carrot and Stick

Guardian Weekly/Learning English, (2002), 166/5, 6.

Language teachers frequently use the term 'motivation' when they describe successful or unsuccessful learners. This reflects our intuitive belief that during the lengthy and often tedious process of mastering a foreign/second language (L2), the learner's enthusiasm, commitment and persistence are key determinants of success or failure. In the vast majority of cases learners with sufficient motivation can achieve a working knowledge of an L2, regardless of their language aptitude, whereas without sufficient motivation even the brightest learners are unlikely to persist long enough to attain any really useful language. This being the case, teacher skills in motivating learners should be seen as central to teaching effectiveness. Indeed, research has shown that for many teachers problems about motivating pupils are the second most serious source of difficulty (after maintaining classroom discipline), preceding other obviously important issues such as the effective use of different teaching methods, a knowledge of the subject matter, and the suitable use of textbooks and curriculum guides. If you have ever tried to teach a language class with reluctant, lethargic or uncooperative students, you will know from bitter personal experience that researchers got it right this time.

In the light of the importance attached to motivation, it is hard to believe that until the end of the 1980s there had been hardly any attempts in the psychological literature to design motivational strategies for classroom application, and in language teaching methodology it was not until the mid-1990s that the first descriptions of practical classroom techniques started to appear in print. Obviously, researchers had been far more interested to find out what motivation was than how it could be promoted. During the past six years, however, things have finally started to change. More and more articles and books have been published with the word 'motivating' in their title, as if a new spirit had entered the profession, urging scholars to 'stick their neck out and see what we've got'. Fortunately, what we've got is nothing to be ashamed of. There is a growing set of core knowledge in motivation research that has stood the test of time and can be safely translated into practical terms. Here, by way of distillation, are what I believe to be the three key principles of motivating learners, plus some concrete motivational strategies and ideas that have worked well for me in the past.

Principle 1: There is much more to motivational strategies than offering rewards and punishment

Although rewards and punishments are too often seen as the only tools present in the motivational arsenal of many teachers, a closer look at the spectrum of other potentially more effective motivational strategies reveals that we have a huge array of varied techniques at our disposal to increase our learners' enthusiasm for language learning. In fact, most educational psychologists would consider rewards and punishment too simplistic and rather undesirable tools. The 'carrot and stick' approach may work in the short run but rarely does it lead to real long-term commitment. Long books have been written, for example, about the potential damage of grades, which are by far the most often used forms of rewards/punishment. Indeed, getting rewards — and good grades in particular — can become more important than learning, and students can easily become 'grade-driven'. Therefore, I would encourage teachers to start experimenting with other motivational techniques. Although there are no magic motivational buttons that can be pressed to 'make' students want to learn, the variety of different ways by which human learning can be promoted is so rich that we may be able to find something that works in most learning situations.

Principle 2: Generating student motivation is not enough in itself — it also has to be maintained and protected

In everyday parlance 'motivating' someone equals generating motivation in the person. However, in educational contexts this is not the whole picture. Although generating motivation is a crucial aspect of any motivational teaching practice, unless motivation is actively maintained and protected during the lengthy process of L2 learning, the natural human tendency to lose sight of the goal, to get tired or bored of an activity and to give way to attractive distractions, will result in the initial motivation gradually petering out. Thus, motivation needs to be actively nurtured, which means that any motivational practice needs to be an ongoing activity.

Principle 3: It is the quality and not the quantity of the motivational strategies we use that counts

Writing a book on motivational strategies made me increasingly aware of the great number of useful techniques mentioned in the literature that I myself had not been applying consistently in my teaching practice. Is this a problem? Not necessarily. There is so much that requires our constant attention in the language classroom that we simply cannot afford to continuously strive to achieve 'supermotivator' status. I have come to believe that what we need is quality rather than quantity:

A few well-chosen strategies that suit both us and our learners may be sufficient to create a positive motivational climate in the classroom. Indeed, some of the most motivating teachers often rely on only a handful of basic techniques.

'SELLING' CONFIDENCE, OWNERSHIP AND SUCCESS

Whetting appetites

The key issue in generating interest in learning is to arouse the learners' curiosity and attention, and to create an attractive image for the L2 course. This is very much a 'selling' task in which you may point out challenging, exotic or satisfying aspects of L2 learning; connect L2 learning with activities that students already find interesting or hold in esteem (e.g. computer-assisted learning); highlight the variety of activities that L2 learning may involve; and provide a demonstration of some particularly enjoyable tasks.

Increasing expectancy of success

The notion of 'expectancy of success' has been one of the most researched factors in motivational psychology, which is due to the undeniable fact that we do things best if we believe we can succeed. Whether or not a student will expect success in a given task is a rather subjective matter. Therefore an effective way of motivating learners is to put them in a more positive or optimistic mood. The best way of ensuring that students expect success is to make sure that they achieve it consistently. It also helps if the success criteria are clear, sufficient advance preparation is provided and students are aware that they can rely on ongoing assistance both from you and their peers.

Making materials relevant

One of the most demotivating factors for learners is when they have to learn something that they cannot see the point of because it has no seeming relevance whatsoever to their lives. This experience is unfortunately more common than many of us would think. Stick to the general principle: find out what your students' goals are and what topics they want to learn about, then build these into your curriculum as much as possible.

Breaking the monotony

Even in classes characterised by a mixture of interesting teaching approaches, there is a danger of settling into familiar routines, which then, can easily turn into a monotonous 'daily grind'. In order to prevent monotony, we need to vary as many aspects of the learning process as possible (e.g. the focus and nature of the tasks, the type of student involvement, the learning materials or the arrangement of the furniture). Of course, trying to continuously change all the aspects of teaching would be the perfect recipe for teacher burn-out. Rather, we may look at these factors as cooking ingredients, and all we need to make sure is that we don't serve exactly the same meal every day.

Increasing self-confidence

Learning a new language is to a large extent a 'confidence game'. Confident learners can communicate with surprisingly limited L2 resources, whereas no amount of vocabulary and grammatical knowledge will help someone to speak if confidence is lacking. Two key aspects of confidence building are providing regular encouragement and reducing language anxiety. We should never forget that the language classroom is an inherently face-threatening environment where even saying a simple sentence carries the danger of making big mistakes. Helping learners to accept that mistakes are a natural part of the learning process is already half the battle.

Positive social image

For most school children the main social arena in life is their school and their most important reference group is their peers. Therefore no student is likely to be keen to do a task that puts them in a situation where they are made to look small in front of their classmates. In contrast, if we can provide an opportunity for everybody to play the protagonist's role in one way or another (e.g. by creating situations in which students can demonstrate their particular strengths), the 'positive hero' image might work as an unprecedented stimulant.

Creating learner autonomy

Parents taking small children to eat out often find that if they order the food there is a good chance that the child will not like it, whereas if the children can choose for themselves, they tend to finish their meal. Translating this into psychological terms, students are more motivated to pursue tasks that they feel some sort of an 'ownership' of. This can be achieved by allowing them real choices about as many aspects of the learning process as possible, handing over various leadership/teaching roles, and adopting the role of a facilitator rather than a 'drill sergeant'. Autonomy and motivation go hand in hand.

Increasing satisfaction

I have noticed in myself and also in many others that we tend to show far less emotion when something goes right than when it goes wrong. The problem with acknowledging accomplishments in such a cool manner and only making failures or difficulties tangible is that we miss out on the celebratory part and reduce the amount of satisfaction we may feel. Celebrations and satisfaction are crucial motivational building blocks because they validate effort, affirm the entire learning process, and in general provide the bright spots along the road towards the ultimate goal. So take time to celebrate any victory!

Offering grades

Although many teachers and researchers would love to get rid of any form of assessment, realistically speaking, grades are likely to remain a fact of life at least for the foreseeable future. Therefore an important task is to find ways of offering grades and rewards in a motivating manner. The following guidelines may take us some way towards this end: (a) Make the assessment system completely transparent, with clear success criteria, and create opportunities for the students to also express their views; (b) Make sure that grades also reflect effort and improvement and not just objective levels of achievement; (c) Apply continuous assessment that does not only take into account scores of pencil-and-paper tests; (d) Encourage accurate student self-assessment by providing various self-evaluation tools.

Chapter 5

New Themes and Approaches in Second Language Motivation Research

Annual Review of Applied Linguistics, (2001), 21, pp. 43-59.

The first three decades of L2 motivation research until about the early 1990s was largely inspired and fuelled by the pioneering work of social psychologists in Canada, most notably Robert Gardner, Wallace Lambert, Richard Clément, and their associates. Applying versions of a standardised motivation test developed by Robert Gardner's research group at the University of Western Ontario, the *Attitude/Motivation Test Battery* (AMTB; for a complete version, see Gardner, 1985a), a great deal of empirical research during this period was directed at measuring the association between various aspects of motivation and L2 learning achievement. The emerging body of research studies established motivation as a principal determinant of second language acquisition, comparable in its impact to another well-researched learner variable, language aptitude.

During these first decades of research, motivation was primarily seen as a relatively stable learner trait that was, to a large extent, a function of (a) the learner's social perceptions of the L2 and its speakers, as reflected by various language attitudes; (b) generalised attitudes toward the L2 learning situation, such as the appraisal of the course or the teacher; and (c) interethnic contact and the resulting degree of linguistic self-confidence. The 1990s extended this conception by adding a number of cognitive and situation-specific variables to the existing paradigm (e.g., attributions and group cohesiveness), and there was a shift by some toward viewing motivation as a more dynamic factor that is in a continuous process of evolution and change according to the various internal and external influences the learner is exposed to (for a recent review, see Dörnyei, 2001a). The traditional approach of computing correlations between motivational and achievement factors gradually gave way to more complex, often qualitative, analyses of motivational antecedents and consequences, resulting in a colourful spectrum of new research directions. This chapter is intended to survey these recent developments and highlight some potentially fruitful areas for future research. First I summarise some general theoretical and research methodological advances, then I describe a number of novel motivational themes emerging in the literature.

THEORETICAL ADVANCES

The 1990s brought an extraordinary boom in L2 motivation research: Dörnyei (1998b) reviewed over 80 relevant L2 studies from the period, including more than ten newly designed theoretical motivation constructs. The extent of the shift in thinking is probably best characterised by the fact that a new motivation model developed by Robert Gardner's research laboratory (Tremblay and Gardner, 1995) in response to calls for the adoption of a wider vision of motivation (p. 505) did not actually include Gardner's best known motivational component, the integrative motive. Approaching the new millennium, the boundaries of L2 motivation were pushed even further, with researchers adopting varied and increasingly complex perspectives. A good cross-section of the emerging new wave of motivational thinking was provided by a colloquium at the annual conference of the American Association for Applied Linguistics (AAAL) in March, 2000 (Vancouver), and by an edited volume partly based on the colloquium proceedings which contains 20 chapters written by researchers from over ten different countries in Asia, Europe, and the Americas (Dörnyei and Schmidt, 2001).

From the point of view of their theoretical novelty, the following five motivational areas appear particularly interesting: social motivation; motivation from a process-oriented perspective; the neurobiological basis of motivation (see also Schumann, 2001b); L2 motivation and self-determination theory; and task motivation.

Social motivation

In an article deliberating upon the future of applied linguistics, McGroarty (1998) has argued that in order to be able to address the most intellectually challenging and practically significant aspects of language learning and teaching (p. 592), applied linguists need to understand better how the *social contexts* surrounding language acquisition affect the learning process. This view accords with the recent emergence of a broader perspective in the whole of the social sciences sometimes referred to as an ongoing second cognitive revolution (Hickey, 1997, p. 183) that emphasises the sociocultural roots of learning and cognition in general. Motivational psychology has not remained immune to the new spirit: in a pioneering article, Bernard Weiner (1994) set out to conceptualise *social motivation,* involving the complex of motivational influences that stem from the sociocultural environment rather than from the individual. During the past five years, social goals have been the subject of a great deal of research in psychology (cf., Juvonen and Nishina, 1997; Wentzel, 1999).

Because of the inherently social nature of L2 acquisition, the study of the linguistic impact of various sociocultural factors has, in fact, had a relatively long history in the L2 field. In addition to Gardner's motivation theory, social determinants of L2 learning were the focus of Giles and Byrne's (1982) intergroup model, Schumann's (1978) acculturation theory, and Clément and Noels's (1992; Noels and Clément, 1996) situated language identity theory, although these theories were not always expressed explicitly in motivational terms. In the light of the increasing social awareness in motivational psychology, this line of inquiry is of particular significance and, as emphasised by Clément and Gardner (2001), Dörnyei (1999), and McGroarty (2001), L2 motivation as a *situated construct* will undoubtedly be one of the main targets of future motivation research.

Motivation from a process-oriented perspective

A recent line of investigation that I have been actively involved in has examined the *temporal dimension* of motivation, that is, the way in which motivational processes happen in time. This question is, I believe, particularly important when the target of interest is a sustained learning process, such as the mastery of an L2, that can take several years to be successfully accomplished. During the course of such a lengthy process, student motivation does not remain constant but undergoes continuous changes; as Ushioda (1996a, p. 240) summarises, within the context of institutionalised learning especially, the common experience would seem to be motivational flux rather than stability. In view of this, the study of the dynamics of motivational change and the identification of typical sequential patterns and developmental aspects is likely to be a fruitful area for future research. Examples of a process-oriented conception in L2 motivation research include the separation of the *initiation of motivation* from the process of *sustaining motivation* by Williams and Burden (1997) and Ushioda's (1998, 2001) analysis of how new motivational orientations evolve while the learner is engaged in the L2 learning process.

The most complex process-oriented construct in the L2 field has been put forward by Dörnyei and Ottó (1998; cf. also Dörnyei, 2001a), who devised a *process model of L2 motivation* which organises the various motivational influences along a sequence of discrete actional events in the chain of instigating and enacting motivated behaviour. The model details how initial wishes and desires are first transformed into goals and then into operationalised intentions, which are seen as the immediate antecedents of action; after action has been initiated, an appraisal and an action control process mediate executive motivation, leading (hopefully) to the accomplishment of the goal and concluded by the final evaluation of the process. In a recent paper summarizing theoretical and practical implications of the process-oriented approach, I have argued (Dörnyei, 2000) that focusing on the temporal aspect of motivation is particularly useful because it allows researchers to discuss both preactional choice motivation (i.e., the motives leading to selecting goals and forming intentions) and volitional/executive factors during the actional phase (i.e., motives affecting ongoing learning behaviours) in a unified framework. Although this research perspective is still relatively new, during the past decade it has been adopted by a growing number of scholars within the field of educational psychology (cf., Snow, Corno, and Jackson, 1996), partly driven by recognition that, by accounting for the dynamic evolution of motivation, we can fully accommodate the learner's active role in controlling and shaping the affective foundation of the learning process. This perspective fits in well with the recent emphasis placed on the study of student self-regulation.

A neurobiological explanation of motivation

A novel line of research that has the potential to revolutionise the study of L2 motivation has been pursued by John Schumann (1998, 1999, 2001a), who has examined second language acquisition from a neurobiological perspective. This work has been one of the first attempts in the L2 field to incorporate the findings of neuroscience and to link the study of language to this particularly dynamically developing discipline within cognitive sciences. The key constituent of Schumann's theory is *stimulus appraisal*, which occurs in the brain along five dimensions: *novelty* (degree of unexpectedness/familiarity); *pleasantness* (attractiveness); *goal/ need significance* (whether the stimulus is instrumental in satisfying needs or achieving goals); *coping potential* (whether the individual expects to be able to cope with the event); and *self and social image* (whether the event is compatible with social norms and the individual's self-concept). These appraisals become part of the person's overall value system through a special memory for value and are largely responsible for providing the affective foundation of human action. Recently, Schumann (2001b) has broadened his theory by outlining a conception of learning as a form of *mental foraging* (i.e., foraging for knowledge), which engages the same neural systems as the ones used by organisms when foraging to feed or mate, and which is generated by an incentive motive and potentiated by the stimulus appraisal system.

Motivation and self-determination theory

One of the most influential paradigms in mainstream motivational psychology has been offered by *self-determination theory* (Deci and Ryan, 1985; Vallerand, 1997), which includes the well-known distinction between *intrinsic motivation* (i.e., performing a behaviour for its own sake in order to experience pleasure and satisfaction such as the joy of doing a particular activity or satisfying one's curiosity) and *extrinsic motivation* (i.e., performing a behaviour as a means to an end, that is, to receive some extrinsic reward such as good grades or a raise in salary, or alternatively to avoid punishment). The theory places the various types of regulations on a continuum between self-determined (intrinsic) and controlled (extrinsic) forms of motivation, depending on how internalised they are, that is, how much the regulation has been transferred from outside to inside the individual. Five distinct categories along this continuum have been identified: *external regulation* (i.e., motivation coming entirely from external sources such as rewards or threats); *introjected regulation* (i.e., externally imposed rules that students accept as norms they should follow in order not to feel guilty); *identified regulation* (i.e., engaging in an activity because the individual highly values it and sees its usefulness); *integrated regulation* (i.e., involving choiceful behaviour that is fully assimilated with the individual's other values, needs, and identity); and pure *intrinsic regulation*.

Because learning an L2 almost always contains a combination of external and internal regulatory factors, Noels and her colleagues (Noels, 2001; Noels, Clément, and Pelletier, 1999; Noels, Pelletier, Clément, and Vallerand, 2000) set out to explore how the orientations proposed by self-determination theory relate to various orientations that have traditionally been identified in the L2 field (e.g., instrumental and integrative orientations). Noels argues that applying the intrinsic/ extrinsic continuum can be helpful in organizing language learning goals systematically; she notes, further, that the paradigm is particularly useful for analyzing the classroom climate and the L2 teacher in terms of how much they promote either control or autonomy, a dimension of contrast which has immediate practical implications for educating autonomous, self-regulated L2 learners.

Task motivation

While it is true that certain motivational perceptions and attributes are generalised across learning situations and remain fairly fixed once established, it is also clear that other motivational factors show considerable variation according to the particular learning event with which they are associated, as evidenced by the varying degrees of interest and commitment students demonstrate toward different *learning tasks*. This duality of generalised and situation-specific motives was explicitly addressed by Tremblay, Goldberg, and Gardner (1995) when they distinguished *trait* and *state motivation*, the former involving stable and enduring dispositions, the latter transitory and temporary responses or conditions. The potential usefulness of such a distinction lies in its capacity to explain learners' situational and task preferences. Indeed, from a pedagogical point of view, it would be very beneficial to identify components of *task motivation*, because it would allow curriculum designers and language teachers to systematically select and administer tasks in a motivating manner, thus increasing learner engagement.

In a recent theoretical discussion of task motivation, Julkunen (2001) argues that students' task behaviour is fuelled by a combination of generalised and situation-specific motives according to the specific task characteristics, a position in line with Tremblay, Goldberg and Gardner's (1995) conclusion that trait motivation influences state motivation. In a study focusing on the motivational background of student engagement in communicative L2 tasks, Dörnyei and Kormos (2000) found that the learner's overall disposition toward task performance has at least three distinct layers: (a) generalised motives (e.g., integrativeness); (b) course-specific motives (i.e., the appraisal of the L2 course); and (c) task-specific motives (i.e., attitudes toward the particular task). The need to distinguish between the latter two aspects which have traditionally been lumped together under the situation-specific category was highlighted by the finding that, among the learners in our study who displayed low task-attitudes, those who had a favourable disposition toward the course in general participated more actively than those who had unfavourable attitudes toward both the course and the task. Furthermore, in discussing task motivation from a process-oriented perspective, I have argued elsewhere (Dörnyei, 2000) that in many learning situations there are various levels of increasingly focused task engagement (e.g., taking up studies in general, enrolling in a particular course, attending a particular lesson or carrying out a particular learning task) and that the resulting action-oriented contingencies, or mind sets, interact with each other in an as yet unspecified manner.

Finally, a further feature of task motivation which makes it a particularly intriguing research domain is the fact that the motivation of task participants is not independent of each other. It is easy to see that if one is paired up with a highly motivated or unmotivated partner, this pairing affects the person's own disposition toward the task; in other words, task motivation is *co-constructed* by the participants. I have found two sources of empirical evidence to support this claim in a follow-up to the Dörnyei and Kormos (2000) study (Dörnyei, 2002): First, students with low task attitudes performed significantly better when their partner demonstrated high task attitudes. Second, correlations of the individual students attitudes toward the course and the task with their task engagement index were .32 and .39, respectively, whereas the same correlations computed for the dyads joint performance were .59 and .52, respectively. That is, when the two task participants merged motivational and performance indices were correlated, the positive association was significantly higher.

NEW APPROACHES IN RESEARCH METHODOLOGY

L2 motivation research has traditionally followed the principles of quantitative social psychology, making extensive use of the various rating scales developed for the measurement of attitudes. Data obtained by such scales have been typically processed by means of inferential statistical procedures, such as correlation or factor analysis. While this research tradition is still strong and some particularly large scale investigations have been reported on recently (e.g., Dörnyei and Clément, 2001: 4,765 primary school pupils in Hungary; Schmidt and Watanabe, 2001: 2,089 university students in Hawaii; Inbar, Donitsa-Schmidt, and Shohamy, 2001: 1,690 secondary school students in Israel), I consider it a significant step in motivation research that traditional quantitative research methodologies have been increasingly complemented by qualitative approaches. Interpretive techniques such as in-depth interviews or case studies are in many ways better suited to explore the internal dynamics of the intricate and multilevel construct of student motivation than quantitative methods, and the richness of qualitative data may also provide new slants on old questions (Pintrich and Schunk, 1996). The potential of qualitative research methodology is well evidenced by a series of recent studies in this vein by Ushioda (1998, 2001), Williams and Burden and colleagues (1999, 2001), Nikolov (1999, 2001), and Syed (2001), focusing on issues as diverse as attributions, motivational development, classroom motives, self-motivation, and the motivational impact of the learner's self-concept.

Quantitative research methodology has not remained unchanged either: the most significant advance in this area has probably been the increasing application of structural equation modelling (SEM) to interpret large, multivariate datasets. Although LISREL models have been used in L2 motivation research since the early 1980s, the past five years have seen an increase in the utilisation of the procedure, partly because SEM programs have become easier to handle and more readily available (e.g., as part of SPSS). Recent studies employing SEM techniques include Gardner, Masgoret and Tremblay (1999), Gardner, Tremblay and Masgoret (1997), Laine (1995), Masgoret and Gardner (1999), and Yamashiro and McLaughlin (2000). Paul Tremblay (2001) offers a very useful methodological overview of how to apply the procedure to best effect.

EMERGING NEW MOTIVATIONAL THEMES

In the final section of this chapter, I would like to highlight a number of particularly interesting new research topics that have received attention during the past few years. This selection is necessarily subjective and the coverage of the various topics will be brief.

Teacher motivation

Although there is ample indirect evidence that the teacher's own level of motivation is infectious, that is, it has a significant impact on the students' learning commitment, hardly any research has been done in the past to explore this relationship. Recently, however, a number of theoretical and empirical studies have addressed the issue, providing a firm foundation for future research. Drawing largely on the (limited) work in mainstream psychology and the pioneering research in the L2 field by Pennington (1995) and Doyle and Kim (1999), I devoted a whole chapter in my general overview of L2 motivation (Dörnyei, 2001a) conceptualising and analyzing *teacher motivation*. During the past 18 months, some further data-based studies have contributed to our understanding of what makes teachers motivated and how this motivation is reflected in their students' achievement in work by Jacques (2001), Kassabgy, Boraie, and Schmidt (2001), and Masgoret, Bernaus, and Gardner (2000).

Motivation and learning strategy use

The relationship between learning strategy use and student motivation has been an issue of interest in educational psychology for a decade. Learning strategies are techniques that students apply of their own free will to enhance the effectiveness of their learning; in this sense, strategy use, by definition, constitutes instances of motivated learning behaviour. This close relationship between learning strategies and student motivation has been reflected by the fact that a well-known motivation test in educational psychology, the *Motivated Strategies for Learning Questionnaire (MSLQ*; Pintrich, Smith, and McKeachie, 1989) provides a combined measure of university students' motivational orientations and their use of different learning strategies. Recently Brown, Cunha, Frota, and Ferreira (2001) have produced a Portuguese version of the test for the purpose of administering it in Brazil. In the L2 field, the systematic study of the interrelationship between motivation and learning strategy use was initiated in the mid-1990s by Schmidt, MacIntyre, and colleagues (e.g., MacIntyre and Noels, 1996; Schmidt, Boraie, and Kassabgy, 1996); building on these results, Schmidt and Watanabe (2001) have recently further investigated the topic by obtaining data from over 2,000 university students.

Demotivation

Motivation research typically conceptualises a motive as a kind of inducement, that is, as a positive force whose strength ranges on a continuum from zero to strong. However, very little is usually said about motivational influences that have a detrimental rather than a positive effect on motivation, that is, which instead of energising action, de-energise it. This gap is all the more surprising because in educational contexts demotivation is a regrettably common phenomenon. In a review of the few relevant L2 studies available (Chambers, 1993; Dörnyei, 1998a; Oxford, 1998; and Ushioda, 1998), I have concluded that demotivation is a salient phenomenon in L2 learning and that teachers have a considerable responsibility in this respect (Dörnyei, 2001a). Of course, when interpreting demotivated student responses, we need to bear in mind Chambers's warning that we are living in an age when it is not 'cool' for students to show enthusiasm for anything and "Boredom is in" (p. 14). In any case, much further research is needed to do this important motivational factor justice.

Willingness to communicate (WTC)

A recent extension of motivation research with both theoretical and practical potential involves the study of the L2 speaker's *willingness* to engage in the act of L2 communication. Originally inspired by research in L1 communication studies (e.g., McCroskey and Richmond, 1991), MacIntyre, Clément, Dörnyei, and Noels (1998) have attempted to conceptualise *willingness to communicate* (WTC) in the L2, thereby explaining the individual's readiness to enter into discourse at a particular time with a specific person or persons, using a L2 (p. 547). The L2 WTC construct we have conceived is made up of several layers and subsumes a range of linguistic and psychological variables, including linguistic self-confidence (both state and trait); the desire to affiliate with a person; interpersonal motivation; intergroup attitudes, motivation and climate; parameters of the social situation; communicative competence and experience; and various personality traits. Thus, the model attempts to draw together a host of learner variables that have been well established as influences on second language acquisition/use, resulting in a construct in which psychological and linguistic factors are integrated in an organic manner. This line of inquiry may well have important educational implications in that generating a willingness to communicate in the foreign language is arguably a central if not *the* most central objective of modern L2 pedagogy. The study of the nature of WTC is an ongoing research effort (cf. e.g., MacIntyre, Babin, and Clément, 1999), and the WTC construct has also been successfully integrated as a predictor variable accounting for a very significant proportion of the variance in learner performance in the Dörnyei and Kormos (2000) study already mentioned.

Motivating language learners

From a practicing teacher's point of view, the most pressing question related to motivation is not *what* motivation is but rather *how* it can be increased. It is an unflattering indication of the detachment of research from classroom practice that very little work has been done in the L2 field to devise and test motivational strategies systematically. To be fair, some practical recommendations have been offered by Alison (1993), Brown (1994), Chambers (1999), Dörnyei (1994a), Oxford and Shearin (1994), and Williams and Burden (1997), but largely without any firm theoretical or empirical basis. The neglect of the study of motivational strategies is due in part to the fact that the experimental research required to test the effectiveness of a strategy is rather labour-intensive, and as Gardner and Tremblay (1994b) summarise, offers many methodological pitfalls. The only published empirical study on motivational strategies that I am aware of in the L2 field is a teacher survey that I conducted with a colleague (Dörnyei and Csizér, 1998) in which we asked 200 teachers to rate the importance of a set of 51 strategies and to estimate how often they used the strategies in their own practice. As a result, we compiled a list of Ten Commandments for motivating language learners. In addition, I have recently completed a systematic overview of all the major motivational strategies that have been documented in the educational psychological and second-language literature and summarised the findings in a teacher's handbook (Dörnyei, 2001a).

There are two further areas related to the question of how to motivate learners: the issues of *motivational change* and *motivational self-regulation*. With regard to the former, there have been a number of empirical studies in L2 motivation research investigating the motivational effects of bicultural excursion programs, methodological interventions, intensive language programs, and study trips abroad (for reviews, see Gardner, 1985a: Ch. 5; MacFarlane and Wesche, 1995; Morgan, 1993). Two recent large-scale investigations conducted in this vein are Inbar, Shohamy, and Donitsa-Schmidt (1999) and Inbar, Donitsa-Schmidt, and Shohamy (2001), both examining how the teaching of spoken Arabic affects the attitudinal/motivational disposition of Israeli school children.

Motivational self-regulation, or *self-motivation*, is an intriguing new area within motivational psychology, exploring ways by which we can endow learners with appropriate knowledge and skills to motivate themselves. Evidence that this idea is not completely naïve has been provided by the fact that in certain classrooms, even under adverse conditions and without any teacher assistance, some learners are more successful in keeping up their goal commitment than others. How do they do it? The only answer is that they apply certain self-management skills to overcome environmental distraction or competing/distracting emotional or physical needs/states. Ushioda (1997, 2001) analyzes several of the positive motivational thinking patterns that help someone to keep going. Based on Kuhl's (1987) and Corno and Kanfer's (1993) pioneering taxonomies, I have suggested (Dörnyei, 2001a) that self-motivating strategies are of five main types: commitment control strategies, metacognitive control strategies, satiation control strategies, emotion control strategies, and environmental control strategies. Some of the actual strategies listed under these categories are, in fact, very similar to the affective learning strategies conceptualised by Oxford (1990) and O'Malley and Chamot (1990).

CONCLUSION

This brief and necessarily sketchy overview has hopefully demonstrated that L2 motivation research is currently flourishing. The pioneers of the field have been joined by a new generation of international scholars and the scope of motivation research has been extended to cover a variety of related issues. As a result, we now have a vibrant mixture of approaches to the understanding of L2 motivation, comparable on a smaller scale to the multi-faceted motivational arena in psychology generally. The renewed interest in L2 motivation is at the same time indicative of a more general trend in applied linguistics whereby an increasing number of scholars combine psychological/psycholinguistic and linguistic approaches in order to better understand the complex mental processes involved in second language acquisition.

Chapter 6

Motivation in Action: Towards a Process-oriented Conceptualisation of Student Motivation

British Journal of Educational Psychology, (2000), 70, pp. 519-538.

Conceptualisations of motivation in the psychological literature show considerable variation both in terms of their scope and their level of analysis, but most researchers would agree that motivation theories in general attempt to explain three interrelated aspects of human behaviour: the *choice* of a particular action, *persistence* with it, and *effort* expended on it. That is, motivation is responsible for *why* people decide to do something, *how long* they are willing to sustain the activity, and *how hard* they are going to pursue it. There is far less agreement on the actual mediating factors and processes by means of which motivation achieves its impact on human behaviour, and the field of motivational psychology is characterised by a great number of competing or partially overlapping theories. This is, of course, no accident. Motivation theories attempt to explain nothing less than why people behave and think as they do, and human nature being as complex as it is, there are simply no cut and dried answers to be offered.

If we consider the history of motivation research during the 20th century, we can identify four principal challenges scholars have had to face which have played an important part in preventing a consensus. These are the challenges of: (a) *consciousness vs. unconsciousness* (i.e., distinguishing conscious vs. unconscious influences on human behaviour; cf. Sorrentino, 1996); (b) *cognition vs. affect* (i.e., explaining in a unified framework both the cognitive and the affective/emotional influences on human behaviour; cf. Weiner, 1992); (c) *context* (i.e., explaining the interrelationship of the individual organism, the individual's immediate environment and the broader sociocultural context; cf. Goodenow, 1992; Wentzel, 1999); and (d) *time* (i.e., accounting for the diachronic nature of motivation, that is, conceptualising a motivation construct with a prominent temporal axis; Heckhausen, 1991; Husman and Lens, 1999). These challenges feature prominently in Eccles, Wigfield, and Schiefele's (1998) recent summary of the field:

> The view of motivation has changed dramatically over the last half of the 20th century, going from a biologically based drive perspective to a behavioural-mechanistic perspective, and then to a cognitive-mediational/constructivist perspective. The conception of the individual as a purposeful, goal-directed actor who must coordinate multiple goals and desires across multiple contexts within both short- and long-range time frames currently is prominent. As we approach the 21st century, the role of affect and less conscious processes is re-emerging as a central theme. Complementing this more complex view of the psychology of motivation, researchers interested in the contextual influences on motivation are also adopting more complex and multicontextual frameworks. (p. 1074)

In this paper, I will focus on one of these challenges, the *challenge of time*, and discuss its particular relevance to the understanding of motivation in educational contexts. First I will provide an overview of past research on the temporal dimension of motivation and analyse the distinction between 'volition' and 'choice motivation'. Then I will describe an attempt at conceptualising a construct of student motivation with a featured temporal axis. Finally I will discuss the practical implications of a process-oriented conception of student motivation.

THE TEMPORAL DIMENSION OF MOTIVATION

In a comprehensive overview of motivation, German psychologist Heinz Heckhausen (1991) points out that a big problem in motivational psychology is the manifold meanings carried by the concept 'motivation', as the term is associated with phenomena as dissimilar as wishes, decision-making and action. He argues that one possible approach to restricting this manifoldness is to try to 'separate the sequence of events involved in being motivated into "natural", i.e., discrete phases' (p. 175), that is, to organise the various motivational factors and components along a temporal axis, reflecting the motivational process as it happens in time. Although motivation has traditionally been treated as a relatively stable emotional or mental state (measurable by tapping into it at one point of time, e.g., by administering a questionnaire), such a process-oriented view has been expressed by other researchers as well. For example, in their summary of motivation in education, Pintrich and Schunk (1996) argue that motivation involves various *mental processes* that lead to the initiation and maintenance of action; as they define the term, 'Motivation is the process whereby goal-directed activity is instigated and sustained' (p. 4). Similarly, goal theorist Martin Ford (1992) has also adopted a dynamic conception of motivation in his comprehensive system of goals, emotions and personal agency:

> Historically, motivation has been viewed either as a variable state that has little enduring significance (e.g., a state produced by a temporarily aroused drive or set of environmental contingencies) or as a stable trait representing a relatively fixed part of an individual's personality (as illustrated by concepts such as need for achievement and

locus of control). A major objective of this book is to add a *developmental orientation* to these traditional perspectives on motivation. (p. 15)

The unique feature of the approach Heckhausen, Kuhl and their associates (Heckhausen, 1991; Heckhausen and Kuhl, 1985; Gollwitzer, 1990; Kuhl, 1985, 1986, 1987, 1992; Kuhl and Beckmann, 1994) have proposed is the conscious attempt to distinguish separate, sequentially ordered phases within the motivated behavioural process, introducing a 'temporal perspective that begins with the awakening of a person's wishes prior to goal setting and continues through the evaluative thoughts entertained after goal striving has ended' (Gollwitzer, 1990, p. 55). A central feature of their theory (often referred to as 'Action Control Theory') is the separation of the *'predecisional phase'* associated with the intention-formation process and the *'postdecisional phase'* associated with the action implementation process within the motivated behavioural sequence:

- The *predecisional phase* can be seen as the decision-making stage of motivation (or 'choice motivation'), involving complex *planning* and *goal-setting* processes during which initial wishes and desires are articulated and evaluated in terms of their desirability and chance of fulfilment.
- The *postdecisional phase* is the implementational stage of motivation (or 'executive motivation'), related to the *volitional* aspects of goal pursuit, involving motivational *maintenance* and *control* during the enactment of the intention. Key issues to be examined here are the phenomena of action initiation, perseverance, and overcoming various internal obstacles to action.

Heckhausen and Kuhl believe that these two phases are energised and directed by largely different motives. 'Why one wants to do something and that one wants to do it is one thing, but its actual implementation and successful completion is another' (Heckhausen, 1991, p. 163). Indeed, only by assuming such a division of motives can we explain, for example, the frequent phenomenon of someone deciding to enrol in a voluntary language course (motivated by 'choice motivation'), then soon dropping out (because the 'executive motives' fail to sustain the instigation force), and then again re-enrolling in the course (since after the action engagement has been terminated, the predecisional forces become activated again).

In their comprehensive summary of affective and conative functions in the *Handbook of educational psychology*, Snow, Corno, and Jackson (1996) highlight the significance of Heckhausen and Kuhl's approach because, as the authors argue, the primary concern of most theories of human motivation in the past has been the 'choice' rather than the 'volitional/ executive' aspect, with little concern for analysing the motivational processes that underlie the progress from plans/goals to outcomes. Indeed, even the few motivation constructs which do include certain time elements typically focus on how broad issues such as past attributions or future goals affect the predecisional phase, rather than detailing sequences or patterns of motivational events and components (cf. Husman and Lens, 1999; Karniol and Ross, 1996; Raynor and Roeder, 1987). We must note that currently there appears to be a marked shift in this respect in motivational psychology, and this ongoing change of priorities has been initiated primarily in the domain of educational psychology. In the spirit of Heckhausen and Kuhl's (1985) 'Action Control Theory', a number of researchers both in Europe and North America have recently highlighted the importance of volitional/executive factors to understanding the conative foundation of learning within educational settings (e.g., Boekaerts, 1994; Corno, 1993, 1994; Corno and Kanfer, 1993; Kanfer, 1996; Snow and Jackson, 1994; Snow, Corno and Jackson, 1996; Wolters, 1998), an issue that will be discussed below.

THE SIGNIFICANCE OF A PROCESS-ORIENTED APPROACH TO UNDERSTANDING STUDENT MOTIVATION

A basic assumption underlying this paper is the belief that a focus on the temporal dimension of motivation is particularly important for the understanding of student motivation, and a process-oriented approach can also have considerable practical implications. This view has been supported by an increasing amount of research in various educational domains during the past decade, targeting two main topics: (a) motivational maintenance and volition, and (b) motivational evolution and fluctuation.

Motivational maintenance and volition

In a recent neurobiological account of foreign language learning, Schumann (1998) argues that 'sustained deep learning' processes, that is, extended processes during which the learner gains expertise in a field by means of skill/knowledge acquisition (e.g., the study of foreign languages, mathematics, or cooking, etc.), show different motivational characteristics from short-term activities or simple learning tasks, partly because in prolonged learning situations a major motivational function is to maintain the motivational impetus for a considerable period (often several years). Arguing in a similar vein, Kanfer (1996) contrasts the motivational basis of complex 'skill acquisition' processes with that of simpler activities that do not require task learning and which, once the commitment has been made, can be carried out swiftly and without difficulty (e.g., choosing between two job offers):

> When goals can be accomplished without task learning, the influence of motivation on behaviour is often largely a matter of choice. For example, the decision about which of two job offers to accept depends primarily on the individual's evaluation of the costs and benefits associated with each offer. Once a decision is made, however, the actions involved in implementing the goal of accepting the job are straightforward ... However, this is *not* the case in skill acquisition. During skill training, goal accomplishment proceeds slowly, as the individual develops an understanding of the task and proficiency in skills relevant to performance ... Continued task practice (i.e., persistence) is necessary to yield improvements in task performance. But for practice

to have a positive effect on performance, additional motivational mechanisms are required to sustain attention and effort over time and in the face of difficulties and failures. (p. 405)

In other words, complex learning contexts reduce the role of the motivational influences associated with the initial decision to pursue the goal, and highlight the importance of motivational influences that affect action during actual task engagement.

The significance of motivational influences that affect learning *during* action engagement rather than *prior to* action initiation in educational settings becomes even more obvious if we consider that in instructional contexts many of the decisions and goals are not really the learners' own products but are imposed on them by the system. This restricted student involvement in designing their own learning schedules or choosing which activities to engage in limits the importance of the 'choice' aspect of student motivation; instead, key motivational issues in the context of instruction involve maintaining assigned goals, elaborating on subgoals, and exercising control over other thoughts and behaviours that are often more desirable than concentrating on academic work (Corno, 1993). Thus, as Corno and Kanfer (1993, p. 305) summarise:

> The point is that motivation, conceptualised as a choice process, can be a necessary but insufficient condition for enhancing learning and performance in many school and work endeavours ... During pursuit of difficult or long-term goals, effective volitional control over action can enhance learning and performance, as well as sustain motivation for goal striving.

Motivational fluctuation and evolution

During the lengthy process of mastering certain subject matters, motivation does not remain constant but is associated with a dynamically changing and evolving mental process, characterised by constant (re)appraisal and balancing of the various internal and external influences that the individual is exposed to. Indeed, even within the duration of a single course, most learners experience a fluctuation of their enthusiasm/commitment, sometimes on a day-to-day basis. In Ushioda's (1996a) words, 'within the context of institutionalised learning especially, the common experience would seem to be motivational flux rather than stability' (p. 240). In order to account for the 'daily ebb and flow' of motivation (i.e., the level of effort invested in the pursuit of a particular goal oscillating between ups and downs), an adequate model of student motivation needs to have a featured temporal dimension that can accommodate systematic patterns of transformation and evolution in time. Berliner's (1989) observation summarises this position well:

> The emphasis by school people, focused as one might expect on daily life in classrooms and schools, almost always leads to an emphasis on the process of motivation and not on motivation as a product. The daily ebb and flow of motivation, while of crucial significance to the classroom teacher, charged as they are with the need to maintain a heterogeneous group's interest in learning, is of only mild interest to the parents, school researcher, and society at large. Teachers and school administrators focus on motivation as process, because they have to; the rest of us more often focus on motivation as product. (p. 326)

Interim summary: Motivation and time

Although motivation theories have traditionally viewed motivation as a rather stable construct, the 'time' dimension is relevant to motivation in at least two crucial areas:

1. Motivation to do something usually evolves gradually, through a complex mental process that involves initial planning and goal setting, intention formation and task generation, and finally action implementation and control.

2. In sustained, long-term activities, such as the mastering of a

school subject, motivation does not remain constant but is characterised by regular (re)appraisal and balancing of the various internal and external influences that the individual is exposed to, resulting in a somewhat fluctuating pattern of effort and commitment.

Thus, a process-oriented model of motivation should be able to account for both the generation and further development of motivation. Past research by Heckhausen, Kuhl, Corno, Kanfer and their associates suggests that an adequate process model should address the preactional and the actional phases of the motivational sequence separately, with the former being associated with 'choice motivation', the latter with 'volition' or 'executive motivation' . In order to account for both of these dimensions, motivation can be defined as *the dynamically changing cumulative arousal in a person that initiates, directs, coordinates, amplifies, terminates, and evaluates the cognitive and motor processes whereby initial wishes and desires are selected, prioritised, operationalised, and (successfully or unsuccessfully) acted out.*

A PROCESS MODEL OF STUDENT MOTIVATION

In order to draw together the results of past research on motivational processing, István Ottó and the author of this paper have devised a model of student motivation that follows through the motivational process from the initial wishes/desires to the completion of action and the subsequent retrospective evaluation (Dörnyei and Ottó, 1998; cf. also Dörnyei, 2000). The model was originally developed within the field of second language education, where, due to the long-lasting nature of mastering a foreign language, accounting for the time element is a particularly pressing issue (cf. Williams and Burden, 1997). It must be noted that our construct does not offer any radically new insights or identify novel motivational factors but rather attempts to synthesise various influential conceptualisations of motivation in a systematic process-oriented framework. Although the purpose of this paper is not to describe this model in detail, because it illustrates the strength and the limitations of the temporal conception of motivation, a brief description of its main components will follow.

Figure 6.1   Schematic Representation of Dörnyei and Ottó's (1998)
Process Model of Student Motivation

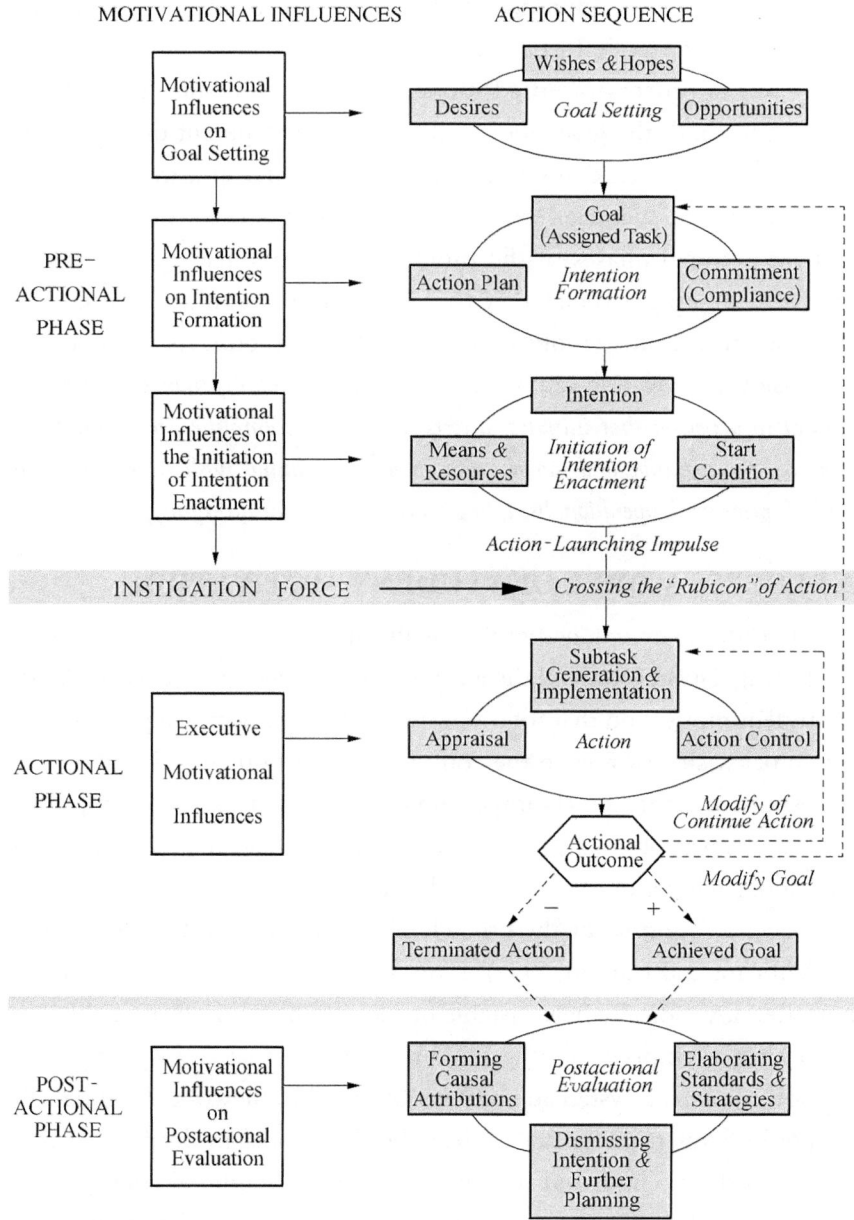

Figure 6.1 presents the schematic representation of our process model of student motivation, which contains two main dimensions: *Action Sequence* and *Motivational Influences*. The first dimension represents the behavioural process whereby initial wishes, hopes, and desires are first transformed into goals, then into intentions, leading eventually to action and, hopefully, to the accomplishment of the goals, after which the process is submitted to final evaluation. The second dimension of the model, motivational influences, includes the energy sources and motivational forces that underlie and fuel the behavioural process.

Following Heckhausen and Kuhl's Action Control Theory, the action sequence process has been divided into three main phases: *preactional phase*, *actional phase*, and *postactional phase*.

Preactional phase

The first stage of the motivated behavioural process is made up of three sub-phases, *goal setting, intention formation*, and the *initiation of intention enactment*. In some cases these follow on from each other very rapidly, almost simultaneously, but often there is a serious time lapse between them and the sequence can also terminate before reaching action. The antecedents of *goal setting* in our model are broad *wishes/hopes*, *desires* and *opportunities* (this last component is included because on occasions the starting point of the motivated behavioural process is not the individual's fantasy land but rather an emerging opportunity). However, it is assumed that every individual entertains a great number of wishes, hopes and desires, and comes across several action opportunities that, for some reason or another, will not be further pursued. Therefore, the first key component of the action sequence in our model is when the goal setting process reaches a concrete outcome, an actual *goal* — it is at this point that the motivated behavioural process begins in earnest.

Because it represents the first concrete decision the learner has taken, the goal is an important element in the motivated action sequence but it does *not* directly initiate action. The immediate antecedent of action in our model is the *intention*, which we see as being qualitatively different from a 'goal' in that it already involves *commitment*. This is an important distinction and it has been made in order to account for the huge difference which exists between the multiple goals and long-term plans the individual may harbour at a given point of time and the far fewer concrete intentions the individual will make actual resolutions to carry out. Commitment making can be a highly responsible personal decision, staking personal prestige and even material resources on the goal, and it may also involve foregoing other possible goals or pastimes, along with the rewards that might have attended them (Baumeister, 1996).

Adding commitment to a goal is a crucial step in the motivational process but it is not sufficient in itself to energise action if the goal is not translated into concrete steps the individual needs to take. Thus, a final necessary step in generating a fully operational intention is to develop a manageable *action plan* which contains the necessary technical details regarding the planned action, namely the

- *action schemata* (i.e., concrete guidelines such as subtasks to implement, and a number of relevant strategies to follow),
- *the time frame* (i.e., temporal specifications regulating the actual timing of the onset of action, e.g., a concrete time — 'I'll get down to it tomorrow' — or a condition — 'I'll do it when I have finished this').

Although a plan of action does not have to be fully completed before initiating an act — it may be (and usually is) finalised while acting — there must be at least a general action plan before one is able to act at all.

An intention is the immediate antecedent of action, but it is important to realise that action does not follow automatically from it. The right opportunity for starting the action may never materialise, or the means and resources may not be made available, leaving the intention unfulfilled. Thus, our model suggests that there are two necessary conditions for issuing an 'action-launching impulse' (Heckhausen and

Kuhl, 1985, p. 137):

- the availability of the necessary *means and resources*,
- the *start condition*.

Actional phase

The onset of action results in significant qualitative changes in one's motivation. Following Heckhausen (1991), we believe that it can be compared to crossing a metaphorical 'Rubicon': by actually embarking on the task (e.g., enrolling in a language course) the individual has committed him/herself to action and now the emphasis shifts from deliberation and decision-making to the implementation of action. In other words, 'choice motivation' is replaced by 'executive motivation'.

During the *actional phase* three basic processes come into effect:

1. *Subtask generation and implementation.* This refers to learning proper. Action initiation starts with implementing the subtasks that were specified by the action plan; however, as mentioned earlier, action plans are rarely complete (particularly not with sustained activities such as school learning) and during the course of action one continuously generates (or is assigned) new subtasks/subgoals.

2. A complex ongoing *appraisal* process. One continuously evaluates the multitude of stimuli coming from the environment and the progress one has made towards the action outcome, comparing actual events with predicted ones or with ones that an alternative action sequence would offer.

3. The application of a variety of *action control* mechanisms. These mechanisms, closely linked with the appraisal process, refer to 'knowledge and strategies used to manage cognitive and noncognitive resources for goal attainment' (Corno and Kanfer, 1993, p. 304). That is, action control processes involve self-regulatory mechanisms that are called into force in order to enhance, scaffold, or protect learning-specific action; active use of such mechanisms may 'save' the action when ongoing monitoring

reveals that progress is slowing, halting, or backsliding.

On the basis of the interplay of the appraisal and control processes, the ongoing action will lead to some kind of *actional outcome*: the optimal scenario is that the actor achieves his/her goal, whereas the other extreme is terminating the action completely. However, arriving at a dead end during the actional phase does not necessarily lead to action abandonment:

- If the motivational foundation of the initial wish or desire was sufficiently powerful, the individual may mentally step back to the preactional phase, revise the concrete goal to be pursued and form a new intention (e.g., by lowering the level of aspiration).
- Alternatively, by maintaining the original intention, the individual may fine-tune or modify the strategies and subtasks applied in the pursuit of the goal during the actional phase.
- Finally, in case of a temporary interruption, action can be continued at a later time.

Postactional phase

The postactional stage begins after either the goal has been attained or the action has been terminated; alternatively, it can also take place when action is interrupted for a longer period (e.g., a holiday). The main processes during this phase entail evaluating the accomplished action outcome and contemplating possible inferences to be drawn for future actions. Postactional evaluation is different from the ongoing appraisal process in that here the actors are not engaged in the actual behaviour any longer (that is, they are no longer in an implementation-oriented mind set), which allows them to adopt a broader perspective on the whole of the motivated behavioural process and its effect on their self-esteem (Heckhausen, 1991). During this phase, the actor compares initial expectancies and plans of action to how they turned out in reality and forms *causal attributions* about the extent the intended goal has been reached. This critical retrospection contributes significantly to accumulated experience, and helps to elaborate on the learner's *internal standards* and the repertoire of *action-specific strategies*; in fact, as Boekaerts (1988) emphasises, it is through this process that an individual can develop a stable identity as a successful learner.

The formation of adequate standards to compare actual and potential performance, and the extension of the repertoire of personalised action-control strategies already serve to prepare the ground for the future, but before further action can be taken, the initial intention has to be *dismissed* to give way to new wishes, goals, and intentions. An accomplished intention may clear the way for a subsequent intention leading to a more distant superordinate goal — in this case the postactional motivation process evolves into a preintentional phase and the cycle begins anew.

Motivational influences on the different action phases of the model

The action sequence dimension described above outlines the sequential pattern of the motivated behavioural process but it is incomplete without a second, complementary motivational dimension which is made up of the various *motivational influences* that fuel the actional sequence. These energy sources can be enhancing or inhibiting, depending on whether they contribute to the successful implementation of the goal or dampen the actor's endeavour. As such, motivational influences encompass the various motivational factors discussed in the motivation literature, including cognitive, affective, and situational variables, conditions, and processes.

As indicated in Figure 6.1, motivational influences form five clusters, according to the five specific phases of the motivated action sequence they affect (i.e., goal setting, intention formation, initiation of intention enactment, action, and postactional evaluation). The motivational influences associated with goal-setting are linked with an arrow to the determinants of intention formation, which are in turn linked to those of the initiation of intention enactment. This indicates that in the preactional phase the relevant motivational influences are assumed to have a cumulative effect, with the preactional motivational system operating like a series of interlinked filters: only those initial wishes/desires will lead to the eventual issue of an action launching impulse which are associated with sufficient cumulative energy sources at each stage of the preactional process to exceed the necessary threshold for stepping further. The overall resultant motivational force associated with the preactional phase is labelled in the figure as the *instigation force,* which determines the intensity of the initial action. Moving further 'down' Figure 6.1, however, the motivational influences associated with the actional phase are seen as not being *directly* related to the motives affecting the earlier and later stages of the process. This is in line with Heckhausen and Kuhl's 'Action Control Theory', which emphasises that 'executive motives' are largely different from the motives making up 'choice motivation'. Similarly, the motivational influences associated with the postactional evaluation phase are also assumed to be relatively independent of the forces affecting earlier phases of the model.

For space limitations the actual motivational influences cannot be elaborated on here (cf. Dörnyei, 2000) but from the perspective of the topic of this paper these are of less importance than the Action Sequence process. In general, motives related to the preactional phase involve factors ranging from the learner's subjective norms and the perceived values associated with the task, through the expectancy of success and various goal characteristics, to various environmental effects and the perceived behavioural control. Executive motives related to the actional phase concern, among other things, the appraisal of the learning experience, a sense of autonomy, the type of the classroom goal structure and the influences of the teacher and the peer group. The main postactional influences include attributional styles, self-concept beliefs and the effects of feedback and other evaluational cues. That is, a process model of the sort presented above can accommodate a variety of motives discussed in different motivation theories.

THEORETICAL PROS AND CONS

From a theoretical point of view, the main strength of a process-oriented approach is that it offers a potentially fruitful method of interpreting and integrating the manifold motivational factors that affect the student's learning behaviour in classroom settings. Using *time* as an organising principle offers a 'natural' way of ordering the relevant motivational influences into various distinct stages of the motivational sequence along a temporal axis. In fact, because the different sub-phases of the motivation process may be associated with different motives (as was argued earlier), ignoring 'time' in motivation models can (and often does) result in a situation when two theories are equally valid and yet contradict — simply because they refer to different *phases* of the motivation process.

A second area where a process-oriented approach might be fruitful is the study of the motivational basis of *learning tasks*. Although from an educational point of view understanding the motivational processes that fuel the quantity and quality of learners' on-task behaviour is particularly relevant, motivational psychology in the past has not generated substantial research on task motivation. Instead, human behaviour has been typically treated in a 'macro-sense', emphasising general action tendencies and their relationship with basic motivational influences rather than the specific motives that underlie the completion of particular tasks. As Winne and Marx (1989) explain in a pioneering study on task motivation, task researchers have traditionally viewed the key factor in task performance to be the 'students' *capability* to exercise cognition rather than the selection, temperament, or persistence of cognition (p. 227). A process-oriented model of motivation, with its inherent emphasis on volitional/executive aspects of goal attainment, offers a useful research paradigm for the micro-analysis of the various factors, conditions, constraints and processes that determine student success in learning tasks, and such a task-based approach also provides an interface for discussing cognitive and affective mechanisms in an integrated manner (Winne and

Marx, 1989).

The main weakness of a process-oriented approach as outlined above is that it implies that the actional process in question is well-definable and occurs in relative isolation, without any interference from other ongoing activities the learner is engaged in. Regrettably, this is rarely true in the strict sense. First of all, where exactly does 'action' start in an institutional context? Consider, for example, a first-year college student: where would be the 'Rubicon', that is, the borderline between preaction and action in his/her case? At the point when he/she decides to study in higher education? Or enrols in a particular university? Or selects his/her specific courses? Or attends a particular class? Or engages in a particular activity within this class? It seems logical that taking all these steps would result in somewhat different, increasingly action-oriented contingencies or 'mind sets' in the student. This, however, means that the 'choice' phase of one actional step might happen simultaneously to the executive phase of another, resulting in complex interferences: for example, with regard to the choice of specific courses, a student is already in the executive stage in terms of having started his/ her university studies and thereby facing the needs to carry out the various tasks associated with the official requirements, but the same student is still in the predecisional phase in the sense that he/she is still involved in contemplating the reasons for and against particular courses.

The second factor that complicates the picture concerns multiple engagement in a number of different activities at the same time, an issue already highlighted by Atkinson and Birch (1974) in their 'Dynamic Action Model' over two decades ago. Although it is true that people pursue only a limited number of actions at a time, various action episodes can be simultaneously active. For example, a new action may be initiated while the success of the previous action is still being evaluated. This is particularly valid for classroom contexts where student motivation and achievement are the product of a complex set of interacting goals and intentions of both academic and social nature (Juvonen and Nishina,

1997; Wentzel, 1999). However, hardly any research has been done to examine how people deal with multiple actions and goals, how they prioritise between them and how the hierarchies of superordinate and subordinate goals are structured. Recently, Boekaerts (1998) has proposed a pioneering action hierarchy framework for studying the complex of student motivation, but as she concludes, such research is still in a rather preliminary stage:

> Interdependent learning situations ... require students to balance many goals and tasks simultaneously. In these social settings students may feel that they have to satisfy incongruent or even mutually exclusive goals, such as acquiring a new cognitive skill (mastery goal), coping with the threat of losing face (well-being goal), pleasing one's friends and pleasing the teacher (social goals). It should be noted that these two social goals may or may not be congruent. We know very little about how students determine goal priority and how they change their learning strategies and goal commitment in function of perceived goal conflict. We also know next to nothing about students' capacity to regulate divergent goals in terms of top-down and bottom-up goal processes (movement in their goal hierarchy) and about the tradeoffs that students make in terms of investing resources. Future research should address these issues. (Boekaerts, 1998, p. 21)

It is likely that a purely cognitive approach will not be adequate for understanding how learners prioritise amongst multiple goals. Although most of the contemporary motivation literature takes it for granted that human behaviour can be explained by factors that the individual is aware of, it requires little justification that this is *not* always so. In fact, early theories of motivation were strongly influenced by Freud's (e.g., 1966) emphasis on deep, pervasive drives and instincts as being powerful directive influences on human behaviour. Classroom learning is an intensely interpersonal process, and psychoanalytic theory has provided ample evidence that interpersonal relations are often affected by unconscious 'scripts' (such as transference, projections, defence mechanisms, etc.; for a review, see Ehrman and Dörnyei, 1998); thus, within classroom contexts unconscious relationship patterns inevitably influence the students' ongoing on-task and social behaviour. In a review of the conscious/unconscious issue, Sorrentino (1996) acknowledges the significance of non-conscious forces and concludes that behaviour *can* happen without reference to conscious thought, although conscious cognitions can inhibit or further instigate such behaviour and can also strengthen or weaken other competing action tendencies.

A further aspect of the conscious/non-conscious issue has been highlighted by Bargh (1990), who argues in his 'auto-motive' model that humans do a lot of things as a matter of routine, and such habitual actions are often not under direct motivational control but are automatically linked with mental representations of the social environment without the individual being aware of the source of goal-directed action. The 'purely cognitive' picture is further muddled if we consider the impact of the individuals' *mood states*. In a thought-provoking article, Schwarz and Bohner (1996) draw attention to the fact that depending on what mood people are in, they tend to find goals more or less attractive, tend to assess their own resources and the situation in a more or less favourable way, and tend to evaluate their performance as more or less satisfactory. This phenomenon is well-known to many classroom practitioners, yet little controlled research has been done to understand the exact nature of such mood-related biases.

The above considerations point to the need to extend cognitive paradigms in future research by including various motivational influences that are not under the individual's direct control. In addition, motivational psychology has recently placed an increasing emphasis on presenting student motivation in a developmental framework (for a review, see Wigfield, Eccles, and Rodriguez, 1998) and, in accordance with this, an adequate process model will also have to incorporate a developmental aspect.

PRACTICAL IMPLICATIONS OF A PROCESS-ORIENTED CONCEPTION OF STUDENT MOTIVATION

As argued earlier, a process-oriented approach can be particularly fruitful with regard to the understanding of student motivation, which is why this line of enquiry has been pursued primarily within the domain of educational psychology during the 1990s. There are two areas where such an approach can have considerable practical implications: (a) the systematic development of *motivational strategies* that the teacher can apply to generate and maintain motivation in his/her learners; and (b) the formulation of *action control* or *self-motivating strategies* that enable learners to take personal control of the affective conditions and experiences that shape their subjective involvement in learning.

Devising motivational strategies

With motivation being a key factor in learning success, teacher skills in *motivating* learners should be seen as central to teaching effectiveness (Galloway et al., 1998). However, as Good and Brophy (1994) summarise, this practical aspect of motivation has not received much scholarly attention until recently, 'so that teachers were forced to rely on unsystematic "bag-of-tricks" approaches or on advice coming from questionable theorising' (p. 212). One reason for this neglect may have been that 'pure' theories of motivation, that is, models that represent a single theoretical perspective and are therefore anchored around a few selected motivational aspects (e.g., around a key concept or process), while largely ignoring research that follows different lines, do not lend themselves to effective classroom application. Several researchers have pointed out that the intricate motivational life of actual classrooms can be best accounted for only by means of detailed and most likely eclectic constructs that represent multiple perspectives. For example, Graham (1994) states that 'classroom motivational life is complex. No single word or principle such as reinforcement or intrinsic motivation can possibly capture this complexity' (p. 47), and the same belief was expressed by Weiner (1984) as follows:

> A theory of student motivation ... will have to include many concepts and their interrelationships. Any theory based on a single concept, whether that concept is reinforcement, self-worth, optimal motivation, or something else, will be insufficient to deal with the complexity of classroom activities. (p. 18)

In accordance with these claims, in the *Handbook of Educational Psychology* Stipek (1996) extends the need for comprehensiveness to classroom teachers' motivational practices:

> Although different factors have been emphasised at different times in the history of research on achievement motivation, all are assumed to play a role. Thus, teachers who want to provide an educational program that maximises student motivation must attend to all of these sets of factors. (p. 86)

A process-oriented framework can offer a solid theoretical background to devising *motivational strategies* because of its comprehensiveness: following through the motivational process from the initial arousal of the motivation to the completion and evaluation of the motivated action allows researchers to integrate various lines of research in a unified construct, with a special emphasis placed on executive motives that energise the implementation of various learning tasks. Taking this approach, I have drawn up a taxonomy of motivational strategies (Dörnyei, 2001a) that contains the following main classes:

- *Creating the basic motivational conditions* (appropriate teacher behaviours and a good relationship with the students; a pleasant and supportive classroom atmosphere; a cohesive learner group with appropriate group norms).
- *Generating initial motivation* (enhancing the learners' subject-

matter-related values and attitudes; increasing the learners' 'goal-orientedness'; increasing the learners' expectancy of success; making the curriculum relevant for the learners; creating realistic learner beliefs).

- *Maintaining and protecting motivation* (setting 'proximal subgoals'; presenting and administering tasks in a motivating way; increasing the quality of the learning experience; increasing the learners' self-confidence; allowing learners to maintain a positive self and social image; creating learner autonomy; promoting self-motivating learner strategies).

- *Rounding off the learning experience: Encouraging positive self-evaluation* (promoting attributions to effort rather than to ability; providing motivational feedback; increasing learner satisfaction, and the issue of rewards, grades and punishment).

Formulating action control/self-motivating strategies

Besides providing a comprehensive framework to guide practical work on devising motivational strategies, a process-oriented approach has a further, somewhat related feature that makes it beneficial for promoting effective, self-regulated learning: its emphasis on *action control mechanisms*. These mechanisms, as conceptualised originally by Kuhl (1985), can be seen as a subclass of *self-regulatory strategies* concerning the learners' self-motivating function. As its name also implies, a central component of Heckhausen and Kuhl' s Action Control Theory is 'action control' , which has been explained by Kuhl (1986, p. 424) as follows:

> We know from everyday experience that we do not always carry out our intentions. Choice of a goal and persistence in striving for it do not guarantee that goal-related intentions will be actually performed. In many cases, a certain amount of effort is needed to enact an intention. It takes effort to maintain an intention, to shield it from the press resulting from competing action tendencies, and to strengthen it if necessary until

it has been carried into effect. I assume that this kind of self-regulatory effort is required not only for enacting 'difficult' intentions (e.g., to quit smoking) but also for enacting seemingly easy intentions (e.g., to make a phone call). Since 'effort' is a phenomenal summary term that probably refers to a variety of mechanisms, our task is to investigate the specific mechanisms that mediate the enactment of intentions. I have proposed the term 'action control' to refer to these self-regulatory mechanisms.

In academic situations action control can be characterised, using Corno's (1993) words, 'as a dynamic system of psychological control processes that protect concentration and directed effort in the face of personal and/or environmental distractions, and so aid learning and performance' (p. 16), and it is particularly important in prolonged learning situations as action control mechanisms help individuals to maintain their priorities in the face of temptation and adversity. Corno (1994) summarises the academic relevance of volitional (i.e., action control) strategies as follows:

> The world is replete with enchanting distractions for even the most eager of students. Schools are complex social networks as well as places of work. Homes provide children with television, computer games, and compact discs. After-school clubs engulf what little spare time children have. To succeed academically, students must learn to cope with the competition between their social and intellectual goals and to manage and control the range of other distractions that arise. Volitional strategies have a promising role to play in achieving these goals. (p. 248)

Kuhl (1985, 1987) proposed a taxonomy of six main types of action control strategies and, being the first of its kind, this taxonomy has been influential in shaping subsequent research into the self-regulatory mechanisms related to self-motivation. Adapting this conceptualisation to educational contexts, Corno and Kanfer (1993, pp. 311-313) distinguish four large classes of 'volitional control strategies':

1. *Metacognitive control strategies*: intentionally ignoring attractive alternatives or irrelevant aspects and adopting a 'let's not ruminate and procrastinate any longer but get down to doing it' attitude (e.g., 'Think of first steps to take and get started right away' or 'Set contingencies for performance that can be carried out mentally, such as self-reward; self-imposed penance').

2. *Emotion control strategies*: managing emotional states that might disrupt or inhibit action (e.g., 'Generate useful diversions' or 'Recall your strengths and your available resources; remember, you've done this kind of thing before').

3. *Motivation control strategies*: enhancing the motivational basis of intentions to pursue a goal (e.g., 'Add a twist to make this project more interesting' or 'Escalate goals by prioritising and imagining their value').

4. *Environmental control strategies*: manipulating aspects of the individual's environment in a way that the resulting socio-environmental pressure or control makes the abandoning of the intention more difficult or by creating safeguards against undesirable environmental temptations (e.g., 'Move away from noise and distraction' or 'Make a social commitment of doing something, e.g., preparing all your home assignments or not being late').

The issue of motivational self-regulation has attracted increasing attention by other researchers as well during the past few years. Baumeister (1996), for example, emphasised action maintenance strategies that enable people to regulate the cognitive and emotional impact of ego threats. By consciously ignoring face-threatening stimuli, by adopting 'defensive preoccupation' (i.e., focusing on an alternative stimulus that can absorb attention), by summoning positive feelings/happy memories to defuse the threat, or by constructing their narratives of events so as to place themselves in a more positive light, people may self-regulate cognitive processes and thus protect their self-esteem from threatening implications. Garcia and Pintrich (1994) highlight one particular strategy that serves to maintain self-worth: 'self-affirmation'. If an individual experiences a negative evaluation of the self in a valued domain, a self-affirmative process is initiated, and the individual will 'seek to affirm a positive global evaluation of the self by activating positive conceptions of the self (those in other, equally valued domains)' (p. 137).

In sum, the analysis of self-motivating strategies appears to be one of the most promising domains of applied motivation research. Much of past research on self-regulated learning has focused on students' knowledge and control of cognitive and metacognitive strategies, and work by Corno, Kanfer, Pintrich and their colleagues has evidenced that motivational self-regulation, or 'metamotivational skills' in Boekaerts's (1995) term, constitute an important aspect of academic self-regulation skills. Recent empirical support to this claim has been provided by Wolters (1998), who found that college students regulated their effort in academic tasks by using a variety of cognitive, volitional and motivational strategies.

CONCLUSION

In this paper I have argued that an increased attention to the temporal aspect of motivation (i.e., how motivational processes operate in time) can have important theoretical and practical implications for the study of student motivation. A process-oriented approach shifts the emphasis from preactional 'choice motivation' (which has been the traditional concern of motivation research) to volitional/executive aspects of goal attainment during the actional phase; that is, it addresses motivation in ongoing social activities such as classroom learning. The process model of student motivation that I have presented was intended to illustrate the potential of such an approach for integrating various, generally independent research trends into a unified framework, but it also highlighted a number of theoretical challenges that will need to be responded to in future research. I have argued that it is not at all clear at present where predecisional deliberation ends and 'action' starts in complex, prolonged learning activities such as mastering school subjects.

In many learning situations there are various levels of increasingly focused task engagement (e.g., taking up studies in general, enrolling in a particular course, attending a particular lesson or carrying out a particular learning task) and the resulting action-oriented contingencies or mind sets interact with each other in an as yet unspecified manner. A related issue concerns how simultaneous action that the learner is engaged in affects task motivation, that is, how multiple goals are prioritised and how the hierarchy of superordinate and subordinate goals is structured. This question is unlikely to be addressed adequately from a purely cognitive perspective, because non-conscious motives and scripts, as well as automated action schemata and various mood states, appear to have a considerable impact on ongoing social behaviour.

Although the line of research presented in this paper is still relatively new, during the past decade it has been adopted by an increasing number of scholars within the field of educational psychology. This reflects a growing awareness of the benefits of looking at motivation as being associated with a process that can account for the dynamic evolution of motivation and which can also fully accommodate the learner's and the teacher's active role in controlling and shaping the affective foundation of the learning process. This paper was intended to provide an integrative review of past research efforts along these lines and to demonstrate the educational relevance of a process-oriented conceptualisation of student motivation.

Chapter 7

The Motivational Basis of Language Learning Tasks

In Robinson, P. (Ed.). (2002). Individual differences in second language acquisition (pp. 137-158). Amsterdam: John Benjamins.

INTRODUCTION

The study of *language learning tasks* offers a particularly fruitful research direction towards the understanding of how instructed second language acquisition (SLA) actually takes place. By focusing on tasks, researchers are able to break down the complex, prolonged learning process into discrete segments with well-defined boundaries, thereby creating researchable behavioural units that have a well-definable profile in terms of the L2 input/output and the language processing operations involved. Thus, tasks can be seen as primary instructional variables or building blocks of classroom learning, and for research purposes they can be used as "logical models that describe what students are doing in classrooms and the context of their actions" (Winne and Marx, 1989, p. 224). For this reason, during the past decade SLA research has paid increasing attention to the analysis of tasks, looking at them both from a theoretical (language processing) and a methodological (instructional design) perspective (e.g. Bygate, 1999; Bygate, Skehan and Swain, 2001; Crookes and Gass, 1993a, 1993b; Dörnyei and Kormos, 2000; R. Ellis, 2000; Foster, 1998; Foster and Skehan, 1996; Long and Crookes, 1992; Robinson, 1995a, 2001a, 2001b; Skehan, 1998a, 1998b; Skehan and Foster, 1997, 1999; Swain and Lapkin, 2000; Willis, 1996; Yule and Powers, 1994).

Taking tasks as the basic level of analysis is also a logical step in the study of motivation to learn a foreign/second language (L2). Traditionally, L2 motivation was examined in a broad sense, by focusing on the learners' overall and generalised disposition towards learning the L2, but the 1990s shifted the emphasis towards a more situated approach, with more and more studies investigating how student motivation is reflected in concrete classroom events and processes (for a recent review, see Dörnyei, 2001c). While the former macro perspective is more relevant from a social psychological perspective as it allows researchers to characterise and compare the motivational pattern of whole learning communities and then to draw inferences about intercultural communication and affiliation, the latter micro perspective is more in line with an educational approach whereby the significance of motivation is seen in its explanatory power of why learners behave as they do in specific learning situations. This emerging new perspective of motivation has often been referred to as the 'situation-specific' approach (cf. Dörnyei, 1996; Julkunen, 1989, 2001), and the study of *task motivation* can be seen in many ways as the culmination of this approach: motivation can hardly be examined in a more situated manner than within a task-based framework.

In the light of these considerations, the purpose of this paper is to examine the main characteristics of task motivation. As a preliminary, we should note that although the understanding of the motivational processes fuelling the quantity and quality of learners' on-task behaviour is highly relevant both from a theoretical and a practical point of view, motivational psychology in the past has not generated substantial research on the subject (for a valuable exception, see Winne and Marx, 1989). This paper will address one key aspect of task motivation, its *dynamic nature*, examining how motivation is shaped by various internal and external forces/conditions in an interactive and ongoing manner. I will argue that the actual degree of motivational force associated with an individual's specific on-task behaviour is the composite outcome of a number of distinct motivational influences, many of which are related to the various broader 'contexts' each task is surrounded with, such as:

- the language class the task takes place in;
- the language course the class is part of;
- the school that offers the language course; and
- the particular language that the course is targeting.

I believe that all these 'contexts' function as *'motivational contingencies'* in that they have some bearing on the final task motivation. I will propose a process-oriented approach that is suited for an analysis of such dynamic relationships, and I will also present empirical data from a task-based classroom study that examined the motivational basis of L2 learners' task engagement.

MAIN ASPECTS OF TASK MOTIVATION

In order to study the motivational characteristics of instructional tasks, we first need a definition of what a 'task' is. In view of the conception proposed above whereby instructional tasks are discrete units of situated learning behaviours, the most important specification for a 'task' is the identification of its boundaries, that is, determining when a particular task starts and ends. For the purpose of this study I will conceive a learning task as a complex of various goal-oriented mental and behavioural operations that students perform during the period between the teacher's initial task instructions and the completion of the final task outcome1. Accordingly, learning tasks constitute the interface between educational goals, teacher and students.

Let us start the examination of task motivation by considering a basic distinction proposed by Tremblay, Goldberg and Gardner (1995), who distinguished *trait* and *state motivation*, the former involving stable and enduring dispositions, the latter transitory and temporary responses or conditions. The trait/state distinction has been applied in psychology with regard to a number of different individual difference variables (e.g. anxiety; cf. MacIntyre, 1999, this volume) and from the point of view of motivation this dichotomy makes good sense: It is highly likely that, when confronted with a particular task, a learner will be motivated both by generalised, task-independent factors (e.g. overall interest in the subject matter) and situation-specific, task-dependent factors (e.g. the challenging nature of the task). Task motivation would then be the composite of these two motivational sources (cf. Julkunen, 2001).

Although the trait/state approach is a possible way of conceptualising task motivation, its weakness is that it suggests a rather static conception. Instructional tasks involve a series of learner behaviours that can last for a considerable period (e.g. up to several hours) and it is unlikely that the learner's motivation during this period will remain constant. Thus, instead of assuming a simple and stable 'state motivation' component to account for the situation-specific aspect of task motivation, a more accurate characterisation may be provided by taking a *process-oriented approach* that, as the term suggests, looks at the dynamic motivational processes that take place during task completion. The validity of such a conception has received empirical confirmation in a recent study by MacIntyre, MacMaster and Baker (2001), who found a clear factor analytic distinction between what they termed "attitudinal motivation" (associated with Gardner's approach) and "action motivation" (associated with Kuhl's process-oriented *'action control'* approach — see below).

MOTIVATION FROM A PROCESS-ORIENTED PERSPECTIVE

A *process-oriented approach* attempts to account for the ongoing changes of motivation over time. From this perspective, motivation is not seen as a static attribute but rather as a dynamic factor that displays continuous fluctuation, going through certain ebbs and flows. In 1998, István Ottó and I attempted to draw up a process model that would describe this evolution (Dörnyei and Ottó, 1998), outlining how initial wishes and desires are first transformed into goals and then into operationalised intentions, and how these intentions are enacted, leading (hopefully) to the accomplishment of the goal and concluded by the final evaluation of the process. Drawing on the work of German psychologists Heinz Heckhausen and Julius Kuhl (e.g. Heckhausen, 1991; Heckhausen and Kuhl, 1985; Kuhl and Beckmann, 1994), we suggested that from a temporal perspective at least three distinct phases of the motivational process should be separated (see Figure 7.1, for a schematic representation):

- *Preactional stage*: First, motivation needs to be *generated* — the motivational dimension related to this initial phase can be referred to as *choice motivation*, because the generated motivation leads to the selection of the goal or task that the individual will pursue.

- *Actional stage*: Second, the generated motivation needs to be actively *maintained* and *protected* while the particular action lasts. This motivational dimension has been referred to as *executive motivation*, and it is particularly relevant to learning in classroom settings, where students are exposed to a great number of distracting influences, such as off-task thoughts, irrelevant distractions from others, anxiety about the tasks, or physical conditions that make it difficult to complete the task.

- *Postactional stage*: Finally, there is a third phase following the completion of the action — termed *motivational retrospection* — which concerns the learners' *retrospective evaluation* of how things went. The way students process their past experiences in this retrospective phase will determine the kind of activities they will be motivated to pursue in the future.

Figure 7.1.   A Process Model of Learning Motivation in the L2 Classroom

Preactional Stage	**Actional Stage**	**Postactional Stage**
CHOICE MOTIVATION	EXECUTIVE MOTIVATION	MOTIVATIONAL RETROSPECTION
Motivational functions:	**Motivational functions:**	**Motivational functions:**
• Setting goals • Forming intentions • Launching action	• Generating and carrying out subtasks • Ongoing appraisal (of one's performance) • Action control (self-regulation)	• Forming causal attributions • Elaborating standards and strategies • Dismissing intention & further planning
Main motivational influences:	**Main motivational influences:**	**Main motivational influences:**
• Various goal properties (e.g. goal relevance, specificity and proximity) • Values associated with the learning process itself, as well as with its outcomes and consequences • Attitudes towards the L2 and its speakers • Expectancy of success and perceived coping potential • Learner beliefs and strategies • Environmental support or hindrance	• Quality of the learning experience (pleasantness, need significance, coping potential, self and social image) • Sense of autonomy • Teachers' and parents' influence • Classroom reward- and goal structure (e.g. competitive or cooperative) • Influence of the learner group • Knowledge and use of self-regulatory strategies (e.g. goal setting, learning and self-motivating strategies)	• Attributional factors (e.g. attributional styles and biases) • Self-concept beliefs (e.g. self-confidence and self-worth) • Received feedback, praise, grades

Because students are rarely in the position of choosing the tasks they would like to engage in, with regard to the understanding of task motivation it is the second, actional, stage that is of the greatest importance for us. According to a process-oriented conception, the learner enters this actional stage with a certain level of motivation (which can be called the 'instigation force'), but very soon a new set of motivational influences — associated with the immediate learning situation — come into force, and a complex process of 'motivational processing' commences (Winne and Marx, 1989).

This involves two interrelated submechanisms: *ongoing appraisal* and *action control*. While learners are engaged in a task, they continuously *appraise* the multitude of stimuli coming from the environment and the progress they have made towards the action outcome, comparing actual performances with predicted ones or with ones that alternative action sequences would offer. This appraisal process is closely linked with a second mechanism, *action control*, which refers to "knowledge and strategies used to manage cognitive and noncognitive resources for goal attainment" (Corno and Kanfer, 1993, p. 304). That is, action control processes denote self-regulatory processes that are called into force in order to enhance, scaffold or protect learning-specific action; active use of such mechanisms may 'save' the action when ongoing monitoring reveals that progress is slowing, halting or backsliding.

'Motivational processing', then, is seen as the interplay of the appraisal and the action control systems. Following Winne and Marx's (1989) reasoning, negative signals from the appraisal system may trigger the need to activate action control strategies, and if appropriate schemata are available, certain mental or behavioural adjustments are made and the motivational level necessary for sustaining action is restored. The effective operation of executive motivational processing is, therefore, the function of the learner's willingness to activate action control mechanisms and the availability of these (cf. Dörnyei, 2001c, for more detail).

In a recent paper (Dörnyei, 2000), I have concluded that the main strength of a process-oriented approach with regard to the understanding of student motivation is that it makes it possible to interpret and integrate the manifold motivational factors that affect the student's learning behaviour in classroom settings. Using *time* as an organising principle provides a natural way of ordering the relevant motivational influences into various distinct stages of the motivational sequence along a temporal axis. However, one problematic aspect of such an approach is that it implies that the actional process in question is well-definable and occurs in relative isolation, without any interference from other ongoing activities the learner is engaged in. Regrettably, this is rarely true in the strict sense. Where exactly does 'action' start in an educational context? Consider, for example, first-year college students: Where would be the borderline between pre-action and action in their case? At the point when they decides to study in higher education? Or enrol in a particular university? Or select the specific courses they will take? Or attend a particular class? Or engage in a particular activity within this class?

It seems logical to assume that taking all these steps will result in somewhat different, increasingly action-oriented contingencies or 'mind sets' in the students. This, however, means that the 'choice' phase of one actional step might happen simultaneously with the executive phase of another, resulting in complex interferences: For example, a British secondary school pupil is in the actional/executive stage of learning in the sense that he/she is actively attending school and trying to meet various curricular requirements, but at the same time he/she may still be in the preactional/choice phase in the sense that he/she may still be contemplating which 'A' level courses to take for specialisation.

Although I believe that the conception of task motivation as a complex of motivational influences associated with various levels of action-oriented contingencies or mind sets provides a more elaborate description than that offered by the trait/state approach, this conception is still incomplete if it does not take into account the *dynamic nature* of motivational processing. It is very likely that the various motivational influences *interact* with each other; for example, certain general orientations (such as an instrumental orientation) may cause the learner to perceive or responded to certain situation-specific motivational features differently from the perceptions/ reactions associated with other orientations. In other words, an IF-THEN contingency can occur whereby motives of different levels of generalisation activate each other. Indeed, it is not difficult to find evidence for such IF-THEN contingencies in the L2 motivation literature. For example, in a study conducted by Noels, Clément and Pelletier (1999) focusing on the motivational impact of the language teacher's communicative/ instructional style, the researchers have found that — quite logically — the degree of the teachers' support of student autonomy and the amount of informative feedback they provided were in a direct positive relationship with the students' sense of self-determination (autonomy) and enjoyment. However, this directive influence did not reach significance with students who pursued learning primarily for extrinsic (instrumental) reasons, which indicated that those learners who studied a language primarily because they had to were less sensitive to this aspect of teacher influence than those who did it of their own free will.

In my own research, in a study conducted together with Judit Kormos (Dörnyei and Kormos, 2000) we found that students with a more positive versus a more negative attitude towards a particular task displayed significant differences from each other in a number of respects. Their linguistic self-confidence only affected their task engagement among students with a positive attitude towards the task, and social factors such as the learners' social status (i.e. social standing/position in class) affected task engagement positively amongst students with positive and negatively amongst students with negative task attitudes. In addition, when we changed the language of the tasks from English as a second language to the students' mother tongue (L1), we obtained a strikingly different motivational pattern, with several significant *negative* correlations emerging between motivational variables and task engagement factors: in the L1 version learners who did not particularly like the English classes and did not see much point in learning English in general appeared to be more active than their motivated peers. These findings suggested to us that the predictor variables of task performance constituted a complex, multi-level and hierarchical construct.

RESEARCH QUESTION AND DESIGN

The study reported in this paper is a follow-up to the Dörnyei and Kormos (2000) investigation and uses data from the same large-scale British-Hungarian research project conducted together with Martin Bygate (University of Leeds) and Anita Csölle, Dorottya Holló, Krisztina Károly and Nóra Németh (all from Eötvös University, Budapest). The research objective was to examine a yet uncharted aspect of motivational processing, the motivational impact of the fellow-participant in a task. It has been suggested by several scholars in the past that peer influences constitute an important motivational factor (for a review, see Dörnyei, 2001c), but I am not aware of any concrete research that would have examined this relationship in actual terms. Thus, the main research question of this study is to examine the extent to which task motivation is *co-constructed*, that is, shaped by the dynamic interplay of the task participants' motivation. ①

The design of this study was relatively straightforward: Following a correlational research design, a number of individual difference (mainly motivational) and language variables were identified and assessed, and then correlations were computed between them. The language variables were objective measures of the participants' actual language output in a communicative language task (performed in dyads): the *size of speech* produced (measured by the number of words) and the *number of turns*

---

① We must note, however, that the teacher's and the students' views concerning these task boundaries might not coincide (MacIntyre, personal communication, 8 May 2001), which raises the broader question as to whether we can speak about the 'task' in general, without separating different task perceptions according to the teacher, the students and perhaps even the task designer (cf. Winne and Marx, 1989).

the participants' exchange comprised. These were taken as an index of the learners' *task engagement*, which is a central issue in instructed SLA because it is a prerequisite to any language processing to take place; to put it broadly, if students are not actively involved in the instructional tasks and do not produce a certain amount of language output, L2 learning is unlikely to be effective in developing communicative skills. Therefore, all the cognitive and linguistic processes discussed in the L2 task literature depend, to some extent, on this initial condition. This importance attached to task engagement is consistent with findings in educational psychology; as Winne and Marx (1989, p. 225) summarise:

> In order to promote, facilitate, or develop students' knowledge and skills in any subject, contemporary research about learning converges on at least one clear prescription: Teachers must arrange for students to engage in cognitive activities in which they manipulate and transform information.

The individual difference variables included various attitudinal/motivational measures related to learning English in general and to the language course the students were attending in particular. Because the language measures concerned the quantity of the speech produced by the participants, one further individual difference variable was added to the research paradigm, the learners 'willingness to communicate' (WTC) in the L1, which refers to the person's general readiness to enter into discourse. According to McCroskey and Richmond (1987), WTC is a personality trait that is responsible for the "regularity in the amount of communication behaviour of an individual across situations" (p. 138) and it is related to a number of enduring personality variables such as introversion/extroversion, self-esteem and communication apprehension (for more details, see MacIntyre, Clément, Dörnyei and Noels, 1998, who conceptualised WTC in the L2 to be an important language learning variable).

In order to assess participant effects, I correlated the interlocutor's predictor and the speaker's criterion variables, that is, looked at the association between an individual's language output and his/her interlocutor's motivational disposition. Finally, correlations were also computed between the motivational and language measures with the dyads as the basic units of analysis, that is, with the communication partners' scores pooled.

METHOD

Participants

The participants of the investigation were 44 Hungarian students (aged 16–17) studying English at an intermediate level in five classes in two Budapest secondary schools. The two schools were of the same type, "gimnázium" (similar to the former British grammar schools), providing general instruction and preparing students for further studies in higher education. The English curriculum involved teaching integrated skills with an emphasis on developing communicative competence and students in all five groups used coursebooks published in Great Britain. The group sizes ranged from 12 to 16 (but not every student participating in the large-scale longitudinal project was present when the data reported here were gathered).

Task

The task used in the study was an *oral argumentative task*. This task was designed as an interactive problem-solving activity, aimed at eliciting arguments concerning everyday school matters (see Appendix). Students (working in pairs) were given a list of items and they were asked to select and rank-order some of these individually, based on an imaginary situation. Following this, they were to compare with their partners their preferences and come to a compromise by means of a negotiation process.

Data collection and processing

All the data collection for the study was carried out during the students' regular English classes. The students' performance on the research task was recorded and then transcribed. As mentioned above, we used two measures to describe the quantity of learner engagement, the *speech size* measured by the number of words produced and the *number of turns* generated by the participants. This second measure was included because it was assumed that the successful completion of a problem-solving, negotiation-based task such as the one we had used would require a considerable amount of turn-taking to take place. In contrast, a hasty and unmotivated solution in which no real arguments or attempts at persuading the interlocutor are involved can be achieved by using very few turns. Therefore, the number of turns used by a speaker can be seen as an indicator of the level of student involvement. We must note that there is a difference between the two language measures in that the number of turns depends more directly on the quality of the joint interaction than the number of words does. For example, if the interaction itself is not very productive but one person offers lengthy monologues, this will result in a high word count but a low turn number on his/her part. Indeed, turn number is a function of the interlocutor's active contribution, since in turn-taking the number of turns produced by the two speakers is by definition roughly equal.

Students also filled in a *self-report questionnaire*, which focused on various attitudinal/motivational issues, based on Clément, Dörnyei and Noels's (1994) instrument specifically developed for Hungarian learners. The data from the questionnaire were computer coded and the number of variables was reduced by computing six multi-item scales (summarised below) by summing the thematically corresponding items. As mentioned before, a seventh background variable was added to these six scales, the learners' *willingness to communicate* (WTC) in their L1, in order to account for their general communication orientation. This scale was obtained by another self-report questionnaire and the actual items used in our study were adapted from an instrument developed by the originators of the construct, McCroskey and Richmond (1991).

Because there was considerable between-group variation in the learners' language output (recall that the learners came from five class groups in two schools), we computed standard scores within each class for both the motivational and language variables and used these rather than the raw scores for the computations. This involved mathematically converting the distribution of the scores within each class sample in a way that the mean was 0 and the standard deviation 1, which is an established statistical method for compensating for within-sample differences before pooling the data from various subgroups (see Dörnyei, 2001c; Gardner, 1985a).

Variables in the study

The following list summarises the seven individual difference variables used in the study, with their description, the number of items they were made up of and the Cronbach Alpha internal consistency reliability coefficient for each scale. The mean Cronbach Alpha coefficient across the six attitudinal/motivational scales is .76, which is adequate for such scales. The coefficient for WTC is lower because the scale deliberately sampled responses concerning different social situations[2].

Integrativeness

A broad positive disposition towards the L2 speaker community, including an interest in their life and culture and a desire for contact with them (7 items, Cronbach α = .80)

Incentive values of English proficiency

A broad factor associated with the various benefits — pragmatic and L2 use-related — of L2 proficiency; e.g. "Learning English is important for me because I may need English in the future (work, further education)" (8 items, Cronbach α = .80)

---

[2] Students were to indicate on a six-point scale the extent to which they would engage in an L1 conversation in the following five situations: standing in the bus stop with friends; asking questions in a public "teacher-student forum" at school; at a party where one doesn't know anybody; meeting a (not too close) acquaintance at the post office; and in the lift with a stranger.

Attitudes towards

E.g. "I like the English classes"; "I wish we had more English classes *the English course* at school" and "The things we learn in the English classes will be useful in the future" (3 items, Cronbach α =.83)

Linguistic self-confidence

Factor associated with a favourable self-conception of language aptitude, a satisfaction with progress and a belief in one's ability to succeed in L2 learning; e.g."I am sure I'll be able to learn English" (6 items, Cronbach α = .76)

Language use anxiety

Anxiety experienced while using the L2; e.g. "I usually feel ill at ease when I have to speak English" and "I often become uncertain when I have to speak in the English classes" (2 items, Cronbach α = .73)

Task attitudes

E.g. "I have found the tasks used in the project useful for L2 learning" and "I liked the tasks used in the project" (2 items, Cronbach α =.61)

Willingness to Communicate (WTC)

The learners' readiness to enter into discourse with people in different social situations; e.g. "Standing in the bus stop with friends" (5 items, Cronbach α = .48; see also Note 2)

RESULTS AND DISCUSSION

Correlations between task attitudes and the other individual difference measures

Let us first look at the correlations between task attitudes and the other individual difference measures (see Table 7.1). Of the five correlations with motivational variables three are significant, indicating that — in accordance with Tremblay, Goldberg and Gardner's (1995) and Julkunen's (2001) claims — the appraisal of the specific task was related to more general motivational variables. The strong correlation with *Course attitudes* was expected because task and course attitudes both concern classroom learning in a situated manner, and the significant correlation with *Integrativeness* is consistent with Gardner's (1985a) theory (see MacIntyre, 2002) as well as past findings in Hungarian student samples (e.g. Clément, Dörnyei and Noels, 1994; Dörnyei and Clément, 2001). The positive association with *L2 use anxiety* is somewhat unexpected; it indicates that those learners who take the task more seriously experience more nervousness about speaking in the L2. Recent research by Dewaele (2002a; Dewaele and Furnham, 2000) suggests that certain personality variables (e.g. psychoticism, extraversion and neuroticism) are directly related to the amount of language anxiety one experiences. We can speculate that the same personality variables might also affect one's attitudes towards a communicative task, which then would imply that the association between L2 anxiety and task attitudes is due to mediating personality effects. With regard to WTC, the non-significant correlation indicates that there is no evidence of a relationship between the learners' attitude towards the communicative task used in the study and their WTC orientation.

Table 7.1   Correlations between 'Task Attitudes' and the Other Individual Difference Variables

	Task attitudes
Integrativeness	.40**
Incentive values	.26
Course attitudes	.58***
Self-confidence	.07
L2 use anxiety	.37*
WTC	.21

* = *p*<.05; ** = *p*<.01; *** = *p*<.001

Correlations between the motivational and language variables

Table 7.2 presents the correlations between the seven individual difference and two language variables. The table reveals significant positive correlations between the language variables and the two most situation-specific variables, *Course attitudes* and *Task attitudes*, and presents a further significant correlation between *Self-confidence* and speech size. As the multiple correlations show, the motivational variables together explain roughly 35-40 per cent of the variance in the language measures. Although the overall magnitude of the coefficients in Table 7.2 is similar to correlations reported in the motivation literature, it is lower than what I originally expected. This is because, unlike most studies on L2 motivation in which the criterion measure is some sort of course achievement or standardised language proficiency score, in this investigation the obtained attitudinal/motivational variables were correlated with objective measures directly reflecting the participants' actual language behaviours in a concrete learning task. And since the relationship between motivation and learning behaviours is by definition stronger than that between motivation and learning achievement (because the latter is also influenced by other, non-motivational factors such as the learners' ability, learning opportunities and instructional quality), this stronger relationship was expected to show up in the correlations.

Table 7.2   Correlations between the Language and the Individual Difference Variables

	Words	Turns
Integrativeness	.16	.07
Incentive values	−.10	.28
Course attitudes	.39**	.35*
Self-confidence	.34*	.23
L2 use anxiety	−.10	.00
Task attitudes	.32*	.48***
Multiple correlations	*.59*	*.61*
WTC	.25	.38*
Multiple correlations with WTC	*.63*	*.70*

* = $p<.05$; ** = $p<.01$; *** = $p<.001$

With regard to WTC, it shows a significant positive correlation with the number of turns but not with the number of words produced. This is in accordance with the construct of WTC, since it is more a measure of whether someone will initiate talk rather than how much the person actually speaks. Looking at the multiple correlations that include the WTC measure (explaining 46 per cent of the variance), it is clear that WTC explains a considerable amount of unique variance in the language measures.

Separating high-task-attitude and low-task-attitude subsamples

One possible reason why some correlations reported in Table 7.2 are not as high as expected might be related to the diversity in the learners' task attitudes. Let us, for a moment, look at the task situation from the students' perspective. Although the language tasks were administered during the learners' regular English classes (as mentioned earlier, the study was part of a larger-scale task-based investigation), they were not part of the official syllabus but instead served research purposes. And even though we placed a great emphasis on 'selling' our project to the students, that is, on creating positive task attitudes, it was inevitable that not everybody took the activities equally seriously. We can guess, for example, that some of the students may have looked at our project as a welcome break from the serious, 'real' school activities, whereas others may have found our tasks pointless or a nuisance. This is, in fact, quite understandable and to a certain extent inevitable with a classroom-oriented investigation such as this; however, if this assumption is true, it would mean that the behaviour of some of the students (the ones who did not take the task seriously for some reason) was somewhat disinterested/random and not necessarily reflecting their motivation to learn the L2. Such disinterested task behaviour would, in turn, depress the motivation-behaviour correlation coefficients.

In order to test this hypothesis, I divided the sample into two subgroups based on the *Task attitudes* variable, by assigning learners to the 'high-task-attitude' subsample (LowS) if their score was lower than 4; this resulted in groups of 21 and 23, respectively. Following this, I repeated the correlation analysis reported above in the two subsamples separately (see Table 7.3)

Table 7.3   Correlations between the Language and the Individual Difference Variables in the High- and Low-Task-Attitude Subsamples

	High-task-attitude learners		Low-task-attitude learners	
	Words	Turns	Words	Turns
Integrativeness	.18	−.10	.06	−.13
Incentive values	−.47*	.22	.10	.25
Course attitudes	−.04	−.07	.47*	.29
Self-confidence	.45*	.12	.24	.29
L2 use anxiety	−.33	−.02	−.17	−.31
Task attitudes	.17	.30	−.07	.08
WTC	.46*	.63***	.01	.11

*= p<.05; ** = p<.01; *** = p<.001*

The results in Table 7.3 confirm the assumption that the two subsamples show different characteristics in terms of the relationship between the motivational and language variables. In the HighS, speech size correlates highly significantly with *Integrativeness* and *Self-confidence*, and the number of turns shows a significant positive correlation with *Incentive values*; the same correlations in the LowS are non-significant. This means, firstly, that amongst the learners who had positive task attitudes, the confident ones outperformed the less confident ones, which makes sense. Secondly, the significant correlations also indicate that learners who had more positive generalised motives to accompany their high situation-specific motives (i.e. task attitudes) also tended to perform better, which is in accordance with the suggestion presented in the Introduction that task performance is fuelled by a combination of situation-specific and generalised motives.

In the LowS we find only one significant correlation with a language measure, which is consistent with the hypothesis that because these learners failed to take the task sufficiently seriously, their performance would be somewhat disinterested/random. However, the single emerging significant relationship, between *Course attitudes* and speech size, is very important: it shows that among the learners who displayed low task-attitudes, those who had a favourable disposition toward the language course in general participated more actively in the task than those who had unfavourable attitudes toward both the course and the task. In other words, the generalised positive disposition toward the whole course neutralised some of their negative attitudes towards the particular task. This finding indicates that situation-specific motives in educational settings involve at least two distinct levels — task-related and course-related — which provides evidence for the assumption that the complex of task motivation can be better described as a composite of multiple motivational influences related to the various actional/engagement contingencies than as a composite of trait and state motivation.

The most dramatic difference between the HighS and LowS occurs between WTC and the language measures. In the HighS, this relationship is indeed very strong: it explains 36% of the variance in the number of turns (as indicated by the correlation coefficient of .60), and even the somewhat lower (but still significant) correlation with the size of the learner's speech (.46) accounts for 21% of the variance. In contrast, the same correlations in the LowS are non-significant, which again attests to the disinterested/random nature of the performance of low-task-attitude students.

The motivational influence of the interlocutor

The results reported so far have generally supported a process-oriented conception of task motivation, and further support for this perspective would be gained if we could find indications of any impact of the interlocutor's level of motivation on his/her communication partner's task performance. That such an influence exists is a logical assumption because two interacting people affect each other in many ways, and it would also highlight the dynamic, negotiated nature of task motivation. To test this assumption, correlations were computed between the interlocutors' motivational variables and speaker's language output measures (see Table 7.4); in other words, if Sally and Johnny were paired, Table 7.4 presents the correlation between Sally's motivation and Johnny's language output.

Table 7.4   Correlations between the Speakers' Language Measures and the Interlocutors' Attitudinal/Motivational Measures

	Whole sample		High-task-att.		Low-task-att.	
	Words	Turns	Words	Turns	Words	Turns
Integrativeness	−.06	.08	−.23	−.02	.19	−.31
Incentive values	.11	.24	−.22	.01	.23	.28
Course attitudes	.22	.40**	−.28	.17	.50*	.45*
Self-confidence	.11	.29	.06	.20	.16	.41
L2 use anxiety	−.13	−.05	−.45*	.01	.31	−.01
Task attitudes	.22	.34*	−.11	.37	.65***	.48*
WTC	−12	.35*	−.22	.47*	.05	.35

* = p<.05; ** = p<.01; *** = p<.001

The results shown in the table are noteworthy. For the whole sample, we find four significant correlations between the individual difference variables and the number of turns and only two with the number of words, which is in line with the more 'mutual' nature of the former language variable (discussed earlier). The overall pattern provides strong evidence that the interlocutor's motivational disposition is related to the speaker's performance. If we break down the whole sample into HighS and LowS subgroups, we can see that interlocutor effects primarily concern the LowS, where they serve as a 'pulling force': if someone with a low task attitude is matched up with a more motivated peer, the chances are that the person's performance will improve. Although there are only three significant positive correlations in the Lows, we can find here four other correlations of .37, which is significant at the $p < .10$ level, indicating trends. All this points to a very consistent pattern.

These interlocutor influences can be explained in two ways:

1. One might argue that the influence is primarily *linguistic* — the partner's motivational disposition affects only the partner's own performance and it is only this increased (or decreased) performance that will indirectly affect the speaker's language output in that if someone's partner initiates more (or less) speech, this will make it easier (or more difficult) for the speaker to produce speech. In other words, if Johnny speaks more, one can argue that his partner, Sally, may also produce more speech simply by reacting to Johnny and completing adjacency pairs.

2. The alternative explanation centres around *motivation* and states that the actual task motivation of the task participants is not independent from each other. If one is paired up with a highly motivated or unmotivated partner, this will affect the person's own disposition toward the task; that is, task motivation will be *co-constructed* by the task participants, with the interlocutor either pulling 'up' or 'down' the speaker.

I am more inclined towards the second explanation, primarily because I have found in the past that L2 learner interaction can be very uneven, with someone often speaking a great deal more than his/her interlocutor without being much affected by this imbalance. The real impact of the interlocutor on his/her communication partner is, I believe, caused by the 'spirit' he/she brings into the exchange, which functions as a motivational 'turn-on' or 'turn-off'. Looking at Table 7.4, we can also find some indirect support for this speculation in that the interlocutor's WTC does *not* affect the speaker's speech size. This shows that the fact that one's interlocutor is more talkative does not automatically increase one's language output — which is the basis of the linguistic explanation.

The motivation of the dyads

If it is true that task motivation is (at least partially) co-constructed, this would imply that looking at the communicating dyads — rather than the individual speakers — as the basic level of analysis will produce results of increased explanatory power with regard to the motivation-behaviour relationship. Table 7.5 presents correlations between the motivational and language variables for the 21 dyads that participated in the study. These correlations were obtained by pooling the data for the two people in each dyad.

Table 7.5   *Correlations between the Language and the Individual Difference Variables for the 21 dyads (i.e. with the Speaker's and the Interlocutor's Data Pooled)*

	Words	Turns
Integrativeness	.29	.19
Incentive values	.24	.44*
Course attitudes	.52*	.45*
Self-confidence	.25	.35
L2 use anxiety	.09	.00
Task attitudes	.59**	.66***
Multiple correlations	*.68*	*.75*
WTC	.48*	.71***
Multiple correlations with WTC	*.83*	*.95*

$* = p<.05;$ $** = p<.01;$ $*** = p<.001$

The coefficients in Table 7.5 are considerably higher than the corresponding correlations for the individual students reported in Table 7.2. Although some of the correlations do not reach statistical significance, this may in fact be due to the limited sample size caused by halving the number of cases when pooling the communication partners' data. The multiple correlations indicate that the motivational variables together explain 72 per cent of the variance in the total speech size and 69 per cent of the variance in the number of turns generated. These coefficients are over 30 per cent higher than the corresponding figures at the individual level (cf. Table 7.2), which provides strong support for the thesis of motivational co-construction. Furthermore, if we add the variance explained by WTC to that explained by the six motivational measures, we find that 76 per cent of the variance in speech size and 81 per cent of the variance in the number of turns are explained by the individual difference variables. These unusually high figures mean that at the dyad level the motivational variables accompanied by the WTC personality trait do an excellent job in explaining the bulk of the variance in the language performance measures.

CONCLUSION

Admittedly, this study has several limitations, the most notable ones being the small sample size and the fact that correlations do not indicate causation (and therefore we cannot take it for granted that the individual difference factors were the independent and the language measures the dependent variables). However, I believe that the results are consistent and powerful enough to suggest some valid patterns and tendencies.

Motivation-behaviour relationship and task based research

The results in this study support the assumption that when the relationship between motivation and concrete learning behavioural measures is assessed we can obtain considerably higher correlations than when motivation is related to global achievement measures. The magnitude of the multiple correlations in Table 5 indicates that if we take into account both communication partners' motivation at the same time, we can achieve highly satisfactory explanatory power, and if we also add an index of the participants' general communicational characteristics (i.e. WTC) to the equation, the individual difference variables account for the bulk of the variance in the language measures. This also confirms, in a more general sense, the suitability of adopting a task-based framework for the purpose of motivation research. Looking at the impact of motivation on concrete learning behaviours in a situated manner will result in a clearer and more elaborate understanding of L2 motivation than the traditional research practice whereby the most common criterion variable was a general achievement of proficiency measure. On the other hand, it must also be pointed out that such a situated approach will make motivation studies more difficult to compare to each other, especially if very different tasks were used.

The relationship between general and situation-specific motives

The findings confirm that both situation-specific and more general motives contribute to task motivation but the overall construct is more complex than the composite of state and trait motivation. It was argued that on-task behaviour is embedded in a series of broader actional contexts (e.g. going to a specific school, attending a particular class, taking up the study of a particular L2) and each of these contexts exert a certain amount of unique motivational influence. That is, it may be insufficient to assume that the learner enters the task situation with some 'trait motivation baggage' and to obtain task motivation this 'baggage' needs to be pooled with the motivational properties of the instructional task. Instead, engaging in a certain task activates a number of different levels of related motivational mindsets and contingencies, resulting in complex interferences.

Motivational processing and the dynamic co-construction of task motivation

The findings also support the conception of 'motivational processing' during task completion. The outcome of this processing is a function of a multitude of perceived information and stimuli, and in communicative L2 tasks that involve several participants, the interlocutors' motivational disposition is a key factor affecting the learner's appraisal and action control processes. In other words, task motivation is *co-constructed* by the task participants.

In sum, the main thesis of this paper is that the full complexity of task motivation becomes apparent only when we consider it within a larger context of dynamically interacting synchronic and diachronic factors and actions. This perspective requires a process-oriented approach which recognises that motivation is never static but is constantly increasing or decreasing depending on the various social influences surrounding action, the learner's appraisal of these influences and the action control operations the learner carries out on such motivational content.

APPENDIX

The task used in the study

You are a member of the school student committee. Your school wants to participate in the district's social life and asks students to offer their help. The following possible options have been suggested:

- Delivering lunch to elderly people in the district
- Publishing a local newsletter
- Helping out in the library
- Providing tourist information
- Performing for children in the kindergarten
- Collecting newspaper/wastepaper
- Feeding birds
- Maintaining the park
- Performing for elderly people
- Organising sports events

First, look at the list alone for three minutes and choose 5 activities you would find interesting or useful. Put them on these lines *in the order of your preference.*

    1. _____
    2. _____
    3. _____
    4. _____
    5. _____

Second, compare your list with your partner's. The lists are probably different. Your task is to find the best compromise with your partner and *prepare a final list of 3 activities* you together will recommend to the school management.

    1. _____
    2. _____
    3. _____

You have 10 minutes to convince your partner about your ideas. Make sure you give reasons but remember that you *MUST come to an agreement on the best proposal.*

Chapter 8

Individual Differences in Second Language Acquisition

AILA Review, (2006), 19, pp. 42-68.

Individual differences (IDs) refer to dimensions of enduring personal characteristics that are assumed to apply to everybody and on which people differ by degree. In other words, they concern stable and systematic deviations from a normative blueprint. IDs are important: In psychology there is a whole subdiscipline, traditionally termed *differential psychology* but recently more frequently referred to as *individual difference research*, with a focus on exploring the uniqueness of the individual mind. There is a plethora of studies to show that IDs significantly affect human thinking and behaviour (for reviews, see e.g. Cooper, 2002; De Raad, 2000; Eysenck, 1994) and this impact has been well documented in educational contexts as well (e.g. Snow, Corno and Jackson, 1996). IDs have also been found to be consistent predictors of success in second language acquisition (SLA), yielding multiple correlations with language attainment in instructed settings within the range of .50 and above (see Dörnyei and Skehan, 2003; Sawyer and Ranta, 2001). However, in a recent comprehensive overview of the field (Dörnyei, 2005), I was surprised to find that each main ID area is currently undergoing a fundamental transition/restructuring in second language (L2) research. In this article I address this transformation process with regard to the five most important L2 ID domains, *personality, aptitude, motivation, learning styles* and *learning strategies*. The following discussion will be based on Dörnyei (2005) and readers are referred to this summary for further details.

PERSONALITY TRAITS

Personality is the most individual characteristic of a human being and therefore it may be surprising that from an educational perspective personality factors appear to play a far less important role than some other ID variables such as aptitude and motivation. In accordance with this, the amount of research targeting personality in L2 studies has also been minimal compared to the study of most other ID variables and, as we will see below in more detail, the available results are typically weak or non-conclusive. One reason for the ambiguous position of personality in educational research lies in the fact that personality has traditionally been conceptualised in diverse ways: Personality is such a crucial aspect of psychology that every main branch of psychology has attempted to contribute to the existing knowledge in this area and thus the scope of theorising can be as broad as the differences among the various paradigms in psychology.

The good news, however, is that over the past 15 years personality psychology has reached a growing consensus in the conceptualisation of the main dimensions of human personality. Current research in the field is dominated by only two taxonomies focusing on personality traits, Eysenck's three-component construct (e.g. Eysenck and Eysenck, 1985) and the 'Big Five' model (e.g. Goldberg, 1992, 1993; McCrae and Costa, 2003). Furthermore, the two models overlap considerably: Eysenck's model identifies three principal personality dimensions, contrasting (1) *extraversion* with *introversion*, (2) *neuroticism* and *emotionality* with *emotional stability*, and (3) *psychoticism* and *toughmindedness* with *tender-mindedness*. The Big Five construct retains Eysenck's first two dimensions, but replaces psychoticism with three additional dimensions: *conscientiousness, agreeableness* and *openness to experience*. This convergence in categorisation makes the use of personality factors as independent variables in research studies easier and more reliable for non-psychologists.

In educational psychology several studies have attempted to identify the personality correlates of academic achievement but the emerging overall picture is rather mixed, if not bleak: Although past research has provided evidence that personality factors are implicated in educational achievement, including success in SLA, no coherent picture has emerged. There are at least four reasons to account for this ambiguity:

(1) *Interaction with situation-specific variables.* There is some evidence that personality factors interact with various variables inherent to the social context of the learning situation, which prevents generalised linear associations (such as correlations) from reaching overall significance. Several studies have shown that the nature of the actual tasks students engage in imposes a personality bias. For example, extraverts tend to perform well under conditions of high stimulation or arousal, whereas the same task might impair introverts' performance (Matthews, Davies, Westerman, and Stammers, 2000), and students relatively high on Openness to Experience should thrive in educational settings that promote and reward critical and original thought (Farsides and Woodfield, 2003). Thus, it appears that the relationship between personality factors and learning achievement is often not direct and linear but rather indirect, mediated by various situation-specific variables.

(2) *Need for less simplistic models.* In spite of the often non-linear nature of the relationship between personality factors and learning achievement, the typical research design reported in the literature is still correlational, testing for simple personality- learning outcome relationships. An example of a more complex model that includes a featured personality component in the L2 field is the Willingness to Communicate (WTC)

construct by MacIntyre, Clément, Dörnyei and Noels (1998), in which personality forms an important part of the basic layer of the construct, with four further layers of variables conceptualised between personality traits and communicative behaviour.

(3) *Supertraits or primary traits.* The Big Five construct consists of five main dimensions, or 'supertraits,' which are further broken down to 30 facets, or 'primary traits.' Although the rationale for clustering the primary traits into supertraits was that the facets in one dimension were interrelated, when it comes to their relationship with academic success we find differences among the interrelated primary traits in terms of their impact on learning. For example, Matthews et al. (2000) highlighted that some of the strongest links between personality and performance had been obtained at the primary trait level (notably between anxiety and performance). Such intra-trait differences obviously reduce the supertraits' predictive capacity, but the alternative, that is, to examine the personality-learning relation at the primary trait level, would in effect mean giving up the Big Five construct with all its merits.

(4) *Methodological issues.* The inconclusive results in the literature are also partly due to various methodological limitations or inconsistencies. Different studies have used different criteria for academic success (ranging from exam marks, grade point average and final degree results to situated course-specific evaluations such as course grades), have permitted considerably different time lapses between the collection of predictor and criterion data (with a range of a few weeks to several years) and have employed convenience samples (the most typical being psychology majors at the university of the researchers) in which the variance in ID variables can be so restricted that it may in some (but not all) cases prevent correlation-based coefficients from reaching statistical significance.

Personality factors in SLA research

The most researched personality aspect in language studies has been the extraversion-introversion dimension, which is understandable because this trait is fundamental to a number of personality theories, from the MBTI typology to Eysenck's model and the Big Five construct. Furthermore, as Furnham (1990) points out, it is relatively easy to produce a reliable measure of this trait and there are also several obvious commonsense relationships between extraversion and language use. Yet, the emerging picture about the role of extraversion-introversion in SLA has been rather negative, with scholars either concluding that the relationship between this trait and learning was insignificant or mixed. Dewaele and Furnham (1990) argued that this bad reputation is partly due to not distinguishing properly between written and oral language criteria and in studies where extraversion scores are correlated with linguistic variables extracted from complex verbal tasks (i.e. conversation), a clear pattern emerges: Extraverts are found to be more fluent than introverts both in L1 and L2 and particularly in formal situations or in environments characterised by interpersonal stress. Dewaele (2004) also found that extraverted L2 speakers tended to use colloquial words freely whereas introverts tended to avoid them. This is in accordance with Skehan's (1989) proposal that within SLA we should be able to observe a more prominent positive effect of extraversion than in other educational domains, where introverts have usually been found to have an advantage. On the other hand, Skehan also pointed out that SLA involves many learning tasks and processes which go beyond learning-by-doing or talking-to-learn (e.g. memorising vocabulary or preparing written assignments), and these aspects of learning would seem to relate more easily to the introvert.

Space limitations do not allow us to look at the L2 impact of other personality factors; instead, let me conclude this section by describing briefly Verhoeven and Vermeer's (2002) investigation because, to my knowledge, this study has been the first to use the Big Five personality construct in L2 research. The purpose of the investigation was to examine the communicative competence of young teenage language learners in the Netherlands in relation to their personality characteristics (and also to compare these learners with a native-speaking sample). Communicative competence was operationalised in terms of three main constituents: *organisational competence* (measured by standardised discrete-point tests of vocabulary, grammar and reading), *strategic competence* (measured by two rating scales for teachers to judge the children's planning of communicative behaviour and monitoring communication), and *pragmatic competence* (measured by student performance on eight different role-play tasks). It was found that only Openness to Experience correlated substantially with the linguistic abilities of the children across all the three competencies (with a mean correlation of .43). Extraversion was associated only with strategic competence (r = .51) and Conscientiousness had a moderate correlation with organisational competence (r = .28). These findings are interesting in themselves and they also indicate that if scholars include in their research paradigm a more elaborate conception of L2 proficiency than a global L2 proficiency measure, stronger and more meaningful relationships can be identified.

LANGUAGE APTITUDE

The concept of *language aptitude* is related to the broader concept of *human abilities*, or *intelligence*, covering a variety of cognitively-based learner differences. Ever since the beginnings of ID research at the end of the 19th century, intelligence has been closely associated with learning success — explaining, according to Sternberg (2002) as much as 25% of individual-difference variation in school performance — and therefore it was only a question of time that attempts were made to conceptualise the specific ability to learn a foreign language. This ability has been referred to under a variety of names, ranging from 'language aptitude' and a special 'propensity' or 'talent' for learning an L2 to more colloquial terms such as a 'flair' or 'knack' for languages. Indeed, language aptitude is one of those psychological concepts that are readily recognisable for researchers and laypeople alike, and nobody would question that the innate ability to learn a language other than one's mother tongue varies significantly from individual to individual. Yet, when we give the concept a closer scrutiny, it also becomes clear that what lies behind the popular surface meaning is rather ambiguous: Even language teaching experts would find it difficult to define what exactly this 'language flair' involves and, similarly to their colleagues in mainstream psychology, scholars specialising in language aptitude research display considerable diversity in the conceptualisation of the construct.

The crux of the problem is that, strictly speaking, there is no such thing as 'language aptitude.' Instead, we have a number of cognitive factors making up a composite measure that can be referred to as the learner's overall capacity to master a foreign language. In other words, foreign language aptitude is not a unitary factor but rather a complex of "basic abilities that are essential to facilitate foreign language learning" (Carroll and Sapon, 1959, p. 14). While this definition has been adequate for several decades, recent research into specific cognitive skills and capacities related to learning, such as 'working memory' or 'phonological coding/decoding,' makes it questionable as to whether it is still useful to use the umbrella-term of 'language aptitude' and, in fact, several recent studies on cognitive abilities have abandoned using the term (e.g. Ellis, 2001; Robinson, 2003). However, because standard measures of language aptitude remain relatively good indicators of learning success, the concept is still widely used in the general sense.

Although language aptitude tests were constructed in the US as early as the 1920s, the 'golden age' of scientific language aptitude testing took place in the 1950s and 1960s, heralded by two systematic test development programmes by John Carroll and Stanley Sapon on the one hand and by Paul Pimsleur on the other. Two commercial aptitude batteries for use with adolescents and adults stem from this early work: the *Modern Language Aptitude Test* (MLAT; Carroll and Sapon, 1959), and the *Pimsleur Language Aptitude Battery* (PLAB; Pimsleur, 1966). Ever since the MLAT and the PLAB were introduced, language aptitude has been equated in most research studies with the scores of one of these (or some other, similar) tests and the tacit understanding in the L2 research community has been that language aptitude is what language aptitude tests measure.

Based on results obtained by the MLAT, Carroll (1981, p. 105) proposed a theoretical construct of language aptitude that comprised four constituent abilities: (1) *Phonetic coding ability*, which is considered the most important component and is defined as "an ability to identify distinct sounds, to form associations between these sounds and symbols representing them, and to retain these associations". (2) *Grammatical sensitivity*, which is "the ability to recognize the grammatical functions of words (or other linguistic entities) in sentence structures". (3) *Rote learning ability*, which is the "ability to learn associations between sounds and meaning rapidly and efficiently, and to retain these associations". (4) *Inductive language learning ability*, which is "the ability to infer or induce the rules governing a set of language materials, given samples of language materials that permit such inferences".

Carroll's (1962, 1981) aptitude theory dominated the field for three decades but the past 15 years brought a new boom in language aptitude research. The 1990s started with the publication of an ambitious anthology entitled '*Language Aptitude Reconsidered*,' edited by Thomas Parry and Charles Stansfield (1990) and including a contribution by Carroll (1990), and as if this volume had given the field some fresh momentum, there followed a renewed interest in the concept (for reviews, see Dörnyei, 2005; Robinson, in press; Skehan, 2002; Sparks and Ganschow, 2001; Spolsky, 1995). What caused this revival? There are at least two main reasons: First, advances in cognitive psychology allowed for a more accurate representation of the various mental skills and aptitudes that make up the composite language learning ability. Second, scholars started to explore ways of linking language aptitude to a number of important issues in SLA research. Thus, the common theme in the various post-Carroll research directions has been the examination of the SLA-specific impact of specific cognitive factors and subprocesses, going beyond the use of the language aptitude metaphor as an umbrella term. By way of illustration, let me highlight four particularly interesting lines of research.

Grigorenko, Sternberg and Ehrman's research

Perhaps the most traditional in the new approaches has been the development of a novel language aptitude test — the *Cognitive Ability for Novelty in Acquisition of Language as applied to foreign language test* (CANAL-FT) — by Grigorenko, Sternberg and Ehrman (2000) in the sense that these authors still focused on the composite aptitude concept, although conceptualised it rather differently from the Carroll-tradition. In contrast to the MLAT or the PLAB, which had emerged from the tradition of psychometric test development, the CANAL-FT has been theory driven, drawing on Sternberg's triarchic theory of human intelligence (Sternberg, 2002). The main emphasis in the CANAL-FT is on measuring how people cope with novelty and ambiguity in their learning. This is done in a naturalistic context by gradually introducing an artificial language, Ursulu, and testtakers are to perform a number of mini-learning tasks so that by the end of the test they have mastered enough lexical, morphological, semantic and syntactic knowledge to cope with a small story in Ursulu.

Research on LI literacy

A systematic line of research by Richard Sparks, Leonore Ganschow and their associates has focused on what they have labelled the Linguistic Coding Differences Hypothesis (LCDH; e.g. Sparks and Ganschow, 1991, 2001; Sparks, Javorsky, Patton, and Ganschow, 1998). According to the hypothesis, one's capacity to learn an L2 is closely related to the individual's L1 learning skills, and L2 learning difficulties stem in part from native language difficulties. The central cognitive factor the theory focuses on is *'linguistic coding,'* which refers to L1 literacy skills such as phonological/orthographic processing and word recognition/decoding (i.e. single-word reading). The LCDH proposes that these abilities serve as the foundation for learning an L2, and an insufficient level of development in linguistic coding skills has a profound impact on L2 learning ability, resulting in a serious handicap. The significance of L1 literacy skills in L2 studies has also been highlighted in an important longitudinal study conducted by Dufva and Voeten (1999), investigating 160 Finnish elementary school children from the first to the third grade. The researchers examined two cognitive areas, L1 literacy acquisition and phonological memory (the latter being part of 'working memory' — see below) in terms of their impact on learning English as a foreign language. The authors found that both L1 literacy and phonological memory had positive effects on L2 learning, together explaining as much as 58% of the variance in English proficiency. Thus, in agreement with Sparks and Ganschow (2001), Dufva and Voeten (1999) concluded that native language word recognition formed the basis of learning an L2. Finally, the importance of L1 skills have also been emphasised recently by Tarone and Bigelow's (2005; Bigelow and Tarone, 2004) research on literacy. These scholars present evidence that alphabetic literacy has a significant impact on oral language processing tasks that require an awareness of linguistic segments. The authors argue that the acquisition of the ability to decode an alphabetic script changes the way in which the individual processes oral language in certain kinds of cognitive tasks, which supports the claim that literacy should be seen as a human capacity central to SLA.

Working memory and language aptitude

Research into the relationship between *working memory* and SLA appears to be one of the most promising current directions in language aptitude studies, and as Miyaki and Friedman (1998, p. 339) conclude, "working memory for language may be one (if not the) central component of this language aptitude." Working memory involves the "temporary storage and manipulation of information that is assumed to be necessary for a wide range of complex cognitive activities" (Baddeley, 2003, p. 189); thus, it underpins our capacity for thinking and has important specific implications for language processing. It appears to be an ideally suited memory construct for SLA purposes because besides its phonological short-term memory constituent it also comprises a featured 'attention' component, and the role of attention and attentional capacity has been a key research target in recent SLA research (see Robinson, 2003). For this reason, Ellis (2001) emphasised that the concept deserves much more consideration than it has been thus far given in L2 studies, a conclusion also echoed by others (see Sawyer and Ranta, 2001).

Miyake and Friedman (1998) also emphasised that although working memory plays a central role in all forms of higher-level cognition, its role is particularly featured in language processing because both the production and the comprehension of language requires the processing of sequences of symbols over time in a linear manner. This linearity inherently necessitates a temporal storing capacity and the ability to integrate information from the stream of successive discourse. According to the current conceptualisation, working memory matches these simultaneous processing and storage requirements perfectly. The authors therefore conclude that individual differences in L1 working memory capacity for language are closely related not only to L2 working memory capacity and L2 language comprehension skills but also to the speed and efficiency of the acquisition of L2 knowledge.

Robinson's research on the Aptitude-Treatment Interaction

A central issue in ID research, and one that has emerged in aptitude research in particular, is the question as to whether there are any optimal combinations of ID variables that are especially conducive to efficient learning. One researcher in particular, Richard Snow, was influential in highlighting the potential importance of such ID variable clusters, or as he called them, *aptitude complexes*. His initiative has been taken up by several of his colleagues and students (see Ackerman, 2003; Corno et al., 2002) because, "Although isolated traits often have ... substantial impact on learning outcomes, it may be that combinations of traits have more predictive power than traits in isolation" (Ackerman, 2003, p. 92). Furthermore, the concept of 'aptitude complexes' can also be combined with Cronbach's 'aptitude-treatment interaction' approach that concerns the ways by which mental abilities interact with learning conditions, resulting in a powerful situated ID paradigm for learning. This is the theoretical foundation that Peter Robinson (e.g. 2001a, 2002a, in press) drew on when he launched his pioneering research program on language aptitude-treatment interaction.

The significance of Robinson's aptitude research lies in the fact that this was the first attempt in the L2 field to describe concrete sets of cognitive demands that can be associated with some basic learning types/tasks, and then to identify specific aptitude complexes to match these cognitive processing conditions. He conceptualised language aptitude as the sum of lower level abilities (e.g. pattern recognition or processing speed), which can be grouped into higher-order cognitive factors (e.g. noticing the gap, or metalinguistic rule rehearsal), which differentially support learning in various learning situations/conditions. Thus, Robinson has been the first scholar to create viable links between ID research and aspects of SLA, and his suggestions and initial framework will hopefully inspire much future research in this direction.

Skehan's conception of language aptitude and SLA

The fourth line of research that has great potential for future developments is Peter Skehan's (1998a, 2002; Dörnyei and Skehan, 2003) attempt to relate various aptitude components to the different phases of the SLA process. Not unlike Robinson, Skehan argued that by taking a componential approach to analysing aptitude we may identify certain aptitudinal constituents that are relevant not simply to formal classroom learning but also to various general aspects or stages of SLA processing. Table 8.1 presents Skehan's proposal of theoretical matches between stages of SLA and aptitude components. In the aptitude column the components that have not as yet been explicitly addressed by existing aptitude tests are printed in italics. This is an interesting example of SLA research serving as a driving force for extending aptitude research and therefore the table also suggests a research agenda regarding areas where new aptitude sub-tests could beneficially be developed.

Table 8.1   Skehan's Proposal of SLA Stages and Aptitude Constructs

SLA Stage	Corresponding Aptitude Constructs
Input processing strategies, such as segmentation	*Attentional control* *Working memory*
Noticing	Phonetic coding ability *Working memory*
Pattern identification	Phonetic coding ability *Working memory* Grammatical sensitivity Inductive language learning ability
Pattern restructuring and manipulation	Grammatical sensitivity Inductive language learning ability
Pattern control	*Automatization* *Integrative memory*
Pattern integration	*Chunking* *Retrieval memory*

LANGUAGE LEARNING MOTIVATION

It is universally accepted that *motivation* plays a vital role in academic learning in general, and this is particularly true of the sustained process of mastering a second language. L2 motivation has been conceptualised as a multi-faceted construct that comprises a number of more general, trait-like and more situation-specific, state-like components that direct and energise learning behaviour (for reviews, see Dörnyei, 2001c, 2005; Gardner, 1985a, 2001; Clément and Gardner, 2001; MacIntyre, 2002; Noels, 2003; Ushioda, 2003).

Research on language learning motivation was first initiated and then consistently pursued by Robert Gardner and his associates in Canada (e.g. Clément and Gardner, 2001; Gardner and Lambert, 1972; Gardner and MacIntyre, 1991, 1993; Masgoret and Gardner, 2003; Tremblay and Gardner, 1995). These researchers have adopted a social-psychological perspective and developed a motivational theory that was centred around language attitudinal variables and was firmly grounded in empirical data obtained through scientific research procedures using standardised assessment instruments. The key component of Gardner's (1985a) motivation theory was the *integrative motive*, which concerns a positive interpersonal/affective disposition toward the L2 group and the desire to interact with and even become similar to valued members of that community. It implies an openness to and respect for other cultural groups and ways of life; in the extreme, it might involve complete identification with the community and possibly even withdrawal from one's original group.

In the 1990s there was a broadening of perspectives in L2 motivational research, exploring a number of different motivational dimensions originally introduced in educational psychological research (for a review, see Dörnyei, 2001c). This 'cross-fertilisation' led to an unprecedented boom in L2 motivation studies and a variety of new models and approaches were put forward in the literature, resulting in what Gardner and Tremblay (1994b) have called a "motivational renaissance". A common feature of these new research attempts was the move toward a more *situated approach* to the study of motivation, examining how the immediate learning context influences the learners' overall disposition and how motivation, in turn, effects concrete learning processes within a classroom context. It was argued by several researchers (e.g. Brown, 1990; Crookes and Schmidt, 1991; Dörnyei, 1994; Julkunen, 1989; Oxford and Shearin, 1994) that the classroom environment had a much stronger motivational impact than had been proposed before, highlighting the significance of motives associated with the L2 course, the L2 teacher and the learner group. It is interesting to note that this change in thinking in the L2 field was parallel to a similar shift in educational psychology toward a more grounded and contextualised approach to motivation research (e.g. Hickey, 1997; Wentzel, 1999).

Thus, by the end of the 1990s motivation research was characterised by a colourful variety of various approaches and constructs and scholars often followed a 'pick-and-mix' method in conceptualising motivation for their particular research purposes. This eclectic background provided fertile ground for theoretical developments, of which I consider three particularly forward-pointing: the process-oriented conceptualisation of motivation, the reinterpretation of the integrative motive and finally the reframing of L2 motivation as part of the self system.

Motivation and time

The situated approach emerging in the 1990s soon drew attention to a rather neglected aspect of motivation: its *dynamic character* and *temporal variation*. As I have argued elsewhere (Dörnyei, 2000, 2001c), when motivation is examined in its relationship to specific learner behaviours and classroom processes, there is a need to adopt a *process-oriented approach* that can account for the daily 'ups and downs' of motivation to learn, that is, the ongoing changes of motivation over time. Looking at it from this perspective, motivation is not seen as a static attribute but rather as a dynamic system that displays continuous fluctuation, going through certain ebbs and flows. Indeed, even during a single L2 course one can notice that language-learning motivation shows a certain amount of changeability, and in the context of learning a language for several years, or over a lifetime, motivation is expected to go through very diverse phases.

The most elaborate conceptualisation of the motivational process to date has been offered by Dörnyei and Ottó's (1998) process model (see also Dörnyei, 2000, 2001c). This model synthesises a number of different lines of research in a unified framework, detailing how initial wishes and desires are first transformed into goals and then into operationalised intentions, and how these intentions are enacted, leading (hopefully) to the accomplishment of the goal and concluded by the final evaluation of the process. Within this process we can distinguish at least three distinct phases: (1) *Preactional Stage*, concerning the selection of the goal or task that the individual will pursue; (2) *Actional Stage*, concerning learning-situation-specific 'executive' motives related to the L2 course, the L2 teacher and the learner group; (3) *Postactional Stage*, concerning the learners' *retrospective evaluation* of how things went.

There have been few studies to date specifically conducted to examine the temporal dimension of motivation. Motivational changes have been empirically documented in the past by studies investigating how motivation loses its intensity in school contexts over sustained periods (e.g. Chambers, 1999; Gardner, Masgoret, Tennant and Mihic, 2004; Williams, Burden and Lanvers, 2002) and how learners' motivational orientation undergoes changes during the learners' lifespan (e.g. Lim, 2002; Shedivy, 2004). Two studies — by Ushioda (2001) and Shoaib and Dörnyei (2005) — have specifically addressed aspects of motivational change within a process-oriented paradigm. An interesting result of the latter study was the identification of a number of salient recurring temporal patterns and *motivational transformation episodes* in the learners' lives that resulted in the profound restructuring of their motivational disposition.

The reinterpretation of the integrative motive

Recently Gardner's (1985a) classic concept of '*integrative motivation*' has been questioned because of its lack of applicability to several learning contexts. In situations where an L2 is used as an international language, and especially in the case of 'Global English', it is less and less clear who 'owns' the L2 and this absence of a well-specified target language community undermines the attitudinal base of Gardner's theory of L2 motivation (see Dörnyei, Csizér and Németh, 2006). For example, investigating language learning in Japan, McClelland (2000) called for a definition of 'integrativeness' that focuses on "integration with the global community rather than assimilation with native speakers" (p. 109), highlighting a "need to reappraise Gardner's concept of integrativeness to fit a perception of English as an international language" (ibid.), a view that has been echoed by several other scholars (e.g. Chen, Warden and Chang, 2005; Csizér and Dörnyei, 2005; Irie, 2003; Lamb, 2004; Ryan, 2006; Yashima, 2000).

In broad terms, an integrative motivational orientation concerns some sort of a psychological and emotional *identification* with the L2 community. One way of extending the concept is to talk about some sort of a virtual or metaphorical identification with the sociocultural loading of a language rather than with the actual L2 community (Dörnyei, 1990b), and in the case of the undisputed world language, English, this identification would be associated with a non-parochial, cosmopolitan, globalised world citizen identity. In several parts of the world there is a clear indication that such a 'global identity' exists, and it is merely a terminological issue as to whether we label this a modified version of integrativeness or in some other way. Besides integrativeness, the Global English identity is also related to instrumental aspects because the English-speaking world coincides with several of the technically most developed industrialised nations and therefore English has become the language associated with technological advances, for example computing and the Internet. This may explain the frequently observed blending of integrative and instrumental motives.

At this stage it is important to introduce the intriguing concept of the '*imagined community*' proposed by Bonny Norton (2001). Based on Wenger's (1998) notion of 'imagination' as a mode of belonging to a community, Norton conceptualises the concept of 'communities of imagination' as being constructed by a combination of personal experiences and factual knowledge (derived from the past) with imagined elements related to the future. It appears that the notion of 'imagined community' lends itself to be used with regard to the international or Global English identity described above as this identity concerns membership in a virtual language community. Indeed, Norton explicitly states that a learner's imagined community invites an "imagined identity" (p. 166). Looking at integrative motivation from this perspective, it can be viewed as the desired integration into an imagined L2 community.

The L2 Motivational Self System

While the concept of extended or metaphorical or imaginary integration does help to explain findings that are in many ways similar to the Canadian 'integrative' results but have been obtained in contexts without any realistic opportunity for direct integration, I would suggest that we can get an even more coherent picture if we leave the term 'integrative' completely behind and focus more on the identification aspects and on the learner's self-concept. I have recently proposed a new approach to the understanding of L2 motivation (Dörnyei, 2005), conceived within an 'L2 Motivational Self System', which attempts to integrate a number of influential theoretical L2 approaches (e.g. Gardner, 1985a; Noels, 2003; Norton, 2001; Ushioda, 2001) with findings in 'self' research in psychology. The central theme of this new conception is the equation of the motivational dimension that has traditionally been interpreted as 'integrativeness/ integrative motivation' with the *Ideal L2 Self*'. The latter refers to the L2-specific facet of one's 'ideal self', which is the representation of all the attributes that a person would like to possess (e.g. hopes, aspirations, desires): If one's ideal self is associated with the mastery of an L2, that is, if the person that we would like to become is proficient in the L2, he/she can be described — using Gardner's terminology — as having an 'integrative' disposition.

Following the work of Higgins (1987, 1998), we can postulate another self dimension, the *Ought-to L2 Self*', which concerns the more extrinsic (i.e. less internalised) types of instrumental motives: This self guide refers to the attributes that one believes one *ought to* possess (i.e. various duties, obligations or responsibilities) and which therefore may bear little resemblance to the person's own desires or wishes. Although the ideal and the ought-to selves are similar to each other in that they are both related to the attainment of a desired end-state, Higgins (1998) emphasises that the predilections associated with the two types of future selves are motivationally distinct from each other: Ideal self-guides have a *promotion* focus, concerned with hopes, aspirations, advancements growth and accomplishments; whereas ought-to self-guides have a *prevention* focus, regulating the absence or presence of negative outcomes, concerned with safety, responsibilities and obligations. Thus, from a self perspective, L2 motivation can be seen as the desire to reduce the perceived discrepancies between the learner's actual self and his/her ideal or ought-to L2 selves.

The L2 Motivational Self System also contains a third major dimension of the L2 motivation complex labelled '*L2 Learning Experience*', which concerns situated 'executive' motives related to the immediate learning environment and experience, corresponding to the motives activated in the actional stage of the process model of motivation described earlier.

An important future research task with regard to the L2 Motivational Self System is to establish its compatibility with the process-oriented conception of L2 motivation described earlier. As we have seen, the L2 Learning Experience dimension is related to executive motives associated with the actional stage of motivated behaviour, and the Ideal and Ought-to L2 Selves are by definition involved in preactional deliberation. It needs to be specified, however, how the latter two components relate to motivational processing occurring during the actional and post-actional phases of the motivational process. That is, it is not clear how our Ideal and Ought-to L2 Selves affect the actual learning process. Ushioda (2001) suggests that motivational change entails the evolving nature of goal-orientation, that is, achieving a clearer definition of L2-related personal goals. Within a self framework this would correspond to the elaboration of the Ideal L2 Self and perhaps the internalisation of the

Ought-to L2 Self.

A possible promising inroad into understanding the interface of the Ideal L2 Self and the actional phase of motivation opens up if we consider Norton's (2001) concept of 'imagined communities' mentioned earlier. Norton highlighted Wenger's (1998) proposal of three modes of belonging to a community: *engagement, imagination* and *alignment*. The conceptualisation of imagination and alignment can lead us to a better understanding of how ideal self images are realised in concrete situations, because, as Norton explained, "imagination does not necessarily result in the coordination of action. It is here that the notion of alignment becomes central, because it is through alignment that learners do what they have to do to take part in a larger community" (p. 164). The author further argued that the concept of 'investment' deserves special attention in this respect because this can capture the learner's active process of promoting belonging to the imagined community (see also Pittaway, 2004).

LANGUAGE LEARNING STYLES

There is a considerable body of literature discussing the role of *learning styles* in SLA and most of these studies treat the concept as an important, although somewhat under-researched, topic. However, the uninitiated reader would find only very few clues in the published L2 literature pointing out the fact that the area is a real quagmire: There is a confusing plethora of labels and style dimensions; there is a shortage of valid and reliable measurement instruments; there is a confusion in the underlying theory; and the practical implications put forward in the literature are scarce and rather mixed, and rarely helpful. Furthermore, this situation is not confined to L2 research only but a similar picture emerges in the field of educational psychology; as Snow, Corno and Jackson (1996) concluded in their summary of individual differences in the *Handbook of Educational Psychology*, "No category we have covered contains a more voluminous, complex, and controversy-laced literature than that of personal styles" (p. 281). The reason why researchers have not given up on learning styles is that there is something genuinely appealing about the notion and what scholars are hoping is that the current confusion is merely due to our insufficient knowledge rather than the scientific inadequacy of the concept.

According to the standard definition, *learning styles* refer to "an individual's natural, habitual and preferred way(s) of absorbing, processing and retaining new information and skills" (Reid, 1995b, p. viii); thus, they are "broad preferences for going about the business of learning" (Ehrman, 1996, p. 49). In other words, the concept represents a profile of the individual's approach to learning, a blueprint of the habitual or preferred way the individual perceives, interacts with and responds to the learning environment. This sounds straightforward, yet subsequent research has uncovered at least three areas of theoretical ambiguity with regard to the notion:

The first problem area concerns the relationship between learning styles and learning strategies. The two concepts are thematically related since they both denote specific ways learners go about carrying out learning tasks. According to Snow et al. (1996), the main difference between the two concepts lies in their breadth and stability, with a style being a "strategy used consistently across a class of tasks" (p. 281). In agreement with this claim, Riding (2000) added that styles probably have a physiological basis and are fairly fixed for the individual, whereas strategies may be learned and developed in order to cope with situations and tasks. On the whole, the argument that styles are stable and have a cross-situational impact sounds convincing but if we take a closer look we find that there is a definite interaction between styles and situations (Ehrman, 1996). The stability aspect of styles has also been questioned when researchers observed that early educational experiences do shape one's individual learning styles by instilling positive attitudes toward certain sets of learning skills and, more generally, by teaching students how to learn (Kolb, Boyatzis and Mainemelis, 2001).

Second, we also get on shaky ground when we try to analyse what exactly the term 'preference' means when we talk about styles being 'broad learning preferences.' How much do these 'preferences' determine our functioning? Ehrman (1996) suggested a relatively soft interpretation of 'preference' by equating it with 'comfort zones.' As she explained, however, for a minority learning styles are more firmly set and are therefore more than mere preferences: They do not have the flexibility to change or shift their employed style according to the demands of the situation, and this may land them in trouble. Accordingly, a learning style can range from a mild preference to a strong need.

The third source of controversy concerns the relationship between learning styles and personality, as reflected by the fact that some well-known psychological constructs are sometimes referred to as learning styles and sometimes as personality dimensions. The dimension of extraversion-introversion is a good example, as this popular dichotomy, first brought into wide use by Swiss psychologist Carl Jung, can be found in almost every personality and learning style taxonomy. In fact, Ehrman (1996) has characterised certain learning styles as 'personality-based learning styles,' which are personality dimensions that have cognitive style correlates. While this may be a subtle and precise definition, the popular perception often mixes up personality and styles, as manifested in the use of the Myers-Briggs Type Indicator (MBTI), which is the most widely employed personality test in the world, but which has been often used in L2 learning styles studies as the main research instrument.

Thus, learning styles are elusive, 'halfway' products: They refer to preferences, but these can be of varying degree; they are related to learning strategies but are somewhat different from them as they fall midway between innate abilities and strategies; they appear to be situation-independent but they are not entirely free of situational influences; and some style dimensions are also listed as major components of personality. Indeed, learning styles appear to have very soft boundaries, making the category rather open-ended, regardless of which perspective we approach it from. (For a critical summary of learning styles in educational psychological research, with a special focus on assessment, see Coffield, Moseley, Hall and Ecclestone, 2004.)

Learning styles in second language research

Styles research in the L2 field offers a mixture of good and bad news. On the positive side is the fact that there has been a longstanding research interest in language learning styles and several instruments have been developed and used to understand the role of learning styles in SLA (for reviews, see Ehrman and Leaver, 2003; Leaver, Ehrman and Shekhtman, 2005; Reid, 1995a, 1998). The negative aspect is that hardly any attempt has been made to address the issue of the various conceptual ambiguities and difficulties associated with the notion, as if authors had been oblivious to the problematic nature of the concept. Furthermore, empirical studies conducted on L2 learning have typically produced weak, mixed or at best moderate results, as a consequence of which there has been a gradual loss of interest in language learning style research in the second half of the 1990s. However, this situation may be changing for the better because there has been a renewed interest since the late 1990s in designing learning style constructs in several parts of the world.

Two instruments in particular are noteworthy: Cohen, Oxford and Chi's (2001) *Learning Style Survey* and the *Ehrman and Leaver Learning Style Questionnaire* (Ehrman and Leaver, 2003). The latter was based on a novel theoretical construct put forward by Ehrman and Leaver, the *E and L Construct*, which offers a systematic and comprehensive summary of the state of the art in language learning style research. It reorganises 10 established style dimensions under a new, comprehensive and parsimonious construct along one superordinate style dimension, with the two poles labelled *ectasis* and *synopsis*. The main difference between the two extremes is that an *ectenic* learner wants or needs conscious control over the learning process, whereas a *synoptic* learner leaves more to preconscious or unconscious processing. The style dimensions range from the classic concept of *field dependence-independence* to *impulsiveness-reflectiveness*, but do not include sensory preferences (e.g. visual vs. aural styles) even though these have constituted the best established learning style dimension in L2 research (see e.g. Reid, 1995a, 1998).

LANGUAGE LEARNING STRATEGIES

Intuitively, I have always believed in the existence and significance of learning strategies and yet I became increasingly puzzled over the years about the lack of an unambiguous theoretical definition of the learning strategy construct. And, similarly to learning styles, most of the relevant literature in the L2 field seems to ignore this problem. So let us first examine the definition issue.

According to a comprehensive definition of learning strategies offered by Oxford (1999, p. 518), the construct refers to "specific actions, behaviours, steps, or techniques that students use to improve their own progress in developing skills in a second or foreign language. These strategies can facilitate the internalisation, storage, retrieval or use of the new language." Definitions of learning strategies do not come any better than this, as indicated by the fact that a recent definition from educational psychology by one of the most influential American strategy experts, Claire Weinstein, covered the same aspects: "Learning strategies include any thoughts, behaviours, beliefs or emotions that facilitate the acquisition, understanding or later transfer of new knowledge and skills" (Weinstein, Husman and Dierking, 2000, p. 727).

Although these definitions appear to be logical and exhaustive, they leave several issues open. The most fundamental one is this: What exactly is the difference between engaging in an ordinary learning activity and a strategic learning activity? That is, what is the difference between the processes of *learning* and *learning strategy use*? In Dörnyei (2005) the following illustration of this problem is given: If someone memorises vocabulary by simply looking at a bilingual vocabulary list, most people would say that this is an example of learning. But if the person applies some colour marking code to highlight the words in the list which he or she still does not know, suddenly we can start talking about strategic learning. But what is the difference? The colour code?

So what are the distinguishing features of learning strategies? Weinstein et al. (2000) offered three critical characteristics: *goal-directed*, *intentionally invoked* and *effortful*. The problem with these intuitively appealing attributes is that they can also be true about *hard* and *focused* learning in general. Does that mean that hard and focused learning is by definition strategic? This is not an unreasonable question, because Macaro (2001) also raised the same issue: "An interesting practice-related avenue to pursue is whether what we mean by *effort* when doing a language task simply means the effective deployment of a range of strategies in a task" (p. 264). However, if we define the strategic quality of learning with goal-oriented, intentionally evoked and effortful behaviour then we, in effect, equate 'strategic' with 'motivated,' because goal-oriented, intentionally evoked and effortful are three key features of motivation.

Cohen (1998) highlighted a further important aspect of learning strategies, the *element of choice*. He argued that it is an essential feature of these strategies that they are voluntarily employed by the learner. Although this is clearly important in distinguishing learning strategies from creative teacher-owned tasks, choice is still not enough to distinguish strategies from non-strategies because students tend to make several choices concerning their learning process that are not strategic in the strict sense, that is, which do not necessarily involve purposeful attempts to enhance the effectiveness of learning. Examples include choosing the time to do home assignments; selecting a pen for doing a writing task; choosing a partner for pairwork whom one likes; performing a classroom task in a way that it will impress one's peers, etc.

I believe the best way of distinguishing between normal learning activities and learning strategy use has been proposed by Riding and Rayner (1998). They argued that an activity becomes strategic when it is particularly *appropriate* for the individual learner, in contrast to general learning activities which a student may find less helpful. Accordingly, learners engage in strategic learning if they exert purposeful effort to select and then pursue learning procedures that they believe will increase their individual learning effectiveness. The same idea has been expressed more technically, from an information-processing perspective, by Winne (2001), who distinguished between *tactics* and *strategies*. A tactic, according to Winne, is a "particular form of schema that is represented as a rule in IF-THEN form, sometimes called a condition-action rule" (p. 159). A strategy is a broader design or plan for approaching a high-level goal and it coordinates a set of tactics. Winne argued that the actual student response only becomes strategic if it matches the IF condition in the pursuit of a goal, that is, if it is appropriate for the particular purpose.

Although defining learning strategies in terms of *appropriateness* appears to be simple and comprehensive, we must note that strategies conceptualised in this vein can only be defined relative to a particular agent, because a specific learning technique may be strategic for one and non-strategic for another depending on the person's IF condition and how the specific strategy offers a personally effective response to that. This relativity is not necessarily a problem but it does go against the standard view in the field; for example, this conception would disqualify several learning strategy inventories which start out with a list of preconceived strategies and learners are asked about the extent of their use of these; however, questionnaire items of this sort do not make sense as they usually posit a rating scale with 'not used or endorsed' at one end, which simply does not apply to strategies conceived in this way (for a new approach to assessing strategic learning, see Tseng, Dörnyei and Schmitt, 2006).

Learning strategies in L2 studies

Although the theoretical inconsistencies surrounding the learning strategy literature in general had been known since the early days, it was not at all unreasonable that the L2 field showed remarkable tolerance of these shortcomings. After all, learning strategies represented one of the most promising topics in the broader field of educational psychology in the 1980s and — what was just as important — research studies that included language learning strategies as either dependent or independent variables tended to produce interesting results (for reviews, see Chamot, 2001; Cohen, 1998; Oxford, 1996). There was an increasing body of research evidence that learning strategies played an important role in L2 attainment and their study offered a glimpse into the subtle mechanisms that constituted the complex process of learning. Any doubts about the validity of the construct were shrugged off by saying that significant developments are often accompanied by a theoretical muddle that will eventually be cleared away by the subsequent restructuring of our existing knowledge.

Regrettably, the necessary theoretical clarification about the nature of the learning strategy concept has not taken place, which resulted in a marked shift in the evolution and application of the notion both in L2 research and educational psychology. In the former field, the concept has increasingly shifted from the basic research domain into the more applied realm of language teaching methodology. In educational psychology the term *learning strategy* was first marginalised and then virtually abandoned by the research community in favour of the more versatile concept of *self-regulation*.

Interestingly, Joan Rubin (2001, 2005) has recently introduced the concept of *"learner self-management"* in L2 studies, and this construct parallels the 'self-regulation' construct established in psychology. This is an important development because the new concept, proposed by one of the leading language learning strategy experts, outlines a future research direction that accommodates some of the concerns outlined above. Rubin's construct of learner self-management refers to the ability to deploy *metacognitive strategic procedures* and to access relevant *knowledge and beliefs*. The former involves planning, monitoring, evaluating, problem-solving and implementing, whereas the latter consists of task knowledge, self knowledge, beliefs, background knowledge and strategy knowledge. Only the last component, strategic knowledge, concerns traditionally conceived learning strategies, and therefore Rubin's construct can be seen as a major extension of the traditional conceptualisation of L2 strategic learning. It will be interesting to see to what extent other strategy experts will embrace Rubin's ideas and how useful the new construct will be with regard to practical strategy training.

Strategy training in L2 studies

Although the amount of research on language learning strategies has been on the decrease in general, there is one area which is a striking exception: language teaching methodology. When it comes to examining how to train students to be more effective strategic learners, there is a healthy supply of summaries, policy papers and various sorts of training materials. Is this not a contradiction to the previous suggestion that learning strategies have contestable validity as a concept? I do not believe so. If we think about it, even if the notion *learning strategy* does not exist as a distinctive aspect of learning but only indicates creative and personalised learning behaviours, the training of these 'strategies' would be a highly desirable activity as it would amount, in effect, to the teaching of learners ways in which they can learn better. And no one would question the fact that most learners would benefit from an improvement of their study skills.

The notion of *learning to learn* in L2 studies has a history of over two decades, starting with Ellis and Sinclair's (1989) famous coursebook, *Learning to Learn English: A Course in Learner Training*, and with more recent books highlighting the specific training of learner strategies (e.g. Chamot, Barnhardt, El-Dinary and Robbins, 1999; Grenfell and Harris, 1999; Macaro, 2001). In educational psychology we can find the same type of publications, with titles highlighting either 'learning to learn' or 'learning strategies' (e.g. Dembo, 2000; VanderStoep and Pintrich, 2003).

Although the various strategy training frameworks differ in detail, they aim to achieve the same overall goals: to raise the learners' awareness about learning strategies and model strategies overtly along with the task; to encourage strategy use and give a rationale for it; to offer a wide menu of relevant strategies for learners to choose from; to offer controlled practice in the use of some strategies; and to provide some sort of a post-task analysis which allows students to reflect on their strategy use. Arguably the most inspiring and instructive part of strategy training is the 'sharing session,' where students are asked to share their learning discoveries and self-generated learning strategies as a regular part of class. Students who are directly involved in the learning process often have fresh insights that they can share with fellow learners in simplified terms, and personal learning strategies are often quite amusing and therefore students usually enjoy discussing them. (For summaries of strategy training, see e.g. Chamot et al., 1999; Cohen, 1998; Harris, 2003; Macaro, 2001; McDonough, 1999). An ambitious recent initiative to integrate learning strategies into language instruction has been provided by Andrew Cohen in his *Styles and Strategies-Based Instruction* (Cohen, 2002; Cohen and Weaver, 2004), which is a learner-focused approach that combines strategy training with awareness raising about the learners' style preferences and the fit between strategies and styles.

Learning strategies and self-regulation in educational psychology

Although the construct of learning strategies has continued to be used for practical purposes in educational psychology, researchers have increasingly found the notion unhelpful when conducting in-depth analyses of the antecedents and ingredients of strategic learning; as a consequence, the concept had been sidelined and marginalised by the 1990s. This does not mean that scholars developed second thoughts about the virtues and benefits associated with learning strategies that made this line of research so popular in the 1980s. Far from it: the learners' proactive and informed contribution to increasing the effectiveness of their own learning was seen as more important than ever before. What had changed was the research perspective: It was realised that strategic learning was a far more complex issue than it was thought before and therefore simply focusing on the 'surface manifestations' — that is, the tactics and techniques that strategic learners actually employ — did not do the topic justice. Scholars recognised that the important thing about proactive strategic learners is not necessarily the exact nature of the strategies, tactics or techniques they apply, but rather the fact that they *do apply* them. That is, what makes strategic learners special is not so much what they do as the fact that they choose to put creative effort into improving their own learning and that they have the capacity to do so. As a consequence, a new construct, 'self-regulation' or 'self-regulated learning,' was introduced in the educational psychological literature.

One may feel that this change has been a mere face-lift and research into self-regulation carried on doing the same kind of investigations as before by simply replacing the term *strategy* (which seemed to cause most of the confusion) with a new metaphor. Although for some scholars this may have indeed been the case, and they merely jumped from one band wagon onto another at the beginning of the 1990s, there are at least two aspects of this conceptual shift that turned out to be truly significant:

a. By shifting the focus from the *product* (strategies) to the *process* (self-regulation), researchers have created more leeway for themselves: Although the so-called 'self-regulatory mechanisms' are very similar to 'learning strategies' and carry the same problems, these mechanisms are not the only important elements within the self-regulatory process and therefore their insufficient understanding does not necessarily prevent researchers from making headway in understanding other aspects of self-regulation.

b. The new perspective on self-regulation also offers a broader perspective than the previous focus on learning strategies, allowing scholars to make links with aspects of self-regulation that are not confined to the area of learning but concern other types of cognitive and behavioural processes (e.g. in clinical, health and organisational psychology); an excellent summary of this cross-disciplinary effort is provided by Boekaerts, Pintrich and Zeidner's (2000) *Handbook of Self-Regulation.*

As a result of this paradigm shift, by the beginning of the 1990s the study of self-regulation had come of age, causing a "virtual explosion of work in this area" (Zeidner Boekaerts and Pintrich, 2000, p. 750), thereby becoming a "natural and organic part of the landscape of psychology and education" (p. 749).

CONCLUSION

If we consider the existing research on the various ID variables together, we can find three intriguing parallels (Dörnyei, 2005): The most striking aspect of the contemporary ID literature is the emerging theme of *context*: It appears that cutting-edge research in all the diverse areas has been addressing the same issue, that is, the situated nature of the ID factors in question. Scholars have come to reject the notion that the various traits are context-independent and absolute, and are now proposing new dynamic conceptualisations in which ID factors enter into some interaction with the situational parameters rather than cutting across tasks and environments (see also Ellis, 2004).

The second common aspect of much of the best research in the field is the suggestion that instead of trying to detect linear relationships between certain ID factors and corresponding outcome/performance variables in isolation, researchers should work with more complex theoretical paradigms. In these, the various ID factors are seen either to operate in concert or to interfere with each other in a clearly delineated manner and there is a growing conviction amongst scholars that combinations of traits have more predictive power than traits in isolation.

The third important theme that connects the various bodies of research is the recent attempt in the literature to try and relate ID variables to specific SLA processes. This, of course, has been made possible by the increasingly elaborate mapping of the mental mechanisms underlying SLA during the past decade and it seems that ID researchers have welcomed the opportunity to integrate their field into mainstream SLA research. I believe that the future of L2 studies in general lies in the integration of linguistic and psychological approaches in a balanced and complementary manner, and it seems that the study of individual differences has taken this forward-pointing route.

Chapter 9

Creating a Motivating Classroom Environment

In Cummins, J. and Davison, C. (Eds.). (2007). International handbook of English language teaching (Vol. 2, pp. 719-731). New York: Springer.

Researchers analyzing the effectiveness of second language (L2) education usually focus on issues such as the quality and quantity of L2 input, the nature of the language learning tasks, and the teaching methodology applied, as well as various learner traits and strategies. These are undoubtedly central factors in L2 learning, and they significantly determine the effectiveness of the process, particularly in the short run. If, however, we consider learning achievement from a longer-term perspective, other aspects of the classroom experience, such as a motivating classroom climate, will also gain increasing importance. Wlodkowski (1986) points out that although boring lessons can be very unpleasant and sometimes excruciatingly painful, boredom itself does not seem to affect the short-term effectiveness of learning. After all, much of what many of us currently know has been mastered while being exposed to some uninspiring presentation or dull practice sequence. Yet, no one would question that attempts to eliminate boredom from the classroom should be high on every teacher's agenda. Why is that? What is the significance of trying to create a more pleasant classroom environment?

The basic assumption underlying this chapter is that long-term, sustained learning — such as the acquisition of an L2 — cannot take place unless the educational context provides, in addition to cognitively adequate instructional practices, sufficient inspiration and enjoyment to build up continuing motivation in the learners. Boring but systematic teaching can be effective in producing, for example, good test results, but rarely does it inspire a lifelong commitment to the subject matter. This chapter will focus on how to generate this additional inspiration, that is, how to create a motivating classroom environment.

The characteristics of the learning context can be studied from a number of different perspectives. In educational psychology there has been an established line of research focusing on a multidimensional concept describing the psychological climate of the learning context, termed the *classroom environment* (cf. Fraser and Walberg, 1991). Educational researchers have also focused on aspects of classroom management as an antecedent of the overall classroom climate (e.g., Jones and Jones, 2000). Adopting a different perspective to describe classroom reality, social psychologists have looked at the dynamics of the learner group as part of the vivid discipline of group dynamics (e.g., Schmuck and Schmuck, 2001). Motivational psychologists have taken yet another approach by focusing on the motivational teaching practices and strategies employed in the classroom (for example, Pintrich and Schunk, 2002). While all these lines of investigation represent slightly different priorities and research paradigms, in the end they concern the same larger picture and therefore show a considerable overlap. In the following overview, I will synthesise the various approaches by focusing on the different psychological processes that underlie and shape classroom life.

TOWARD A COHESIVE LEARNER GROUP

One of the most salient features of the classroom environment is the quality of the relationships between the class members. The quality of teaching and learning is entirely different depending on whether the classroom is characterised by a climate of trust and support or by a competitive, cutthroat atmosphere. If learners form cliques and subgroups that are hostile to each other and resist any cooperation, the overall climate will be stressful for teachers and students alike, and learning effectiveness is likely to plummet. How do such negative relationship patterns develop? And, once established, how can they be changed? These questions have been studied extensively within the field of group dynamics (for a review, see Forsyth, 1999), and recent work on the topic in the L2 field has produced detailed recommendations on how to develop cohesiveness in the language classroom (e.g., Dörnyei and Malderez, 1999; Dörnyei and Murphey, 2003; Ehrman and Dörnyei, 1998; Senior, 1997, 2002).

Intermember relations within a group are of two basic types: *attraction* and *acceptance*. Attraction involves an initial instinctive appeal, caused by factors such as physical attractiveness, perceived competence, and similarities in attitudes, personality, hobbies, living conditions, etc. An important tenet in group dynamics is that despite their initial impact, these factors are usually of little importance for the group in the long run, and group development can result in strong cohesiveness among members regardless of, or even in spite of, the initial intermember likes and dislikes. In a "healthy group," initial attraction bonds are gradually replaced by a deeper and steadier type of interpersonal relationship, acceptance.

Acceptance involves a feeling toward another person which is non-evaluative in nature, has nothing to do with likes and dislikes, but entails an unconditional positive regard toward the individual (Rogers, 1983), acknowledging the person as a complex human being with many (possibly conflicting) values and imperfections. One of the most important characteristics of a good group is the emergence of a high level of acceptance between members that is powerful enough to override even negative feelings between some. This accepting climate, then, forms the basis of a more general feature of the group, group cohesiveness.

Group cohesiveness refers to the closeness and "we" feeling of a group, that is, the internal gelling force that keeps the group together. In certain groups it can be very strong, which is well illustrated by reunion parties held even several decades after the closure of the group. Cohesiveness is, obviously, built on intermember acceptance, but it also involves two other factors that contribute to the group's internal binding force: the members' commitment to the task/purpose of the group and group pride, the latter referring to the prestige of group membership (cf., elite clubs).

How can we promote acceptance and cohesiveness? There are a variety of methods, and from an L2 teaching perspective, Dörnyei and Murphey (2003) list the following main factors:

1. Learning about each other: This is the most crucial and general factor fostering intermember relationships, involving the students' sharing genuine personal information with each other. Acceptance simply does not occur without knowing the other person well enough — enemy images or a lack of tolerance very often stem from insufficient knowledge about the other party.

2. Proximity, contact, and interaction: Proximity refers to the physical distance between people, contact to situations where learners can meet and communicate spontaneously, and interaction to special contact situations in which the behaviour of each person influences the others'. These three factors are effective natural gelling agents, which highlight the importance of classroom issues such as the seating plan, small group work, and independent student projects.

3. Difficult admission: This explains why exclusive club membership is usually valued very highly, and the same principle is intuitively acted

upon in the various initiation ceremonies for societies, teams, or military groups.

4. Shared group history: The amount of time people have spent together and "Remember when we..." statements usually have a strong bonding effect.

5. The rewarding nature of group activities: Rewards may involve the joy of performing the activities, approval of the goals, success in achieving these goals, and personal benefits (such as grades or prizes).

6. Group legend: Successful groups often create a kind of group mythology that includes giving the group a name, inventing special group characteristics (for example, dress code), and group rituals, as well as creating group mottoes, logos, and other symbols such as flags or coats of arms.

7. Public commitment to the group: Group agreements and contracts as to common goals and rules are types of such public commitment, and wearing school colours or T-shirts is another way of achieving this.

8. Investing in the group: When members spend a considerable amount of time and effort contributing to the group goals, this increases their commitment toward these goals. That is, psychological membership correlates with the actual acts of membership.

9. Extracurricular activities: These represent powerful experiences— indeed, one successful program is often enough to "make" the group, partly because during such outings students lower their "school filter" and relate to each other as "civilians" rather than students. This positive experience will then prevail in their memory, adding a fresh and real feel to their school relationships.

10. Cooperation toward common goals: Superordinate goals that require the cooperation of everybody to achieve them have been found to be the most effective means of bringing together even openly hostile parties.

11. Intergroup competition (that is, games in which small groups compete with each other within a class): These can be seen as a type of

powerful collaboration in which people unite in an effort to win. You may want to group students together who would not normally make friends easily, and mix up the subteams regularly.

12. Defining the group against another: Emphasizing the discrimination between "us" and "them" is a powerful but obviously dangerous aspect of cohesiveness. While stirring up emotions against an outgroup in order to strengthen ingroup ties is definitely to be avoided, it might be OK to occasionally allow students to reflect on how special their class and the time they spend together might be, relative to other groups.

13. Joint hardship and common threat: Strangely enough, going through some difficulty or calamity together (for example, carrying out some tough physical task together or being in a common predicament) has a beneficial group effect.

14. Teacher's role modelling: Friendly and supportive behaviour by the teacher is infectious, and students are likely to follow suit.

TOWARD A PRODUCTIVE NORM AND ROLE SYSTEM IN THE CLASSROOM

When people are together, in any function and context, they usually follow certain rules and routines that help to prevent chaos and allow everybody to go about their business as effectively as possible. Some of these rules are general and apply to everybody, in which case we can speak about group norms. Some others, however, are specific to certain people who fulfil specialised functions, in which case they are associated with group roles.

Group norms

In educational settings we find many classroom norms that are explicitly imposed by the teacher or mandated by the school. However, the majority of the norms that govern our everyday life are not so explicitly formulated, and yet they are there, implicitly. Many of these implicit norms evolve spontaneously and unconsciously during the interactions of the group members, for example, by copying certain behaviours of some influential member or the leader. These behaviours then become solidified into norms, and these "unofficial" norms can actually be more powerful than their official counterparts. The significance of classroom norms, whether official or unofficial in their origin, lies in the fact that they can considerably enhance or decrease students' academic achievement and work morale. In many contemporary classrooms, for example, we come across the norm of mediocrity that refers to the peer pressure put on students not to excel or else they will be called names such as "nerd", "swot", "brain", and so on.

One norm that is particularly important to language learning situations is the norm of tolerance. The language classroom is an inherently face-threatening environment because learners are required to take continuous risks as they need to communicate using a severely restricted language code. An established norm of tolerance ensures that students will not be embarrassed or criticised if they make a mistake and, more generally, that mistakes are seen and welcomed as a natural part of learning. How can we make sure that the norms in our classroom promote rather than hinder learning? The key issue is that real group norms are inherently social products, and in order for a norm to be long-lasting and constructive, it needs to be explicitly discussed and accepted as right and proper. Therefore, Dörnyei and Malderez (1997) have proposed that it is beneficial to include an explicit norm-building procedure early in the group's life. They suggest formulating potential norms, justifying their purpose in order to enlist support for them, having them discussed by the whole group, and finally agreeing on a mutually accepted set of class rules, with the consequences for violating them also specified. These class rules can then be displayed on a wall chart.

Our norm-building effort will really pay off when someone breaks the norms, for example, by misbehaving or not doing something expected. It has been observed that the more time we spend setting, negotiating, and modelling the norms, the fewer people will go astray. And when they do, it is usually the group that brings them back in line. Having the group on your side in coping with deviations and maintaining discipline is a major help: members usually bring to bear considerable group pressure on errant members and enforce conformity with the group norms.

Group roles

Role as a technical term originally comes from sociology and refers to the shared expectation of how an individual should behave. Roles describe the norms that go with a particular position or function, specifying what people are supposed to do. There is a general agreement that roles are of great importance with regard to the life and productivity of the group: if students are cast in the right role, they will become useful members of the team, they will perform necessary and complementary functions, and at the same time they will be satisfied with their self-image and contribution. However, an inappropriate role can lead to personal conflict and will work against the cohesiveness and effectiveness of the group. Thus, a highly performing class group will display a balanced set of complementary and constructive student roles.

Although listing all the possible roles is impossible (partly because some of them are specific to a particular group's unique composition or task), some typical examples include the leader, the organiser, the initiator, the energiser, the harmoniser, the information-seeker, the complainer, the scapegoat, the pessimist, the rebel, the clown, and the outcast. How do these roles emerge? They may evolve naturally, in which case it is to some extent a question of luck whether the emerged roles add up to a balanced and functional tapestry. Alternatively, by their own communications or through using certain teaching structures, teachers might encourage students to explore and assume different roles and adopt the ones that suit them best for strategies and activities. The most subtle way of encouraging role taking is to notice and reinforce any tentative role attempts on the students' part, and sometimes even to highlight possible roles that a particular marginal learner may assume. Alternatively, teachers can make sure that everybody has something to contribute by assigning specific roles for an activity, such as chair, time-keeper, task-initiator, clarifier, provocateur, synthesiser, checker, and secretary (Cohen, 1994; Dörnyei and Murphey, 2003). Having explicitly marked roles in the lessons has the further advantage that teachers can prepare the students to perform these roles effectively, including providing the specific language routines that typically accompany a role.

TOWARD AN OPTIMAL LEADERSHIP STYLE

Language teachers are by definition group leaders and as such they determine every facet of classroom life. The study of various leadership styles and their impact has a vast literature, but all the different accounts agree on one thing: leadership matters. As Hook and Vass (2000) succinctly put it, "Leadership is the fabled elixir. It can turn failing schools into centres of excellence...It is the process by which you allow your students to become winners" (p. 5).

The study of group leadership goes back to a classic study more than 60 years ago. Working with American children in a summer camp, Lewin and his colleagues (Lewin, Lippitt, and White, 1939) were interested to find out how the participants would react to three very different group leadership styles:

1. Autocratic (or authoritarian) leadership, which maintains complete control over the group

2. Democratic leadership, where the leader tries to share some of the leadership functions with the members by involving them in decision-making about their own functioning

3. Laissez-faire leadership, where the teacher performs very little leadership behaviour at all

The results were striking. Of the three leadership types, the laissez-faire style produced the least desirable outcomes: the psychological absence of the leader retarded the process of forming a group structure, and consequently the children under this condition were disorganised and frustrated, experienced the most stress, and produced very little work. Autocratic groups were found to be more productive, spending more time on work than democratic ones, but the quality of the products in the democratic groups was judged superior. In addition, it was also observed that whenever the leader left the room, the autocratic groups stopped working whereas the democratic groups carried on. From a group perspective, the most interesting results of the study concerned the comparison of interpersonal relations and group climate in the democratic and autocratic groups. In these respects democratic groups significantly exceeded autocratic groups: the former were characterised by friendlier communication, more group-orientedness, and better member leader relationships, whereas the level of hostility observed in the autocratic groups was 30 times as great as in democratic groups, and aggressiveness was also considerably (eight times) higher in them.

Although leadership studies have moved a long way since this pioneering research, the main conclusion that a democratic leadership style offers the best potential for school learning is still widely endorsed. In educational psychology, therefore, an important research direction has been to operationalise this general style characteristic. Several models for the "democratic" leader/teacher have been offered in the past; the most influential metaphor used in contemporary educational research and methodology is the humanistic notion of the group leader as a *facilitator*.

A Situated Approach to Facilitation

The concept of the teacher as the facilitator highlights the important role the learner is to take in the learning process, while restricting the teacher's role to facilitating learning, that is, providing an appropriate climate and resources to support the student. Thus, the teachers are not so much "drill sergeants" or "lecturers of knowledge" as partners in the learning process. How should they behave to achieve this? It depends largely on the developmental phase of the learner group, that is, on how far the class has progressed toward becoming a mature and cohesive social unit. In *The Complete Facilitator's Handbook*, John Heron (1999) offers a relatively straightforward situated system of operation and control concerning the behaviour of facilitators.

Heron (1999) argues that — contrary to beliefs — a good facilitator is not characterised by a "soft touch" or a "free for all" mentality. He distinguishes three different modes of facilitation:

1. *Hierarchical* mode, whereby the facilitator exercises the power to direct the learning process *for* the group, thinking and acting *on behalf of* the group, and making all the major decisions. In this mode, therefore, the facilitator takes full responsibility for designing the syllabus and providing structures for learning.

2. *Cooperative* mode, whereby the facilitator shares the power and responsibilities with the group, prompting members to be more self-directing in the various forms of learning. In this mode the facilitator collaborates with the members in devising the learning process, and outcomes are negotiated.

3. *Autonomous* mode, whereby the facilitator respects the autonomy of the group in finding their own way and exercising their own judgment. The task of the facilitator in this mode is to create the conditions within which students' self-determination can flourish.

Heron has found that the ideal proportion of the three modes changes with the level of development of the group. He distinguishes three stages:

1. At the outset of group development, the optimal mode is predominantly *hierarchical*, offering a clear and straightforward framework within which early development of cooperation and autonomy can safely occur. Participants at this stage may be lacking the necessary knowledge and skills to orientate themselves, and they rely on the leader for guidance. Within the hierarchical mode there should be, however,

cooperative exchanges with the teacher and autonomous practice on their own. Also, even in this mode the students' consent should be sought for the major leader-owned decisions.

2. Later, in the middle phase, more *cooperation* with group members may be appropriate in managing the learning process. The facilitator can negotiate the curriculum with the students and cooperatively guide their learning activities. The students' acquired confidence will allow them to take an increasing part in making the decisions about how their learning should proceed.

3. Finally, when the group has reached maturity and is thus ready for the *autonomous* mode, more power needs to be delegated to the members so that they can achieve full self-direction in their learning. Learning contracts, self-evaluation, and peer assessment may "institutionalise" their independence.

Thus, to synthesise Heron's (1999) system with the Lewin, Lippitt, and White (1939) study, a group-sensitive teaching practice begins more autocratically to give direction, security, and impetus to the group. Then as the students begin performing, teachers initiate more democratic control of the processes, increasingly relying on the group's self-regulatory resources. When the group further matures and begins to show its initiative, a more autonomy-inviting, almost laissez-faire, leadership style might be the most conducive to encouraging student independence — but of course, this is a well-prepared withdrawal of the scaffolding rather than an abandonment of leadership responsibilities.

ADOPTING A MOTIVATIONAL TEACHING PRACTICE

Although the title of this chapter identifies the motivating aspect of the classroom environment as the focal issue, the term *motivation* has hardly been mentioned in the previous sections. The main reason for this is that so far we have looked at the characteristics of the whole learner group rather than the individual learner. However, the term *motivation* has usually been associated with an individualistic perspective, focusing on the individual's values, attitudes, goals, and intentions. If we want to talk about the motivation of a whole learner group, it is necessary to also use group-level counterparts of the concept, such as group cohesiveness, group norms, and group leadership. After all, these latter factors all play an important role in determining the behaviour of the learner group, and therefore they can be seen as valid motivational antecedents. In other words, when we discuss the learning behaviour of groups of learners, motivational psychology and group dynamics converge. Having covered the most important group features, the rest of this chapter will draw on findings from more traditionally conceived motivation research.

What makes the classroom climate motivating and how can we increase this characteristic? To start with, let me propose that the motivational character of the classroom is largely a function of the teacher's motivational teaching practice, and is therefore within our explicit control. Therefore, the emphasis in the following analysis will be on proactive and conscious strategies that can be used to promote classroom motivation.

After the initial motivational conditions have been successfully created — that is, the class is characterised by a safe climate, cohesiveness, and a good student-teacher relationship — the motivational teaching practice needs to be established.

This process comprises three phases: (a) generating initial motivation; (b) maintaining and protecting motivation; and (c) encouraging positive retrospective self-evaluation.

Generating initial motivation

Although many psychologists believe that children are inherently eager to expand their knowledge about the world and, therefore, the learning experience is by definition a source of intrinsic pleasure for them, classroom teachers tend to have perceptions that are in sharp contrast with this idyllic view. Instead of all those keen pupils, all they can often see is rather reluctant youngsters who are totally unaware of the fact that there should be an innate curiosity in them, let alone a desire to learn. And even if we are fortunate to have a class of students with a high degree of academic motivation, we cannot expect all the students to favour the L2 course over all the other subjects they study. Thus, unless we are singularly fortunate with the composition of our class group, student motivation will not be automatically there, and we will need to try to actively generate positive student attitudes toward L2 learning.

There are several facets of creating initial student motivation. Dörnyei (2001a) has divided these into five broad groups:

1. Enhancing the learners' language-related values and attitudes: Our basic value system greatly determines our preferences and approaches to activities. We can distinguish three types of language-related values: (a) *intrinsic value*, related to the interest in and anticipated enjoyment of the actual process of learning; (b) *integrative value*, related to our attitudes toward the L2, its speakers, and the culture it conveys; and (c) *instrumental value*, related to the perceived practical, pragmatic benefits that the mastery of the L2 might bring about.

2. Increasing the learners' expectancy of success: We do things best if we expect to succeed, and, to turn this statement round, we are unlikely to be motivated to aim for something if we feel we will never get there.

3. Increasing the learners' goal-orientedness: In a typical class, too many students do not really understand or accept why they are doing a learning activity. Moreover, the official class goal (that is, mastering the course content) may well not be the class group's only goal and in extreme cases may not be a group goal at all!

4. Making the teaching materials relevant for the learners: The core of this issue has been succinctly summarised by McCombs and Whisler (1997): "Educators think students do not care, while the students tell us they do care about learning but are not getting what they need" (p. 38).

5. Creating realistic learner beliefs: It is a peculiar fact of life that most learners will have certain beliefs about language learning, and most

of these beliefs are likely to be (at least partly) incorrect. Such false beliefs can then function like time "bombs" at the beginning of a language course because of the inevitable disappointment that is to follow, or can clash with the course methodology and thus hinder progress.

6. Once the main aspects of creating initial student motivation have been identified, it is possible to generate or select a variety of specific classroom techniques to promote the particular dimension (for practical ideas, see Brophy, 1998; Dörnyei, 2001c).

Maintaining and protecting motivation

It is one thing to initially whet the students' appetite with appropriate motivational techniques, but unless motivation is actively maintained and protected, the natural tendency to lose sight of the goal, to get tired or bored of the activity, and to give way to attractive distractions will result in the initial motivation gradually petering out. Therefore, motivation needs to be actively nurtured. The spectrum of motivational strategies relevant to this phase is rather broad (since ongoing human behaviour can be modified in so many different ways), and the following six areas appear to be particularly relevant for classroom application:

- making learning stimulating and enjoyable;
- presenting tasks in a motivating way;
- setting specific learner goals;
- protecting the learners' self-esteem and increasing their self-confidence;
- creating learner autonomy;
- promoting self-motivating learner strategies.

These motivational dimensions, except for the last one, are more straightforward than the facets of initial motivation described above, and due to space limitations I will not elaborate on them here (for a theoretical and methodological discussion, see Dörnyei, 2001a, 2001c). Self-motivating strategies, however, are a relatively unknown and underutilised area, so let us look at them in more detail.

Self-motivating strategies can be characterised, using Corno's (1993) words, "as a dynamic system of psychological control processes that protect concentration and directed effort in the face of personal and/or environmental distractions, and so aid learning and performance" (p. 16). That is, they involve ways for the learners to motivate themselves and thereby sustain the action when the initial motivation is flagging. These strategies are particularly important in second language learning because due to the long-lasting nature of the process, L2 learners need to maintain their commitment and effort over a long period, often in the face of adversity. Let us not forget that failure in language learning is regrettably a very frequent phenomenon worldwide.

Based on the pioneering work of Corno (1993), Corno and Kanfer (1993), and Kuhl (1987), Dörnyei (2001c) has divided self-motivating strategies into five main classes:

- *Commitment control strategies* for helping to preserve or increase the learners' original goal commitment (e.g., keeping in mind favourable expectations or positive incentives and rewards; focusing on what would happen if the original intention failed)
- *Metacognitive control strategies* for monitoring and controlling concentration, and for curtailing unnecessary procrastination (e.g., identifying recurring distractions and developing defensive routines; focusing on the first steps to take when getting down to an activity)
- *Satiation control strategies* for eliminating boredom and adding extra attraction or interest to the task (e.g., adding a twist to the task; using one's fantasy to liven up the task)
- *Emotion control strategies* for managing disruptive emotional states or moods, and for generating emotions that will be conducive to implementing one's intentions (e.g., self-encouragement; using relaxation and meditation techniques)
- *Environmental control strategies* for eliminating negative

environmental influences and exploiting positive environmental
influences by making the environment an ally in the pursuit of a
difficult goal (e.g., eliminating distractions; asking friends to help
and not to allow one to do something)

An important part of a motivational teaching practice that has a
considerable empowering effect is to raise student awareness of relevant
strategies and to remind them at appropriate times of their usefulness.

Encouraging positive retrospective self-evaluation

A large body of research has shown that the way learners feel
about their past accomplishments and the amount of satisfaction they
experience after successful task completion will significantly determine
how they approach subsequent learning tasks. Strangely enough, the
students' appraisal of their past performance depends not only on the
absolute, objective level of the success they have achieved but also on
how they subjectively interpret their achievement (which is why, for
example, we find so many people being regularly dissatisfied despite
their high-quality work). However, by using appropriate strategies,
teachers can help learners to evaluate their past performance in a more
"positive light," take more satisfaction in their successes and progress,
and explain their past failures in a constructive way. This latter area is
related to the role attributions, which is an issue practicing teachers
are usually unfamiliar with even though it has been a central topic in
educational psychology.

The term *attribution* has been used in motivational psychology to
refer to the explanation people offer about why they were successful
or, more importantly, why they failed in the past. Past research had
identified a certain hierarchy of the types of attributions people make
in terms of their motivating nature. Failure that is ascribed to stable and
uncontrollable factors such as low ability has been found to hinder future
achievement behaviour, whereas failure that is attributed to unstable

and controllable factors such as effort is less detrimental in that it can be remedied. Thus, the general recommendation in the literature is to try and promote effort attributions and prevent ability attributions in the students as much as possible. In failure situations, this can be achieved by emphasizing the low effort exerted as being a strong reason for underachievement, and if failure occurs in spite of hard work, we should highlight the inadequacy of the strategies employed.

Finally, no account of classroom motivation would be complete without discussing the controversial but very salient effects of various forms of feedback, rewards, and grades dispensed by the teacher. As these are all forms of external evaluation by authority figures, they have a particularly strong impact on the students' self-appraisal. Feedback has at least three functions:

1. Appropriate motivational feedback can have a gratifying function, that is, by offering praise it can increase learner satisfaction and lift the learning spirit.

2. By communicating trust and encouragement, motivational feedback can promote a positive self-concept and self-confidence in the student.

3. Motivational feedback should be informative, prompting the learner to reflect constructively on areas that need improvement.

However, we should note that one common feature of educational feedback — its controlling and judgmental nature (that is, comparing students against peer achievement or external standards) — is considered very harmful (Good and Brophy, 2002).

While feedback is generally considered a useful motivational tool when applied sensitively, rewards and grades (the latter being a form of rewards) are usually disapproved of by educational psychologists. This is all the more surprising because most teachers feel that rewards are positive things and dispense them liberally for good behaviour and praiseworthy efforts or accomplishments. So what's wrong with rewards?

The problem with rewards and with grades in particular is that they are very simplistic devices and they can do a great deal of damage. Rewards in themselves do not increase the inherent value of the learning task or task outcome, and neither do they concern other important learning aspects such as the learning process, the learning environment, or the learner's self-concept. Instead, all they do is simply attach a piece of "carrot or stick" to the task. By doing so, they divert the students' attention away from the real task and the real point of learning. When people start concentrating on the reward rather than on the task itself, they can easily succumb to the "mini-max principle" (Covington and Teel, 1996), whereby they attempt to maximise rewards with a minimum of effort. Indeed, we find that many students become grade driven, if not "grade grubbing," surprisingly early in their school career (Covington, 1999). Also, due to their ultimate importance in every facet of the education system, grades frequently become equated in the minds of school children with a sense of self-worth; that is, they consider themselves only as worthy as their school-related achievements, regardless of their personal characteristics such as being loving, good, or courageous. This is obviously a complex issue (for a more detailed discussion, see Dörnyei, 2001c; Good and Brophy, 2002; Pintrich and Schunk, 2001), but it is clear that we need to be cautious with rewards and grades and should try and rely on other forms of motivational practices as much as possible.

CONCLUSIONS

This overview has demonstrated that the quality of the classroom environment is made up of a number of varied ingredients. And just as in cooking, achieving an optimal, motivating outcome can be done using different combinations of spices: while some chefs rely on paprika and build the recipe around it, others prefer pepper and the herbs that go with it. The situation is exactly the same in developing a motivating teaching practice. As long as we are aware of the vast repertoire of techniques that are at our disposal, it is up to us to choose the specific ones that we will apply, based on the specific needs that arise in our concrete circumstances. There is only one thing we should not attempt: to try and apply all the techniques we know at the same time. This would be the perfect recipe for teacher burnout. What we need is quality rather than quantity; some of the most motivating teachers often rely on a few well-selected basic techniques.

Chapter 10

Researching Motivation: From Integrativeness to the Ideal L2 Self

In Hunston, S. and Oakey, D. (Eds.). (2010). Introducing applied linguistics: Concepts and skills (pp. 74-83). London: Routledge.

Language teachers frequently use the term 'motivation' when they describe successful or unsuccessful learners. This reflects our intuitive belief that during the lengthy and often tedious process of mastering a foreign/second language (L2), the learner's enthusiasm, commitment and persistence are key determinants of success or failure. Indeed, in the vast majority of cases, learners with sufficient motivation *can* achieve a working knowledge of an L2, *regardless of* their language aptitude, whereas without sufficient motivation even the brightest learners are unlikely to persist long enough to attain any really useful language ('you can lead a horse to water, but you can't make it drink').

Because of the central importance attached to it by practitioners and researchers alike, L2 motivation has been the target of a great deal of research in Applied Linguistics during the past decades. In this chapter

I describe a major theoretical shift that has recently been transforming the landscape of motivation research: the move from the traditional conceptualisation of motivation in terms of an *integrative/instrumental dichotomy* to the recent conceptualisation of motivation as being part of the learner's self system, with the motivation to learn an L2 being closely associated with the learner's *ideal L2 self.* For space limitations I cannot provide a detailed review of the relevant literature (for recent summaries, see Dörnyei, 2005; Dörnyei and Ushioda, 2009); instead, my focus will be on illustrating how such a major paradigm shift has emerged through a combination of theoretical considerations and empirical research findings.

THE STARTING POINT: 'INTEGRATIVENESS' AS A MOTIVATIONAL FACTOR

There has been a long-lived (and inaccurate) understanding in the L2 profession that language learning motivation can be divided into two main dimensions: *integrative motivation* and *instrumental motivation.* The former refers to the desire to learn an L2 of a valued community so that one can communicate with members of the community and sometimes even to become like them. Instrumental motivation, on the other hand, is related to the concrete benefits that language proficiency might bring about (e.g. career opportunities, increased salary). Thus, broadly speaking, it was thought that we learn a language either because we like it and its speakers or because we think it will be useful for us.

The integrative/instrumental distinction has been attributed (again somewhat inaccurately) to the influential work of Canadian social psychologist Robert Gardner (1985a, 2001), who did indeed introduce these terms but whose theoretical motivation construct was much more elaborate than this simplistic duality. Furthermore, Gardner hardly ever discussed the nature and impact of instrumental motivation, because he was almost exclusively interested in the interpersonal/emotional aspect of motivation that he termed 'integrativeness'. He characterised this motivational dimension as follows:

> Integrativeness reflects a genuine interest in learning the second
> language in order to come closer to the other language community. At
> one level, this implies an openness to, and respect for other cultural
> groups and ways of life. In the extreme, this might involve complete
> identification with the community (and possibly even withdrawal
> from one's original group), but more commonly it might well involve
> integration within both communities. (Gardner, 2001, p.5)

The concept of integrativeness/integrative motivation has become a
popular and much researched concept in L2 research, but starting in the
1990s an increasing number of scholars began to raise issues about how
generalizable the term was. In a multicultural setting such as Montreal,
where Gardner first developed his theory, it made sense to talk about
potential 'integration', but in learning situations where a foreign language
is taught only as a school subject without any direct contact with its
speakers (e.g. teaching English or French in Hungary, China, Japan
or other typical 'foreign language learning' contexts), the 'integrative'
metaphor simply did not make sense. In such environments what exactly
would be — to quote Gardner (2001) — 'the other language community'
that the learner would want to 'get closer to'? In many language learning
situations, and especially with the learning of world languages such as
English or French, it is not at all clear who 'owns' the L2, and this lack
of a specific L2 community undermines Gardner's theoretical concept of
integrativeness. This view has been shared by several scholars worldwide
(e.g. Coetzee-Van Rooy, 2006; Lamb, 2004; Yashima, 2000; for a review,
see Dörnyei, 2005), and, as a result, over the past decade I have been
trying to find a broader interpretation of the notion that goes beyond
the literal meaning of the verb 'integrate' but which also builds on the
relevant knowledge and considerable body of research that we have
accumulated in the past.

TOWARDS THE 'L2 MOTIVATIONAL SELF SYSTEM'

In 2005, I proposed a new motivation construct (Dörnyei, 2005) — the 'L2 Motivational Self System' — that builds upon the foundations laid by Gardner (1985a) but which at the same time broadens the scope of the theory to make it applicable in diverse language learning environments in our globalised world. The proposed model, which attempts to synthesise a number of influential new approaches in the field (e.g. Ushioda, 2001; Noels, 2003), has grown out of a combination of empirical research findings and theoretical considerations (for a detailed description, see Dörnyei, 2009b). Let us look at these more closely, starting with the former.

Empirical findings pointing to the need to reinterpret Integrativeness

Over the past 15 years I have been heading a research team in Hungary with the objective of carrying out a longitudinal survey amongst teenage language learners by administering an attitude/motivation questionnaire at regular intervals so that we can gauge the changes in the population's international orientation. So far three successive waves of data collections have been completed (in 1993, 1999 and 2004) involving over 13,000 learners (for a detailed summary, see Dörnyei, Csizér and Németh, 2006). The survey questionnaire targeted attitudes towards five target languages: English, German, French, Italian and Russian. It was originally developed in collaboration with one of Robert Gardner's closest associates, Richard Clement, and therefore integrativeness and instrumentality had a prominent place in it, but we also measured several other attitudinal/motivational dimensions, such as *Direct contact with L2 speakers* (i.e. attitudes towards actually meeting L2 speakers and travelling to their country), *Cultural interest* (i.e. the appreciation of cultural products associated with the particular L2 and conveyed by the media; e.g. films, TV programmes, magazines and pop music), *Vitality of L2 community* (i.e. the perceived importance and wealth of the L2 communities in question),

Milieu (i.e. the general perception of the importance of foreign languages in the learners' school context and in friends' and parents' views) and finally *Linguistic self-confidence* (i.e. a confident, anxiety-free belief that the mastery of an L2 is well within the learner's means).

In an analysis of the first two waves of the survey (Dörnyei and Csizér, 2002), we computed correlations of the various motivation components with a criterion measure, *Language choice*, which referred to the degree of the learners' desire to learn a particular L2 in the next school year. Correlation is a conceptually straightforward statistical procedure: it allows us to look at two variables and evaluate the strength and direction of their relationship or association with each other. To do so, we compute a 'correlation coefficient' between the two variables, which can range from −1 to +1, with a high correlation indicating a positive relationship, zero correlation no relationship, and a negative correlation an inverse relationship (Dörnyei, 2007b). Thus, for example, learners' IQ is expected to have a high positive correlation with their mathematics grades and zero correlation with, say, the love of chocolate. Table 10.1 presents the results.

Table 10.1   Correlations between the Attitudinal/Motivational Scales and Language Choice in the Dörnyei and Csizér (2002) Study

	English/ UK		English/ US		German		French		Italian		Russian	
	1993	1999	1993	1999	1993	1999	1993	1999	1993	1999	1993	1999
Integrative-ness	.43*	.33*	.43*	.33*	.47*	.43*	.42*	.44*	.43*	.43*	.25*	.32*
Instrument-ality	.28*	.25*	.28*	.25*	.30*	.30*	.27*	.30*	.29*	.31*	.20*	.21*
Attitudes towards L2 speakers/ community	.23*	.16*	.17*	.16*	.33*	.30*	.31*	.33*	.32*	.31*	.12*	.21*
Vitality of the community	.12*	.09*	.12*	.09*	.11*	.12*	.13*	.16*	.16*	.18*	.07*	.10*

(continued)

	English/ UK		English/ US		German		French		Italian		Russian	
	1993	1999	1993	1999	1993	1999	1993	1999	1993	1999	1993	1999
Cultural interest	.14*	.09*	.12*	.10*	.20*	.17*	.20*	.21*	.26*	.23*	.12*	.17*
Milieu	.12*	.12*	.12*	.12*	.01	−.00	.03	.04	.01	−.00	−.05*	−.10*
Linguistic self-confidence	.07*	.06*	.07*	.06*	−.00	.01	.03	−.02	−.01	−.02	−.02	−.04
Multiple correlations	.44*	.34*	.44*	.34*	.49*	.45*	.44*	.46*	.45*	.45*	.27*	.34*

p < .001

As can be seen in Table 10.1, three variables stand out consistently across the languages and the data points: *Integrativeness, Instrumentality* and *Attitudes towards L2 speakers/community*. This was, actually, to be expected given our previous understanding of L2 attitudes and motivation, but what surprised us was that when we computed multiple correlations (i.e. correlations between language choice and all the motivational variables together), the joint correlation was hardly higher than the correlation associated only with *Integrativeness*. For example, the correlation of the choice of English (UK) in 1993 was .43 with *Integrativeness* and .44 with all the altitudinal variables together. This suggested that *Integrativeness* played a principal role in determining the extent of a learner's overall motivational disposition.

To test the prominent position of *Integrativeness*, Dörnyei et al. (2006) submitted the data from all the three waves of the survey to a more complex statistical procedure, *structural equation modelling* (SEM). SEM is very useful to interpret the relationship among several variables within a single framework. Its strength is that we can specify directional paths (i.e. cause-effect relationships) amongst the variables and SEM then produces various goodness-of-fit indices to evaluate the feasibility of the whole model. In conducting the analysis, we took each language and each year separately (so we computed separate models for, say, German in 1993 and French in 2004), but the various models converged and with minor variations produced the same overall result. Figure 10.1 presents the schematic representation of the final construct.

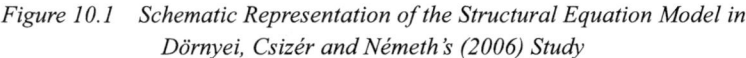

Figure 10.1   Schematic Representation of the Structural Equation Model in Dörnyei, Csizér and Németh's (2006) Study

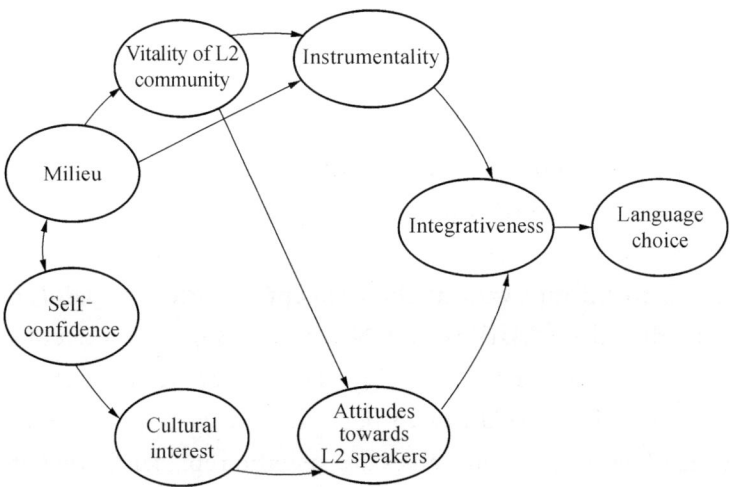

The final model that emerged from our study, presented in Figure 10.1, confirms our earlier observation based on correlation analysis that *Integrativeness* plays a key role in L2 motivation, mediating the effects of all the other attitudinal/motivational variables on the criterion measure *Language choice* (and we obtained exactly the same results with another criterion measure, *Intended effort to study the L2*). Curiously, the immediate antecedents of this latent variable were *Attitudes towards L2 speakers/community* and *Instrumentality*, thus, the three variables that the correlations in Table 7.1 highlighted emerged as the central motivational components in the SEM model as well, and the model also gave us an indication about how these variables related to each other and to the criterion measure. What is more, this was a very consistent finding because it applied to all the different target languages and all the three waves of our survey. The only problem was that what we found did not make much theoretical sense: 'Integrativeness' turned out to be the principal motivation factor in an environment where 'integrating' was not very meaningful (since there was nothing really to integrate into) and, furthermore, integrativeness was closely associated with two very different variables: faceless pragmatic incentives and personal attitudes towards members of the L2 community. It was clear that we needed a new theory to accommodate these findings.

Theoretical considerations

Parallel to conducting the empirical research outlined above, I became familiar with an intriguing new theoretical approach in psychology that looked particularly promising with regard to applying it to L2 motivation: the conceptualisation of *possible selves.* First introduced by Markus and Nurius (1986), the concept of the possible self represents an individual's ideas of what they *might* become, what they *would like* to become and what they are *afraid* of becoming. That is, possible selves are specific representations of one's self in future states, involving thoughts, images and senses, and are in many ways the manifestations of one's goals and aspiration. From a motivational point of view, two types of possible selves — the ideal self and the ought self — seemed particularly relevant (Higgins, 1987). The former refers to the representation of the attributes that someone would ideally like to possess (i.e. representation of hopes, aspirations or wishes), whereas the latter refers to the attributes that one believes one ought to possess (i.e. a representation of someone's sense of duty, obligations or responsibilities) and which therefore may bear little resemblance to desires or wishes. The motivational aspect of these self-guides was explained by Higgins's (1987, 1998) *self-discrepancy theory*, postulating that motivation involves the desire for people to reduce the discrepancy between their actual and ideal/ ought selves.

This self framework not only made intuitive sense to me but it also seemed to offer a good explanation of our Hungarian findings. Looking at 'integrativeness' from the self perspective, the concept can be conceived of as the L2-specific facet of one's ideal self. If our ideal self is associated with the mastery of an L2, that is, if the person that we would like to become is proficient in the L2, we can be described in Gardner's (1985a) terminology as having an integrative disposition. Thus, the central theme of the emerging new theory was the equation of the motivational dimension that has traditionally been interpreted as 'integrativeness/ integrative motivation' with the *Ideal L2 Self.*

Looking back at Figure 10.1, please recall that our Hungarian data showed that the immediate antecedents of the Ideal L2 Self in the model were *Attitudes towards the L2 speakers/community* and *Instrumentality.* Does this make sense? Yes it does: with regard to *Attitudes towards the L2 speakers/community*, we must realise that the actual L2 speakers are the closest parallels to a person's idealised L2-speaking self, which suggests that the more positive our disposition towards these L2 speakers, the more attractive our idealised L2 self. Or, to turn this equation around, it is difficult to imagine that we can have a vivid Ideal L2 Self if the L2 is spoken by a community that we despise. With regard to *Instrumentality*, because the ideal language self is a cognitive representation of all the incentives associated with L2 mastery, it is naturally also linked to professional competence that often requires the knowledge of the L2. Thus, to put it broadly, in our idealised image of ourselves we may want to be not only personally agreeable but also professionally successful.

We should note here, however, that from a self perspective the term 'instrumentality' can be divided into two distinct types. In conceptualizing the ideal/ought self distinction, Higgins (1987, 1998) highlighted a crucial difference between the two dimensions, a contrasting *approach/avoid* tendency: ideal self-guides have a *promotion* focus, concerned with hopes, aspirations, advancements, growth and accomplishments (i.e. approaching a desired end-state); whereas ought-to self-guides have a *prevention* focus, regulating the absence or presence of negative outcomes, concerned with safety, responsibilities and obligations (i.e. avoidance of a feared end-state). With this distinction in mind, we can see that traditionally conceived 'instrumentality/instrumental motivation' mixes up these two aspects. When our idealised image is associated with being professionally successful, instrumental motives with a promotion focus — for example, to learn English for the sake of professional/career advancement — are related to the Ideal L2 Self. In contrast, instrumental motives with a prevention focus — for example, to study in order not to fail an exam or not to disappoint one's parents — are part of the Ought-to L2 Self.

The 'L2 Motivational Self System'

As we have seen above, both the empirical findings and the theoretical considerations seemed to support a reconceptualisation of L2 motivation as part of the learner's self system. I have come to believe that the two elements discussed before, the ideal and the ought selves, are central components of this system, but I also felt that we needed to add a third major component, which concerns the direct impact of the learning environment (and which will not be discussed in this chapter in detail; for reviews, see Dörnyei, 2001c; Manolopoulou-Sergi, 2004). Accordingly, I proposed (Dörnyei, 2005) that the 'L2 Motivational Self System' was made up of the following three components (for more details on the self approach, see Dörnyei, 2009b; Dörnyei and Ushioda, 2009):

- *Ideal L2 Self*, which is the L2-specific facet of one's ideal self. If the person we would like to become speaks an L2, the *ideal L2 self* is a powerful motivator to learn the L2.
- *Ought-to L2 Self*, which concerns the attributes that one believes one *ought to* possess to meet expectations and to *avoid* possible negative outcomes.

- *L2 Learning Experience*, which concerns situated motives related to the immediate learning environment and experience (e.g. the impact of the teacher, the curriculum, the peer group, the experience of success).

VALIDATING THE L2 MOTIVATIONAL SELF SYSTEM

Over the last two years my research students — Stephen Ryan, Tatsuya Taguchi and Michael Magid — and I have been conducting large-scale survey research in Japan and China to validate the L2 Motivational Self System (for details of the surveys, see Ryan, 2009; Taguchi, Magid and Papi, 2009). We believed that if we can support the main tenets of the theory by data coming from foreign language contexts that are very different from the Hungarian learning environment that the L2 self approach originated from, this would be a powerful validity argument of the construct. The studies did indeed confirm that our assumptions were correct; in the following I present some of the key findings: (a) correlations between traditional *Integrativeness* and the *Ideal L2 Self* to check whether the two constructs can indeed be equated; (b) correlations of *Integrativeness* and the *Ideal L2 Self* with criterion measures to see which variable does a better job at explaining motivated behaviour; (c) correlations between aspects of *Instrumentality* and the *Ought-to L2 Self* to check whether traditional instrumentality can indeed be divided into two distinct types.

The relationship between the Ideal L2 Self *and* Integrativeness

Table 10.2 presents correlations between *Integrativeness* and the *Ideal L2 Self*, in three different East Asian surveys involving over 5,300 participants, each consisting of different subsamples. As can be seen, there are substantial positive correlations in every subsample, suggesting that the two variables do indeed tap into the same underlying construct domain. The average correlation across the subsamples is .54, which is very high in L2 motivation research. These consistent results leave no doubt that the two concepts are very closely related.

Table 10.2   Correlations between Integrativeness and the Ideal L2 Self

	Total sample	University students (non-English majors)	University students (English majors)	Secondary school pupils	Adult learners
2,397 Japanese learners (Ryan, 2009)	.59	.54	.53	.61	
1,586 Japanese learners (Taguchi, Magid and Papi, 2009)	.63	.63	.48		
1,328 Chinese learners (Taguchi, Magid and Papi, 2009)	.51	.46	.46	.66	.53

Note: All figures are significant at the p < .001 level.

The correlation of the Ideal L2 Self and Integrativeness with Intended effort

Table 10.3 presents the correlations of *Integrativeness* and the *Ideal L2 Self* with *Intended effort* in the same samples as in Table 10.2. These figures allow us to compare which variable does a better job at explaining the criterion measure, effort. Although *Integrativeness* does a consistently good job at accounting for the variance in the criterion measure, the *Ideal L2 Self* exceeds it in all but one subsample. The average variance (which is the average of the squared correlation coefficients) explained by *Integrativeness* across the different samples is 32 per cent, which can be considered high, but the same figure for the *Ideal L2 Self* is 42 per cent, which is almost 30 per cent higher!

Table 10.3   Correlations of Integrativeness and the Ideal L2 Self with Intended Effort

		Total sample	University students (non-English majors)	University students (English majors)	Secondary school pupils	Adults learners
2,397 Japanese learners	*Ideal L2 Self*	.77	.74	.71	.75	
(Ryan, 2009)	*Integrativeness*	.65	.61	.54	.71	
1,586 Japanese learners	*Ideal L2 Self*	.71	.71	.61		
(Taguchi and Magid, 2009)	*Integrativeness*	.63	.64	.49		
1,328 Chinese learners	*Ideal L2 Self*	.55	.52	.51	.69	.51
(Taguchi and Magid, 2009)	*Integrativeness*	.52	.47	.53	.63	.44

Note: All figures are significant at the p < .001 level.

The case of Instrumentality

Table 10.4 presents correlations that allow us to examine whether *Instrumentality* can indeed be divided into two types as outlined above. The data are drawn from Taguchi et al.'s (2009) Japanese and Chinese samples where the promotion and the prevention aspects of *Instrumentality* were measured separately. If Higgins's (1987, 1998) promotion/prevention distinction applies to our data, then we would expect to find higher correlations of the *Ideal L2 Self* with *Instrumentality-promotion* than with *Instrumentality-prevention*, and the *Ought-to L2 Self* should display the opposite pattern. This is exactly the case in Table 10.4. Furthermore, if the promotion and the prevention aspects are separate from each other then we would not expect a high correlation between them, and indeed both correlations are modest (with even the higher one explaining less than 12 per cent of the variance). Thus, these figures provide unambiguous confirmation that the traditionally conceived 'instrumental motivation' can indeed be divided into two distinct types: one relating to the Ideal L2 Self, the other to the Ought-to L2 Self. These two types are only moderately related to each other and show a distinct correlation pattern with the two self dimensions.

Table 10.4   Correlations between the Ideal L2 Self, Instrumentality and the Ought-To L2 Self in Taguchi, Magid and Papi's (2009) Japanese and Chinese Samples

	Ideal L2 Self		Ought-to L2 Self		Instrumentality – promotion	
	Japan	*China*	*Japan*	*China*	*Japan*	*China*
Instrumentality - promotion	.63*	.46*	.28*	.45*	----	----
Instrumentality - prevention	−.01	−.13*	.53*	.63*	.34*	.26*

* *p < .001*

CONCLUSION

This chapter discussed a major theoretical shift that has been taking place within the field of L2 motivation research. I described how a new paradigm has emerged from both theoretical considerations and research results, and then presented the main components of the newly proposed 'L2 Motivational Self System'. In the second part of the chapter I provided empirical data from three different surveys involving over 5,300 participants to validate the new construct. The correlational results clearly indicated that: (a) *Integrativeness* and the *Ideal L2 Self* tap into the same construct, but the *Ideal L2 Self* does a better job at explaining variance in the criterion measures; (b) the traditionally conceived concept of *Instrumentality* mixes up two types of pragmatic motives (with a promotion vs. a prevention focus) that show a rather different relationship pattern with the *Ideal* and the *Ought-to L2 Selves*. These results are all in accordance with the proposed theory and thus provide a strong validity argument for it. We should reiterate here that in the current study the third main component of the 'L2 Motivational Self System', the *L2 Learning Experience*, was not measured.

Chapter 11

The L2 Motivational Self System

In Dörnyei, Z. and Ushioda, E. (Eds.). (2009). Motivation, language identity and the L2 self (pp. 9-42). Bristol: Multilingual Matters.

> *The space of what might be is a uniquely human domain that is still to be fully mapped. Some is roughly charted, but much more remains to be surveyed.* (Markus, 2006)

In 2005, I outlined the basis of a new approach to conceptualising second language (L2) learning motivation within a 'self' framework (Dörnyei, 2005), calling the new theory the 'L2 Motivational Self System'. The purpose of this chapter is to provide a detailed theoretical description of this construct and to show its foundations and the ways by which I believe it broadens the scope of L2 motivation research. As part of an extended validity argument, I will refer to several empirical studies that tested some tenets of the theory, and I will also discuss how the model is compatible with other influential conceptualisations of motivation by Gardner (2001), Noels (2003) and Ushioda (2001). Finally, I will argue that the new theory has considerable practical implications as it opens up a novel avenue for motivating language learners.

The L2 Motivational Self System represents a major reformation of previous motivational thinking by its explicit utilisation of psychological theories of the self, yet its roots are firmly set in previous research in the L2 field. Indeed, L2 motivation researchers have always believed that a foreign language is more than a mere communication code that can be learnt similarly to other academic subjects, and have therefore typically adopted paradigms that linked the L2 to the individual's personal 'core,' forming an important part of one's identity. Thus, proposing a system that explicitly focuses on aspects of the individual's self is compatible with the whole-person perspective of past theorising.

The actual model has grown out of the combined effect of two significant theoretical developments, one taking place in the L2 field, the other in mainstream psychology. Looking at our own field first, we can conclude that for several decades L2 motivation research had been centred around the highly influential concept of *integrativeness/integrative motivation*, which was first introduced by Gardner and Lambert (1959). However, during the past 20 years there has been growing concern with the theoretical content of this concept, partly because it did not offer any obvious links with the new cognitive motivational concepts that had been emerging in motivational psychology (such as goal theories or self-determination theory) and partly because the label 'integrative' was rather limiting and, quite frankly, did not make too much sense in many language learning environments. The second theoretical development that contributed to the genesis of the L2 Motivational Self System took place in psychological research on the self, leading to a convergence of self theory and motivation theory in mainstream psychology. I will start by describing this movement and the resulting conception of 'possible selves' and 'future self-guides', followed by discussing how these have informed L2 motivation research.

THE CONTRIBUTION OF PSYCHOLOGY: POSSIBLE SELVES AND FUTURE SELF-GUIDES

MacIntyre, MacKinnon and Clément (2009a) are right when they point out that the notion of 'self' is one of the most frequently — and most diversely — used concepts in psychology. A cursory scan of the PSYCHINFO database they conducted revealed more than 75,000 articles with 'self' in their titles and a very long list of self-related concepts used in the literature (e.g. self-esteem, self-concept, self-determination, etc.). Similarly, Higgins (1996, p. 1062) also concluded that 'Psychologists are fascinated with the "self". It headlines more psychological variables than any other concept.'

While there is indeed a confusing plethora of self-related issues, from a motivational point of view one area of self-research stands out with its relevance: the study of *possible selves* and *future self-guides*. The emergence of this subfield has been a direct consequence of the success of personality trait psychology in defining the major and stable dimensions of personality (e.g. the Big Five model; see Dörnyei, 2005). These advances, according to Cantor (1990), have paved the way for paying more attention to questions about how individual differences in personality are translated into behavioural characteristics, examining the '"doing" sides of personality' (Cantor, 1990, p. 735). Thus, over the past two decades self theorists have become increasingly interested in the active, dynamic nature of the self-system, gradually replacing the traditionally static concept of self-representations with a self-system that mediates and controls ongoing behaviour (Markus and Ruvolo, 1989; for a recent review, see Leary, 2007). This move resulted in the introduction of a number of self-specific mechanisms that link the self with action (e.g. self-regulation), and thus an intriguing interface has been formed between personality psychology and motivational psychology.

Markus and Ruvolo (1989, p. 214) explain that although the interwoven nature of the self-system and motivated behaviour is seldom made explicit, 'yet the belief that the two *must be linked* can be inferred from the writing of a variety of personality and motivation theorists' (emphasis mine). One of the most powerful mechanisms intended to make this link explicit and describe how the self regulates behaviour by setting goals and expectations was proposed by Markus and Nurius (1986) in their theory that centred around the concept of 'possible selves'. Due to its versatile character, the possible selves approach also lends itself to various educational applications and, as we will see later, has indeed been successfully applied to a variety of educational contexts.

Possible selves

A person's self-concept has traditionally been seen as the summary of the individual's self-knowledge related to how the person views him/herself at present. Carver, Reynolds and Scheier (1994) emphasise that *possible selves* — representing the individuals' ideas of what they *might* become, what they *would like* to become, and what they are *afraid of* becoming (Markus and Nurius, 1986) — denote a unique self-dimension in that they refer to future rather than current self states. Furthermore, while the self-concept is usually assumed to concern information derived from the individual's past experiences, Markus and Nurius's notion of possible selves concerns how people conceptualise their as-yet unrealised potential, and as such, it also draws on hopes, wishes and fantasies. In this sense, possible selves act as 'future self-guides', reflecting a dynamic, forward-pointing conception that can explain how someone is moved from the present toward the future. At the heart of this movement is the complex interplay of current and imaginative self-identities and its impact on purposive behaviour (Yowell, 2002). Looking back on two decades of research on possible selves, Markus (2006) summarised this as follows:

> Our excitement with the notion of possible selves had multiple sources. Focusing on possible selves gave us license to speculate about the remarkable power of imagination in human life. We also had

room to think about the importance of the self-structure as a dynamic interpretive matrix for thought, feeling, and action, and to begin to theorise about the role of sociocultural contexts in behaviour. Finally, the concept wove together our mutual interests in social psychology, social work, and clinical psychology. (Markus, 2006, p. xi)

We should note that the third point Markus (2006) mentions in the above quote, the inclusion of clinical psychology, is related to the fantasy element of possible selves. As Segal (2006) explains, Markus and Nurius's (1986) conceptualisation meant that social psychology was taking on the subtleties of psychodynamic processes that are so prominent in psychoanalytic theory. His summary is enlightening:

For their contribution to our understanding of the self, Markus and Nurius essentially married a social-cognitive instrument with a projective. Future possible selves are fantasy tempered by expectation (or expectations leavened by fantasy) and so, conceptually, eliciting them invokes two central actions of mental life: The social cognitive act of future planning with the equally human act of generating fantasy. (Segal, 2006, p. 82)

In their seminal paper, Markus and Nurius (1986, p. 954) distinguished between three main types of possible selves: (1) 'ideal selves that we would very much like to become', (2) 'selves that we could become', and (3) 'selves we are afraid of becoming'. The ideal or hoped-for selves might include 'the successful self, the creative self, the rich self, the thin self, or the loved and admired self', whereas the feared selves could be 'the alone self, the depressed self, the incompetent self, the alcoholic self, the unemployed self, or the bag lady self'. While these two extremes are easy to grasp and illustrate, what exactly are the selves of the third type, the 'selves that we could become'? In one sense, this description can be seen as merely a synonym of the generic term 'possible self' (because 'possible' is what 'we can become'), which was surely not the authors' intention.

So, it is more likely that these selves refer to 'expected' or 'likely' selves (Carver et al., 1994), that is, to the default option. Thus, the three main types of possible selves proposed by Markus and Nurius refer to the best case, the worst case and the default scenarios.

There are two important points to note about these self types. First, we should not forget that they all come under the label of *possible* selves, that is, even the ideal, hoped-for self is not completely detached from reality (i.e. it cannot be an utterly implausible fantasy). The second point is that Markus and Nurius (1986) clearly meant this list to provide a broad outline of the scope of possible selves rather than a specific taxonomy, because later in their article they mention hoped-for selves and ideal selves as two separate entries within a list (Markus and Nurius, 1986, p. 957). Interestingly, they also mention 'ought selves' in their paper (which we are going to look at in more detail later), defining it as 'an image of self held by another' (Markus and Nurius, 1986, p. 958). Thus, Markus and Nurius believed in multiple future-oriented possible selves and outlined in their paper the scope of these selves with a number of illustrations but without providing a finite taxonomy.

A final point that needs to be emphasised about Markus and Nurius's (1986) proposal is central to the conception of possible selves yet it tends to be curiously ignored or overlooked in most work on the subject. It concerns the fact that possible selves involve tangible *images* and *senses*; as Markus and Nurius emphasise, possible selves are represented in the same imaginary and semantic way as the here-and-now self, that is, they are a *reality* for the individual: people can 'see', 'hear' and 'smell' a possible self (although I am not that sure about the benefits of the latter). Markus and Ruvolo (1989) argue that it is a major advantage to frame future goals in this way because this representation seems to capture some elements of what people actually experience when they are engaged in goal-directed behaviour. As the authors state, by focusing on possible selves we are 'phenomenologically very close to the actual thoughts and feelings that individuals experience as they are in the process of motivated behaviour and instrumental action' (Markus and Ruvolo, 1989, p. 217). This is a crucial point that I will come back to later.

Future self-guides: Ideal and ought selves

Possible selves are often referred to as 'future self-guides', but strictly speaking, not every type of possible self has this guiding function. As mentioned earlier, the expected, 'could-become' self refers to the default situation and therefore it does not so much guide as predict the likely future scenario. In contrast, the ideal self has a definite guiding function in setting to-be-reached standards and, in a negative way, the feared self also regulates behaviour by guiding the individual *away* from something. It does not need much justification that from the point of view of acting as academic self-guides the learner's ideal self is particularly important, which is an area that has been the subject of a great deal of research by Tory Higgins and his associates (e.g. Higgins, 1987, 1998; Higgins, Klein and Strauman, 1985; Higgins, Roney, Crowe and Hymes, 1994). It is important to know that Higgins's work on selves precedes that of Markus and Nurius (1986), with the latter authors acknowledging Higgins's contribution (by citing, for example, not only Higgins et al., 1985, but also an unpublished manuscript by him from 1983).

The two key components of Higgins's (1987; Higgins et al., 1985) self theory are the *ideal self* and the *ought self*. As we have seen above, Markus and Nurius (1986) also mention these concepts, but Higgins used them as precisely defined technical terms in his more general theory of motivation and self-regulation. The *ideal self* refers to the representation of the attributes that one would ideally like to possess (i.e. representation of hopes, aspirations, or wishes), while the *ought self* refers to the representation of attributes that one believes one ought to possess (i.e. representation of someone else's sense of duties, obligations or moral responsibilities) and which therefore may bear little resemblance to one's own desires or wishes. In his 1987 paper Higgins points out that both the ideal and the ought selves can derive from either the individual's own or someone else's views, which means that the ideal self might represent attributes that another person would like the individual to possess in an ideal case. However, because it is not clear how this meaning would be different from an ought self, it has typically not been included in subsequent uses of the term, and the ideal sense has been usually interpreted in the literature as the individual's own vision for him/herself, while the ought self as someone else's vision for the individual.

An important difference between Higgins's and Markus and Nurius's conceptualisations of the future-oriented self dimensions is that while the latter authors talk about multiple possible selves, including, for example, more than one ideal self, Higgins talks about a single ideal and a single ought self for each individual, viewing these as composite self-guides that sum up all the relevant attributes. However, he also accepts (e.g. Higgins, 1987, 1996) that there are several other types of self-representations beyond the ideal or ought self concepts.

Boyatzis and Akrivou (2006) highlight a potential source of confusion in the distinction between the ideal and the ought selves concerning the level of internalisation of the ought self. They argue that because various reference groups (to which every individual belongs) affect the individual by anticipatory socialisation or value induction, it is not always straightforward to decide at times of social pressure whether an ideal-like self state represents one's genuine dreams or whether it has been compromised by the desire for role conformity. Indeed, group norms, as their name suggests, impose a normative function on group members and because humans are social beings, most of us adhere to some extent to these norms (see Dörnyei, 2007a). This means that there is a pressure to internalise our ought selves to some extent, resulting in various degrees of integration.

The graded internalisation of external motives has been well described in Deci and Ryan's (1985) self-determination theory, which offers an internalisation continuum of extrinsic regulation, identifying four stages of the process: (1) *external regulation,* which refers to the least self-determined form of extrinsic motivation, coming entirely from external sources such as rewards or threats (e.g. teacher's praise or parental confrontation); (2) *introjected regulation*, which involves externally imposed rules that the individual accepts as norms he/she should follow in order not to feel guilty (e.g. some laws of a country); (3) *identified regulation*, which occurs when people engage in an activity because they highly value and identify with the behaviour, and see its usefulness (e.g. learning a language which is necessary to pursue one's hobbies or interests); and (4) *integrated regulation*, which is the most developmentally advanced form of extrinsic motivation, involving choiceful behaviour that is fully assimilated with the individual's other values, needs and identity (e.g. learning English because proficiency in this language is part of an educated cosmopolitan culture one has adopted). At first sight, (1) and (2) appear to be linked to the ought self and (3) and (4) to the ideal self, but where exactly is the boundary? We will come back to this question below when we look at the development of the two self dimensions.

Finally, the ought self raises one more issue. In Higgins's (1987; Higgins et al., 1985) original conceptualisation it referred to a positive reference point (i.e. the person whom I believe I ought to be), but Higgins (1996) suggests that this meaning may be extended to include a negative reference point (i.e. the person I don't want to be), similar to Markus and Nurius's (1986) feared self. This is an important point that I will recall when we look at the motivational capacity of the future self-guides below.

Future self-guides versus future goals

Human action is caused by purpose, and this purpose has often been operationalised in terms of *goals* both in professional and everyday discourse. Thus, goals refer to desired future end-states and this definition is rather close to the definition of future-oriented self-guides. So, are the ideal/ought dimensions merely a subset of goals? The answer is a definite no, and being aware of the difference is a prerequisite to understanding the essence of possible selves. In psychology there is a multitude of cognitive constructs that serve as future-oriented motives, ranging from self-actualisation needs to the different types of goals and orientations in various goal theories. The proponents of each construct present intellectually convincing arguments, which makes it difficult to choose from the wide variety of available constructs. The main attraction of possible self theory for me has been that it goes beyond logical, intellectual arguments when justifying the validity of the various future-oriented self types. As mentioned earlier, possible selves involve images and senses, approximating what people actually experience when they are engaged in motivated or goal-directed behaviour. This is why Markus keeps emphasising that possible selves involve self-relevant imagery (e.g. Markus, 2006; Markus and Nurius, 1986; Ruvolo and Markus, 1992). Thus, possible selves can be seen, according to Markus and Ruvolo (1989, p. 217), as the result of the various motivational factors (e.g. expectances, attributions, value beliefs) 'that is psychologically experienced and that is a durable aspect of consciousness'.

Reading the possible selves literature I have found it remarkable how most authors seem to ignore this crucial distinction between goals and future self-guides in spite of the prominent emphasis on it in Markus's writings. Pizzolato (2006), for example, is quite right when she states that 'Unlike goal theory, possible selves are explicitly related to a long-term developmental goal involving goal setting, volition (via adherence to associated schemas), and goal achievement, but are larger than any one or combination of these constructs' (p. 58), but she could have gone one step further to state that it is the experiential element that makes possible selves 'larger' than any combinations of goal-related constructs. Similarly, Miller and Brickman (2004, p. 14) state that possible selves are examples of long-term, future goals and define these as 'self-relevant, self-defining goals that provide incentive for action', regulating behaviour 'through self-identification with the goals or the integration of the goals into the system of self-determined goals'. Yet, they seem to overlook the key element, namely that possible selves are 'self states' that people experience as reality.

The role of imagination and imagery

Having argued for a prominent place of imagery in possible selves theory, let us examine the notion of imagery/imagination and its motivational impact more closely. Imagination has been known to be related to motivation since the ancient Greeks. Aristotle, for example, defined imagination as 'sensation without matter' and claimed that 'There's no desiring without imagination' (Modell, 2003, p. 108). As McMahon (1973) explains, Aristotle defined the image in the soul as the prime motivating force in human action; he believed that when an image of something to be pursued or avoided was present in imagination, the soul was moved in the same manner as if the objects of desire were materially present.

Interestingly, contemporary definitions of mental imagery are very similar to that of Aristotle. Kosslyn et al. (2002), for example, define it as 'the ability to represent perceptual states in the absence of the appropriate sensory input' and they also confirm the assumption that humans respond to mental images similarly to visual ones. They report on neuroimaging studies that indicate that visual mental imagery and visual perception activate about two thirds of the same brain areas (for a recent summary of relevant research, see Kosslyn, Thompson and Ganis, 2006). These results provide a neuropsychological basis for Markus and Ruvolo's (1989) claim that 'imaging one's own actions through the construction of elaborated possible selves achieving the desired goal may thus directly facilitate the translation of goals into intentions and instrumental actions' (p. 213) and a similar idea has been expressed by Wenger (1998) when he described the concept of 'imagination':

My use of the concept of imagination refers to a process of expanding our self by transcending our time and space and creating new images of the world and ourselves. Imagination in this sense is looking at an apple seed and seeing a tree. It is playing scales on a piano, and envisioning a concert hall. (Wenger, 1998, p. 176)

The motivating power of mental imagery has been well documented in the field of sport psychology as well. Inspired by Paivio's (1985) influential model of cognitive functions of imagery in human performance, hundreds of studies have examined the relationship between mental imagery and sport performance, and as Gregg and Hall (2006) summarise, it has been generally concluded that imagery is an effective performance enhancement technique (see also Cumming and Ste-Marie, 2001, for a similar conclusion). As a result, virtually every successful athlete in the world applies some sort of imagery enhancement technique during training.

Thus, Markus and Nurius's (1986) possible selves concept has opened up a channel to harness the powerful motivational function of imagination (see Taylor, Pham, Rivkin and Armor, 1998), which explains why Markus (2006) emphasised this aspect first in her retrospective summary cited earlier. In the same overview, she added the following:

> We were impressed by the fact that people spend an enormous amount of time envisioning their futures. We now know that this imaginative work has powerful consequences. Possible selves can work to energize actions and to buffer the current self from everyday dragons and many less overt indignities as well. . . In the U.S., it is both a birthright and a moral imperative to tailor one's personal version of the American Dream. The notion that one should 'dream on,' 'keep the dream alive,' and that 'if you dream it, you can become it' is a critical element in the world's cultural imagination about the U.S. ... People across a wide array of contexts are capable and willing to generate possible selves. (Markus, 2006, p. xii)

In summary, let me reiterate that the inclusion of imagery is a central element of possible selves theory. As Segal (2006) emphasises, it is the integration of fantasy with the self-concept construct that marks Markus and Nurius's (1986) work as truly innovative. This is certainly the aspect that grasped my own attention when I first encountered this work, and this is, I believe, what makes the concept of future self-guides such as the ideal and the ought selves suitable to be the lynchpins of a broad theory of L2 motivation. In their analysis of the ideal self, Boyatzis and Akrivou (2006) share Markus's (2006) conclusion that the dream or image of a desired future is the core content of the ideal self. And, as the following quote shows, they also believe that imagination has played a key role in the whole history of the human race:

> Throughout history of mankind, humans are driven by their imagination and their ability to see images of the desired future. Leaders, poets, writers, composers, artists, dreamers, athletes have been able to be inspired, stay inspired and inspire others through such images. These images, once shared, have the power to become a force, and in that sense an inspiration for social development and growth, for intentional change at many levels of social organisation, not just for the individual. (Boyatzis and Akrivou, 2006, p. 633)

The motivational function of future self-guides: Self-discrepancy theory

We saw in the previous section that the imagery component of future self-guides is a powerful motivational tool. Let us examine how this tool fits into a broader theory of the motivational function of the ideal and ought selves. In this respect the most coherent framework has been offered by Higgins's (1987, 1996) *self-discrepancy theory*, which postulates that people are motivated to reach a condition where their self-concept matches their personally relevant self-guides. In other words, motivation in this sense involves the desire to reduce the discrepancy between one's actual self and the projected behavioural standards of the ideal/ought selves. Thus, future self-guides provide incentive, direction and impetus for action, and sufficient discrepancy between these and the actual self initiates distinctive self-regulatory strategies with the aim to reduce the discrepancy — future self-guides represent points of comparison to be reconciled through behaviour (Hoyle and Sherrill, 2006).

An important point to note is that although the ideal and ought selves are similar to each other in that they are both related to the attainment of a desired end-state, Higgins (1998) emphasises that the predilections associated with the two different types of future selves are motivationally distinct from each other: ideal self-guides have a *promotion* focus, concerned with hopes, aspirations, advancements, growth and accomplishments; whereas ought self-guides have a *prevention* focus, regulating the absence or presence of negative outcomes associated with failing to live up to various responsibilities and obligations. As Higgins adds, this distinction is in line with the age-old motivational principle that people approach pleasure and avoid pain.

Conditions for the motivating capacity of the ideal and ought selves

Although the above description of possible selves theory has pointed to the conclusion that future self-guides motivate action by triggering the execution of self-regulatory mechanisms, several studies have found that this does not always happen automatically (e.g. Oyserman, Terry and Bybee, 2006; Yowell, 2002). Past research suggests that there are certain conditions that can enhance or hinder the motivational impact of the ideal and ought selves, the most important of which are the following ones: (1) availability of an elaborate and vivid future self image, (2) perceived plausibility, (3) harmony between the ideal and ought selves, (4) necessary activation/priming, (5) accompanying procedural strategies, and (6) the offsetting impact of a feared self.

Availability of an elaborate and vivid future self image

The primary and obvious prerequisite for the motivational capacity of future self-guides is that they *need to exist*. It has been observed that people differ in how easily they can generate a successful possible self (Ruvolo and Markus, 1992) and, therefore not everyone is expected to possess a developed ideal or ought self guide (Higgins, 1987, 1996). This can explain the absence of sufficient motivation in many people. Furthermore, even if the self image does exist, it may not have a sufficient degree of elaborateness and vividness to be effective. It has been found that the more elaborate the possible self in terms of imaginative, visual and other content elements, the more motivational power it is expected to have. People display significant individual differences in the vividness of their mental imagery (Richardson, 1994), and a possible self with insufficient specificity and detail may not be able to stir up the necessary motivational response.

Perceived plausibility

Ruvolo and Markus (1992, p. 96) argue that it is the individual's 'specific representations of what is possible for the self that embody and give rise to generalised feelings of efficacy, competence, control, or optimism, and that provide the means by which these global constructs have their powerful impact on behaviour'. In other words, possible selves are only effective insomuch as the individual does indeed perceive them as *possible*, that is, realistic within the person's individual circumstances. The significance of the subjective appraisal of future self-guides has been echoed by others as well; for example, Segal (2006, p.91) points out that 'It is well established that the degree to which participants expect their feared or wished for possible selves to come true affects their self-esteem, current mood, and optimism', and MacIntyre, MacKinnon and Clément (2009b, p. 197) also conclude that 'it is also important to find out how *likely* participants consider a possible self to be; a highly unlikely possible self probably will have little relation to motivation'.

Norman and Aron (2003) make an important point when they emphasise the relevance of the individual's perceived control in the context of possible selves. 'Perceived behavioural control' was introduced as a key component in Ajzen's (1988) theory of planned behaviour, referring to the perceived ease or difficulty of performing the behaviour (e.g. perceptions of required resources and potential impediments or obstacles). With regard to possible selves, Norman and Aron argue that perceived control is the degree to which individuals believe their behaviours can influence the attainment, or avoidance, of a possible self. 'If individuals believe they have control over attaining or avoiding a possible self, they will be more inclined to take the necessary steps to do so' (p. 501). Interestingly, Carver et al. (1994) see the main difference between pessimists and optimists exactly in their ability to translate hoped-for possible selves into realistic expectations. As they conclude, because pessimists' hopes 'fail to evolve into expected selves, these hopes may thus be less likely to engage the motivational control systems that cause their realisation in behaviour' (p. 139).

Harmony between the ideal and ought selves

We have seen earlier that the ought self is closely related to peer group norms and other normative pressures (e.g. ethnic community expectations). Thus, learners' (and especially adolescents') ought self may contain certain peer-induced views about academic attainment (e.g. low-achieving expectations that are often called the 'norm of mediocrity') that are in conflict with the individual's ideal self. Put in another way, there can be a clash between a learner's personal and social identity. Oyserman et al. (2006) found that among school children negative group images are often highly accessible, making social group membership feel like it conflicts with academic self-guides, and in such cases teenagers tend to regulate their behaviours to fit in with their peers (Pizzolato, 2006). Thus, an important condition for effective desired possible selves is that they should feel congruent with important social identities, that is, that the ideal and the ought selves should be in harmony.

Necessary activation/priming

Even if the learner does have a well-developed and plausible ideal/ought self image, this may not always be active in the working memory. Hoyle and Sherrill (2006) argue that possible selves become relevant for behaviour only when they are recruited into the working self-concept and for this to happen they need to be activated. This priming of the self image can be triggered by various reminders and self-relevant events, and they can also be deliberately invoked by the individual in response to an event or situation. Ruvolo and Markus (1992), for example, maintain that simulating a desired end-state can activate the future self-guide and they provide empirical evidence that imagery manipulations (in their case, asking participants to imagine themselves as successful or unsuccessful before a task) increased the accessibility of possible selves, as evidenced by the subjects' performance. I come back to the question of the enhancement of self-representations at the end of this chapter when discussing the practical implications of the theory.

Accompanying procedural strategies

Let us consider a learner who is energised by an attractive future ideal self-guide. In order to translate the aroused motivational potential into action, he/she needs to have a roadmap of tasks and strategies to follow in order to approximate the ideal self. For example, it is obviously not enough for an Olympic athlete merely to imagine herself walking into the Olympic stadium or stepping onto the podium if she has no coach or training plan. For this reason, along with many others, Oyserman et al. (2006) argue that future self-guides are only effective if they are accompanied by a set of specific predeveloped and plausible action plans, which are cued automatically by the image. Thus, effective future self-guides need to come as part of a 'package', consisting of an imagery component and a repertoire of appropriate plans, scripts and self-regulatory strategies. This idea of a rich, closely networked package of information about how to achieve their hoped-for possible selves is expressed very clearly by Cross and Markus (1994):

> A possible self may serve as a node in an associative network of experiences, strategies, and self-knowledge. In this way, the possible self

may link effective steps and strategies. . .with beliefs about one's ability and competence in the domain. (Cross and Markus, 1994, p. 434)

A study by Pizzolato (2006) of American minority students provided clear empirical confirmation that without procedural schemas for achieving their educational aspirations the participants could not make specific plans, which jeopardised the achievement of their ideal selves. Miller and Brickman (2004) also emphasise that because future self-guides specify distant goals, people have to create proximal guides themselves, setting concrete courses of action that lead to distal attainments, which is of course a central tenet in goal-setting theory (Locke and Latham, 1990). As Miller and Brickman (2004) argue, it is this system of specific proximal subgoals, or goal-focused strategies, that distinguishes reality-based future goals from empty dreams and fantasies. In their view, the absence of an appropriate system of meaningful paths to pursue the desired selves can be caused by two factors: a lack of sufficient knowledge or experience (e.g. no relevant role models or knowledgeable significant others) and ineffective cognitive skills for planning and problem-solving. On the other hand, if the possible self is accompanied by the necessary procedural knowledge, it will turn from a hoped-for into an expected self (Yowell, 2002).

Offset by feared self

The last condition to be mentioned with regard to the motivational capacity of possible selves concerns an interesting proposal made by Oyserman and Markus (1990). They argued that a desired possible self will have maximal motivational effectiveness when it is offset or balanced by a counteracting feared possible self in the same domain. Indeed, focusing on what would happen if the original intention failed has often been seen in motivational psychology as a powerful source of energy to keep us going (see Dörnyei, 2001a) — in academia, for example, it is often not the imagined success of a paper that makes us get down to writing it but rather the fear of missing the deadline. Thus, according to

Oyserman and Markus (1990), for best effect the negative consequences of not achieving a desired end-state need to be elaborated and be cognitively available to individuals.

In an educational intervention study, Oyserman et al. (2006) demonstrated that positive self-guides and their negative counterparts are not simply inverse factors but have distinct impacts on the students' self-regulatory behaviour: learners with academically focused desired future selves spent more time doing homework and were less disruptive and more engaged in classroom activities, whereas feared possible selves resulted in fewer school absences. This suggests that the most effective condition for future self-guides is a balanced combination of pairs of countervailing selves; in Higgins's paradigm this would suggest a balanced combination of the ideal and the ought selves, which is related to the question of the harmony between the selves mentioned above. Hoyle and Sherrill (2006) argue similarly, stating that the motivation conferred by balanced possible selves is additive, involving both approach and avoid tendencies, and is therefore greater than the motivation conferred by the hoped-for or feared self alone.

THE CONTRIBUTION OF L2 MOTIVATION RESEARCH: GROWING DISSATISFACTION WITH THE INTEGRATIVE MOTIVE

Having described the theoretical advances in psychology that acted as one of the two main sources of inspiration for proposing the L2 Motivational Self System, let us now turn to the second source, which is rooted in developments within L2 motivation research. It concerns a growing dissatisfaction with the concept of *integrativeness/integrative motivation*, which, as I stated in the introduction of this chapter, has been at the centre of L2 motivation research for almost five decades (for reviews, see Dörnyei, 2001c; Gardner, 2001; MacIntyre, 2002; MacIntyre et al., 2009a).

Integrativeness refers to the desire to learn an L2 of a valued community so that one can communicate with members of the community and sometimes even become like them. Gardner (2001) characterised the concept as follows:

> Integrativeness reflects a genuine interest in learning the second language in order to come closer to the other language community. At one level, this implies an openness to, and respect for other cultural groups and ways of life. In the extreme, this might involve complete identification with the community (and possibly even withdrawal from one's original group), but more commonly it might well involve integration within both communities. (Gardner, 2001, p.5)

Integrative motivation is a more complex, multi-componential construct, consisting of three main constituents: 'integrativeness', 'attitudes towards the learning situation' and 'motivation' (see Figure 11.1). The latter is seen as the driving force of motivated behaviour, subsuming effort, desire and affect (Gardner, 2001); that is, it concerns a central motivational engine that needs to be ignited by some specific learning goal such as an integrative orientation.

As I pointed out in my 2005 review (Dörnyei, 2005), a closer look at the L2 motivation literature reveals a certain amount of ambivalence about integrativeness/integrative motivation, amounting sometimes to a kind of 'love–hate' relationship amongst researchers outside Gardner's Canadian circle. The concept is certainly an enigma. It has been without any doubt the most researched and most talked about notion in L2 motivation studies and yet it has no obvious equivalent in any other theories in mainstream motivational and educational psychology. In addition, the label 'integrative' is ambiguous because it is not quite clear what the target of the integration is, and in many language learning environments it simply does not make much sense. In a multicultural setting such as Montreal, where Gardner first developed his theory, we can talk about potential 'integration', but in learning situations where a foreign language is taught as a school subject without any direct contact with its speakers (e.g. teaching English or French in Hungary, China, Japan or other typical 'foreign language learning' contexts) the 'integrative' metaphor does not have any obvious meaning.

Figure 11.1   The Integrative Motive within Gardner's 'Socio-Educational Model of Second Language Acquisition' (Gardner, 2001, p. 4)

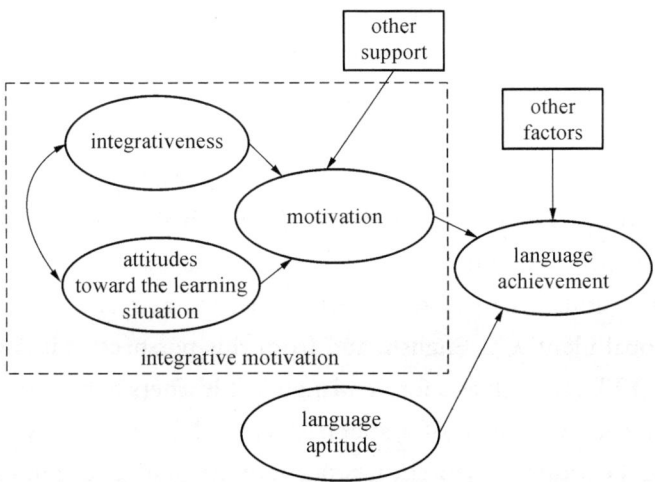

Partly for these reasons and partly because the actual empirical findings did not always fit Gardner's original interpretation of the notion, several scholars in the past have questioned the validity and relevance of integrativeness (e.g. Coetzee-Van Rooy, 2006; Dörnyei, Csizér and Németh, 2006; Irie, 2003; Lamb, 2004; Ushioda, 2006; Warden and Lin, 2000; Yashima, 2000; for a review, see Dörnyei, 2005). Interestingly, this even happened amongst Canadian scholars close to Gardner, as the following quotation shows:

> Although it was originally suggested that the desire for contact and identification with members of the L2 group [i.e. integrative orientation] would be critical for L2 acquisition, it would now appear that it is not fundamental to the motivational process, but has relevance only in specific sociocultural contexts. Rather, four other orientations may be seen to

sustain motivation. (Noels, Pelletier, Clément and Vallerand, 2000, p. 60)

The four orientations — or learning goals — the researchers were advocating are *travel, friendship, knowledge,* and *instrumental orientation,* which echoes the findings of Clément and Kruidenier's (1983) seminal paper in the early 1980s that was the first 'insider challenge' to the integrative construct proposed by Gardner.

The problematic nature of integrativeness has been amplified by the worldwide globalisation process and the growing dominance of Global/World English as an international language (Dörnyei et al., 2006). In the new globalised world order, as Arnett (2002) argues, the pressure for most people is to develop a *bicultural identity,* in which part of their identity is rooted in their local culture while another part is associated with a global identity that links them to the international mainstream. The language of this global identity is English, and from this perspective it is not at all clear who EFL (English as a foreign language) learners believe the 'owner' of their L2 is. This lack of a specific target L2 community, in turn, undermines Gardner's theoretical concept of integrativeness: in Gardner's (2001) definition cited above, for example, what exactly would be — to quote Gardner (2001) — 'the other language community' that the learner would want to 'get closer to'?

As a result of these and other concerns — particularly the under-theorised nature of the concept of integrativeness from a cognitive psychological point of view (see Ushioda, 2007) — integrative motivation has played a rapidly diminishing role in L2 motivation research during the past decade, to the extent that currently few active motivation researchers include the concept in their research paradigms. In a recent article specifically devoted to this issue with regard to the learning of World English, Coetzee-Van Rooy (2006) came to the following summary:

> In conclusion, I want to return to the question posed in the title of this paper: is the notion of integrativeness untenable for world Englishes speakers? Findings from a review of theoretical criticism as

well as empirical projects suggest that the answer is: Yes, the notion of integrativeness is untenable for second-language learners in world Englishes contexts. Researchers who use the construct should at least interrogate its use within the context in which the second language is learnt and the extent of multidimensionality of the learner's identity. (Coetzee-Van Rooy, 2006, p. 447)

THE FORMATION OF THE 'L2 MOTIVATIONAL SELF SYSTEM'

In accordance with the above considerations, at the beginning of the new millennium I was ready to move beyond integrativeness, and possible selves theory seemed to offer the most promising way forward. Consequently, in an article describing the results of a large-scale investigation in Hungary (Dörnyei and Csizér, 2002), we called for a general rethinking of the concept of integrativeness:

> ... the term may not so much be related to any actual, or metaphorical, *integration* into an L2 community as to some more basic *identification process* within the individual's *self-concept*. Although further research is needed to justify any alternative interpretation, we believe that rather than viewing 'integrativeness' as a classic and therefore 'untouchable' concept, scholars need to seek potential new conceptualisations and interpretations that extend or elaborate on the meaning of the term without contradicting the large body of relevant empirical data accumulated during the past four decades. (Dörnyei and Csizér, 2002, p. 456)

As already mentioned briefly, the main personal attraction of possible selves theory for me lay in its imagery component. Language learning is a sustained and often tedious process with lots of temporary ups and downs, and I felt that the secret of successful learners was their possession of a superordinate vision that kept them on track. Indeed, language learning can be compared in many ways to the training of professional athletes, and the literature is very clear about the fact that a successful sports career is often motivated by imagery and vision. The point when this line of thinking went beyond mere speculation was during the reanalysis of our Hungarian motivation data using structural equation modelling (Csizér and Dörnyei, 2005), when I realised that the results supported the possible reinterpretation of integrativeness as the 'Ideal L2 Self'. Let us look at these results in more detail.

Empirical findings pointing to the need to reinterpret integrativeness

Over the past 15 years I have been heading a research team in Hungary with the objective of carrying out a longitudinal survey amongst teenage language learners by administering an attitude/motivation questionnaire at regular intervals so that we can gauge the changes in the population's international orientation. So far three successive waves of data collections have been completed (in 1993, 1999 and 2004) involving over 13,000 learners (for a detailed summary, see Dörnyei et al., 2006). The survey questionnaire targeted attitudes towards five target languages: English, German, French, Italian and Russian. It was originally developed in collaboration with one of Robert Gardner's closest associates, Richard Clément, and therefore integrativeness had a prominent place in it, but we also measured several other attitudinal/motivational dimensions, such as *Instrumentality* (i.e. the pragmatic utility of learning the L2); *Direct contact with L2 speakers* (i.e. attitudes towards actually meeting L2 speakers and travelling to their country); *Cultural interest* (i.e. the appreciation of cultural products associated with the particular L2 and conveyed by the media; e.g. films, TV programs, magazines and pop music); *Vitality of L2 community* (i.e. the perceived importance and wealth of the L2 communities in question); *Milieu* (i.e. the general perception of the importance of foreign languages in the learners' school context and in friends' and parents' views); and finally *Linguistic self-confidence* (i.e. a confident, anxiety-free belief that the mastery of an L2 is well within the learner's means).

We submitted the data from all three waves of the survey to structural equation modelling, treating each language and each year separately (so we computed separate models for, say, German in 1993 and French in 2004) and found that the structure underlying the examined variables was remarkably stable across time and languages: The multiple models we obtained produced the same overall result with only minor variations. Figure 11.2 presents the schematic representation of the final construct, which had excellent goodness of fit indices for all the versions (for details, see Dörnyei et al., 2006).

The most important aspect of the model in Figure 11.2 is, from our perspective, that *Integrativeness* was found to play a key role in L2 motivation, mediating the effects of all the other attitudinal/motivational variables on the two criterion measures *Language choice* and *Intended effort to study the L2*. The immediate antecedents of *Integrativeness* were *Attitudes toward L2 speakers/community* and *Instrumentality*, which indicated that the central component in the motivation paradigm was defined by two very different variables, faceless pragmatic incentives and personal attitudes toward members of the L2 community.

Figure 11.2   Schematic Representation of the Structural Equation Model in Dörnyei, Csizér and Németh's (2006) Study

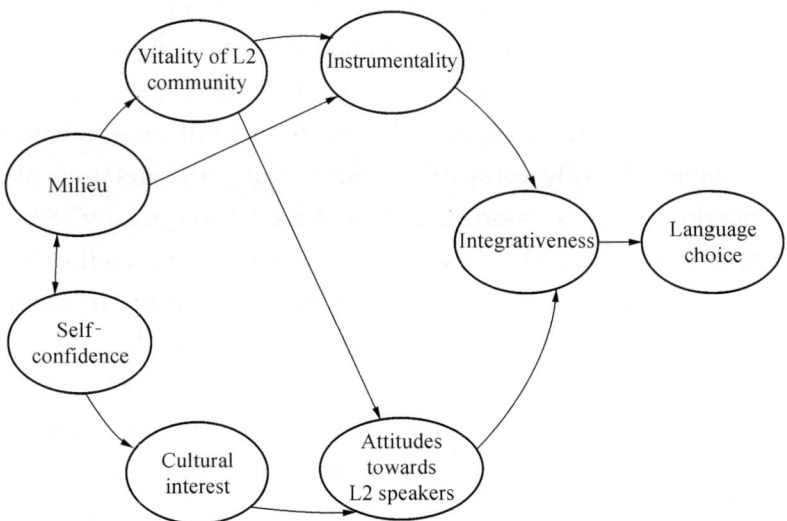

The question was how we could explain these consistent but theoretically far-from-straightforward findings. After some consideration I came to the conclusion that the possible selves approach described earlier offered a good account of the data. Looking at 'integrativeness' from the self perspective, the concept can be conceived of as the L2-specific facet of one's ideal self: if our ideal self is associated with the mastery of an L2, that is, if the person that we would like to become is proficient in the L2, we can be described in Gardner's (1985a) terminology as having an integrative disposition. Thus, the central theme of the emerging new theory was the equation of the motivational dimension that has traditionally been interpreted as 'integrativeness/ integrative motivation' with the *Ideal L2 Self*.

Does the self account explain the two antecedents of integrativeness in Figure 11.2, 'attitudes toward members of the L2 community' and 'instrumentality'? I believe it does, and does it very well:

1. *Attitudes toward members of the L2 community*: There is no doubt that L2 speakers are the closest parallels to the idealised L2-speaking self. This suggests that our attitudes towards members of the L2 community must be related to our ideal language self image. I would suggest that the more positive our disposition toward these L2 speakers, the more attractive our idealised L2 self; or, to turn this equation around, it is difficult to imagine that we can have a vivid and attractive ideal L2 self if the L2 is spoken by a community that we despise. Therefore, the self interpretation of integrativeness is fully compatible with the direct correlation of the concept with 'attitudes toward members of the L2 community'. We find confirmation for this link in the psychological literature. Herbst et al.'s own research and the studies they cite confirm that 'people are attracted to others who emulate the person they want to be rather than the person they actually are' (Herbst Gaertner and Insko, 2003, p. 1206), and, more specifically, 'similarity to the ideal self drives the similarity-attraction association' (p. 1207). Therefore, the correlation in Figure 11.2 not only makes sense but actually validates the reinterpretation of integrativeness

as the ideal L2 self.

2. *Instrumentality*: In our idealised image of ourselves we naturally want to be professionally successful and therefore instrumental motives that are related to career enhancement are logically linked to the ideal L2 self. We should note here, however, that from a self perspective the term 'instrumentality' can be divided into two distinct types. Recall that Higgins (1987, 1998) highlighted a contrasting *approach/avoid* tendency in our future self-guides: ideal self-guides have a *promotion* focus, concerned with hopes, aspirations, advancements, growth and accomplishments (i.e. approaching a desired end-state); whereas ought-to self-guides have a *prevention* focus, regulating the absence or presence of negative outcomes, concerned with safety, responsibilities and obligations (i.e. avoidance of a feared end-state). Looking at it from this perspective, traditionally conceived 'instrumentality/ instrumental motivation' mixes up these two aspects: when our idealised image is associated with being professionally successful, instrumental motives with a promotion focus — for example, to learn English for the sake of professional/career advancement — are related to the ideal self; in contrast, instrumental motives with a prevention focus — for example, to study in order not to fail an exam or not to disappoint one's parents — are part of the ought self. Interestingly, a study by Kyriacou and Benmansour (1997) proposed a data-based five-factor construct that seems to reflect this duality well as it comprises a component labelled 'long-term instrumental motivation,' focusing on acquiring the L2 to enhance one's future professional career, and also a 'short-term instrumental motivation' factor, focusing on getting good grades.

THE L2 MOTIVATIONAL SELF SYSTEM

So far this chapter has described how both empirical findings and theoretical considerations led me to a reconceptualisation of L2 motivation as part of the learner's self system. The good fit between the new theoretical approach and the Hungarian data convinced me that future self-guides — more specifically, the ideal and the ought selves — are central components of this system. However, I also felt that we needed to add a third major constituent, which is associated with the direct impact of the students' learning environment. After all, one of the main achievements of the new wave of motivational studies in the 1990s was to recognise the motivational impact of the main components of the classroom learning situation, such as the teacher, the curriculum and the learner group (for reviews, see Dörnyei, 1994a, 2001c; Ushioda, 2003). For some language learners the initial motivation to learn a language does not come from internally or externally generated self images but rather from successful engagement with the actual language learning process (e.g. because they discover that they are good at it). Thus, in 2005 I proposed that the 'L2 Motivational Self System' was made up of the following three components:

1. *Ideal L2 Self,* which is the L2-specific facet of one's 'ideal self': if the person we would like to become speaks an L2, the *'ideal L2 self'* is a powerful motivator to learn the L2 because of the desire to reduce the discrepancy between our actual and ideal selves. Traditional integrative and internalised instrumental motives would typically belong to this component.

2. *Ought-to L2 Self,* which concerns the attributes that one believes one *ought to* possess to meet expectations and to *avoid* possible negative outcomes. This dimension corresponds to Higgins's ought self and thus to the more extrinsic (i.e. less internalised) types of instrumental motives.

3. *L2 Learning Experience,* which concerns situated, 'executive' motives related to the immediate learning environment and experience (e.g. the impact of the teacher, the curriculum, the peer group, the experience of success). This component is conceptualised at a different level from the two self-guides and future research will hopefully elaborate on the self aspects of this bottom-up process.

Parallels with other conceptualisations of L2 motivation

Although future self-guides may seem rather different in nature from integrativeness, the two theories are not at all incompatible. They both grew out of a social psychological approach to understanding the foundations of action, and both paradigms are centred around identity and identification. With the self system this aspect is obvious, but a closer look at integrativeness also reveals that its core aspect is some sort of a psychological and emotional identification with the L2 community (Gardner, 2001). Indeed, we find several similarities with the L2 Motivational Self System in Gardner's theory. For example, a model put forward by Tremblay and Gardner (1995) as an extension of Gardner's traditional construct includes a broad composite 'Language attitudes' factor at its base, which bears a close resemblance to the proposed concept of Ideal L2 Self in that it subsumes integrative orientation, instrumental orientation, and L2-speaker-related attitudes.

More importantly, Gardner's (2001) socio-educational model described in Figure 11.1 is also compatible with the proposed motivational self system if we consider (1) that the 'motivation' subcomponent in Gardner's construct is, in effect, a measure of motivated behaviour, as indicated by the items that measure it in Gardner's (1985b) Attitude/ Motivation Test Battery (see Dörnyei, 1994b); and (2) that Gardner (2001) attached a possible instrumental motivational link to the Motivation subcomponent in his construct (as the key element of the 'other support' box in Figure 11.1). After these changes, Gardner's motivation construct suggests, in effect, that motivated behaviour is determined by three major motivational dimensions, Integrativeness, Instrumentality, and Attitudes toward the learning situation, which corresponds closely with the proposed L2 Motivational Self System.

Looking at parallels with more recent influential conceptualisations, the proposed self perspective also corresponds with the motivation constructs suggested by Noels (2003) and Ushioda (2001). Noels conceived L2 motivation as being made up of three interrelated orientations: (1) intrinsic reasons inherent in the language learning process, (2) extrinsic reasons for language learning, and (3) integrative reasons. These three components are a close match to the L2 Learning Experience, the Ought-to L2 Self and the Ideal L2 Self, respectively.

Using qualitative rather than quantitative methods, Ushioda identified a more complex motivation construct which, however, is conceptually related both to the one offered by Noels and the L2 Motivation Self System. Her findings pointed to eight motivational dimensions, which in turn can be grouped into three broad clusters: (1) *actual learning process* (subsuming 'Language-related enjoyment/liking', 'Positive learning history' and 'Personal satisfaction'); (2) *external pressures/incentives*; and (3) *integrative disposition* (subsuming 'Personal goals'; 'Desired levels of L2 competence', which consists of language-intrinsic goals; 'Academic interest', which had the greatest contribution from interest in French literature; and 'Feelings about French-speaking countries or people'). Here again the parallels with the L2 Motivational Self System are obvious.

Thus, we can conclude that a number of different L2 motivation theories appear to converge in a common tripartite construct, which is fully compatible with the L2 Motivational Self System. This provides theoretical validation for the new model. Let us examine now whether empirical data also confirm the proposed assumptions.

Empirical validation of the L2 Motivational Self System

Over the last three years several quantitative studies have been conducted to specifically test and validate the L2 Motivational Self System, and the most important of these are included in this volume (Al-Shehri, 2009; Csizér and Kormos, 2009; Ryan, 2009; Taguchi, Magid and Papi, 2009). These investigations took place in five different countries (China, Hungary, Iran, Japan and Saudi Arabia) and involved over 6000 participants in four different sample types: secondary pupils, English-major and non-English-major university students and adult learners. Without wanting to reiterate the findings reported in the specific papers, let me draw five general conclusions:

  1. All these studies found solid confirmation for the proposed self

system.

2. The studies which specifically tested the relationship between Integrativeness and the Ideal L2 Self produced an average correlation of .54 between the two variables across the various subsamples, leaving no doubt that the two concepts are closely related.

3. The Ideal L2 Self was consistently found to correlate highly with the criterion measure (Intended effort), explaining 42% of the variance, which is an exceptionally high figure in motivation studies. In the studies where it was measured, Integrativeness also did a good job at explaining variance in the criterion measure, but the amount of variance it accounted for was considerably less, only 32%.

4. When instrumentality was divided into two types in accordance with Higgins's (1987, 1998) promotion/prevention distinction, all the studies found — in line with the theory — higher correlations of the *Ideal L2 Self* with *Instrumentality-promotion* than with *Instrumentality-prevention*, while Ought-to L2 Self displayed the reverse pattern. Furthermore, the promotion and the prevention aspects were largely independent from each other, with even the highest correlations between the two types of instrumental factors explaining less than 12% of shared variance. Thus, these figures prove that traditionally conceived 'instrumental motivation' can indeed be divided into two distinct types, one relating to the Ideal L2 Self, the other to the Ought-to L2 Self.

5. Structural equation models including the full L2 Motivational Self System displayed fine goodness of fit with the data.

Besides these studies that were specifically conducted for validation purposes, several other empirical investigations reported in this anthology considered some aspect of the validity of the L2 Motivational Self System. We will summarise these in the final chapter in more detail, but as a preliminary it is fair to say that the proposed model came out of these studies in a favourable light. Thus, we can conclude that there exists robust theoretical and empirical confirmation of the soundness of the proposed self-based approach.

PRACTICAL IMPLICATIONS OF THE SELF-BASED APPROACH TO MOTIVATION

One benefit of reinterpreting L2 motivation within the L2 Motivational Self System is that it offers new avenues for motivating language learners. The novel area of motivational strategies concerns the promotion of the first component of the system, the Ideal L2 Self, through generating a language learning vision and through imagery enhancement. Because the source of the second component of the system, the Ought-to L2 Self, is external to the learner (as it concerns the duties and obligations imposed by friends, parents and other authoritative figures), this future self-guide does not lend itself to obvious motivational practices. The third component of the system, the L2 Learning Experience, is associated with a wide range of techniques that can promote motivation, but because these have been described well in past discussions of traditional motivational strategies, I will not focus on them here (for a review, see Dörnyei, 2001a). The new set of motivational techniques associated with the Ideal L2 Self complements these known strategies.

In the first part of this Chapter I summarised the conditions that are necessary for future self-guides to exert their motivational power. Accordingly, the Ideal L2 Self is an effective motivator if (1) the learner has a desired future self-image, (2) which is elaborate and vivid, (3) which is perceived as plausible and is in harmony — or at least does not clash — with the expectations of the learner's family, peers and other elements of the social environment, (4) which is regularly activated in the learner's working self-concept, (5) which is accompanied by relevant and effective procedural strategies that act as a roadmap towards the goal, and finally (6) which also contains elaborate information about the negative consequences of not achieving the desired end-state. Of this list, points (1–4) are specific to the self approach, whereas the final two points involve more general motivational and instructional strategies that have been, in one way or another, part of the traditional conception of motivational teaching practice: point (4)concerns the generation of a realistic and situated action plan while point (5)involves the general idea that we can be both pulled and pushed towards the same goal and the most effective way is to coordinate these forces. Let us look at the strategic implications of these six points.

Construction of the Ideal L2 Self: Creating the vision

We saw earlier that the (obvious) prerequisite for the motivational capacity of future self-guides is that they *need to exist*. It was also mentioned that people differ in how easily they can generate a successful possible self, which means that a major source of any absence of L2 motivation is likely to be the lack of a developed ideal self in general or an Ideal L2 Self component of it in particular. Therefore, the first step in a motivational intervention following the self approach is to help learners to construct their Ideal L2 Self, that is, to *create their vision*.

Strictly speaking, the term 'constructing' the Ideal L2 Self is not really accurate because it is highly unlikely that any motivational intervention will lead a student to generate an ideal self out of nothing — the realistic process is more likely to involve awareness raising and guided selection from the multiple aspirations, dreams, desires, etc. that the students have already entertained in the past. Dunkel, Kelts and Coon (2006) explain that during the formation of their identities, adolescents produce a wide variety of possible selves as potential identity alternatives to explore and 'try on' without full commitment. The origins of these tentative possible selves go back to views held by others, most notably to the ideals that parents hold for themselves and for their children (Zentner and Renaud, 2007). Alternatively, they can also stem from the students' peer groups, which act as powerful reference groups exerting social pressure (Boyatzis and Akrivou, 2006), and a third common route is related to the impact of role models that the students have seen in films, on TV or in real life.

Thus, igniting the vision involves, in effect, increasing the students' mindfulness about the significance of ideal selves, guiding them through a number of possible selves that they have entertained in their minds in the past, and presenting powerful role models. Oyserman et al. (2002) also emphasise the importance of helping students to synthesise the potential hypothetical images with what they know about themselves, their own traits and abilities, as well as their past successes and failures in order to capitalise on existing strengths and avoid weaknesses. In a successful intervention programme with American low-income, minority teenagers, for example, Oyserman et al. (2006) asked students to introduce each other in terms of the skills or ability they possessed, and in the second session participants picked photographs that fitted their adult 'visions'. A different approach was taken in Sheldon and Lyubomirsky's (2006) 'Best Possible Selves' writing project, in which students were directed to outline their 'ideal future life' in as much detail as they could.

In another programme developed by Hock, Deshler and Schumaker (2006) for demotivated elementary to post-secondary students in the US, the first phase included a series of activities designed to help students identify areas in which they have interest and skills and feel good about themselves. This was followed by a semi-structured interview with a teacher or counsellor, either individually or as part of a group, in which the students were asked to identify words or phrases that described them in targeted areas (as a learner, a person, a worker, and in a strength area), and to define their hopes, expectations and fears for the future in each area. The interviews were recorded and students were also encouraged to write down the answers to each question. As a follow-up, in the third phase of the programme they were asked to draw a 'Possible Selves Tree' with branches and other elements (e.g. lightning, termites) representing both their desired and feared possible selves. Interestingly, they were instructed to use the exact words they recorded in the interview to add branches and roots to the tree and the dangers around it.

So far no research has been directed at specifically developing an ideal language self. However, it seems to me that in an era when international holidays are becoming increasingly accessible and cross-cultural communication is a standard part of our existence in the 'global village', it is possible to devise creative ideal-self-generating activities drawing on past adventures, on the exotic nature of encounters with a foreign culture, and on role models of successful L2 learning achievers.

Imagery enhancement: Strengthening the vision

I argued earlier that even if a desired self image exists, it may not have a sufficient degree of elaborateness and vividness in some learners to be effective. The good news is that methods of imagery enhancement have been explored in several areas of psychological, educational and sport research in the past, and the techniques of creative or guided imagery can be utilised to promote ideal L2 self images and thus to *strengthen the students' vision*. (For reviews and resources, see for example, Berkovits, 2005; Fezler, 1989; Gould, Damarjian and Greenleaf, 2002; Hall, Stradling and Young, 2006; Horowitz, 1983; Leuner, Horn and Klessmann, 1983; Singer, 2006; Taylor et al., 1998). The impact of imagery training is evident from an Olympic champion springboard diver's account:

> It took me a long time to control my images and perfect my imagery, maybe a year, doing it every day. At first I couldn't see myself, I always saw everyone else, or I would see my dives wrong all the time. I would get an image of hurting myself, or tripping on the board, or I would 'see' something done really bad. As I continued to work at it, I got to the point where I could feel myself doing a perfect dive and hear the crowd yelling at the Olympics. But it took me a long time. (Gould et al., 2002, p. 70)

As Gould et al. (2002) describe, imagery training for athletes is designed to enhance the vividness and controllability of an athlete's imagery. These can involve a variety of exercises, starting from very simple ones (e.g. imagining one's bedroom and gradually adding details) to complex ones that include controlling and manipulating the content of elaborate image sequences. However, the authors stress that, regardless of which area an athlete is working on, 'imagery is a skill like any other, requiring consistent effort to attain a high level of proficiency' (Gould et al., 2002, p. 70). In psychotherapy, too, there is a number of different approaches, from the 'positive imagery approach' (which involves the use of highly pleasurable, relaxing images to counteract anxiety), to behaviourists' systematic desensitisation or to guided imagery in the treatment of conditions as diverse as anorexia or childhood phobias (see Leuner et al., 1983; Singer, 2006).

Guided imagery is also utilised in medical practice. According to Roffe, Schmidt and Ernst (2005), it has been identified as one of the 10 most frequently recommended complementary cancer therapies on the internet, and Fezler (1989) reports on using imagery successfully even on skin disorders such as acne. Finally, imagery has definite educational potential. Taylor et al. (1998), for example, present evidence that mental simulation was beneficial for university students preparing for an exam, and Berkovits (2005) argues passionately that imagery is the ideal way to work with children:

> When a child uses imagery to find solutions to problems in her current life or from the past, she obtains a sense of autonomy and confidence in her ability to resolve situations she may have felt controlled her. These situations run the gamut of the child's experience, pertaining to her relationship with herself, her peers, her parents, siblings, teachers, authority figures, and learning situations in school, to name a few. Using imagination to find solutions to these situations has the added advantage of improving the child's verbal ability, because the images are clear and precise, and they lend themselves to clarity and precision of expression. (Berkovits, 2005, p. xvii)

Thus, there is a considerable body of literature on the conscious use of imagery to good effect in varied disciplines. What would be needed in applied linguistics now is a systematic review of the techniques utilised with a view of their potential applicability to promoting L2 motivation and the vision to master a foreign language. An intriguing recent publication by Arnold, Puchta and Rinvolucri (2007) has taken the important first step towards introducing mental imagery in the L2 classroom, and although the details of an effective 'language vision programme' are still to be worked out, let there be no doubt about it: 'Our capacity for imagery and fantasy can indeed give us a kind of control over possible futures!' (Singer, 2006, p. 128).

Making the Ideal L2 Self plausible: Substantiating the vision

We saw earlier that possible selves are only effective insomuch as the individual perceives them as possible, that is, realistic within the person's particular circumstances. It is a central tenet in expectancy-value theories of motivation that the greater the perceived likelihood of goal-attainment, the higher the degree of the individual's positive motivation. Indeed, it is obvious that if people are convinced that they cannot succeed no matter how hard they try, they are unlikely to invest effort in the particular task (see Dörnyei, 2001c). This principle also applies to ideal self-images: in order for them to energise sustained behaviour, they must be anchored in a sense of realistic expectations. In other words, they need to be *substantiated*, resulting in the curious mixed aura of imagination and reality that effective images share. As Pizzolato (2006, p. 59) puts it, 'The relation between what students want to become and what students actually become may be mediated by what students feel they are able to become (i.e. expected possible selves).'

In the self-oriented training programme by Oyserman et al. (2006, p. 191) mentioned above, the reality component was added to the desired self image by asking students to draw role models and negative forces, implying the metamessage that 'everyone faces obstacles and difficulties; this does not make the PSs [possible selves] less part of the "true" self'. Then, in the following session students drew timelines into the future, including forks in the road and obstacles, thus reinforcing this message.

In the 'Possible Selves Tree' programme described briefly earlier, Hock et al. (2006) also included a reality check component called 'Reflecting', which encouraged students to evaluate the condition of their Possible Selves Tree and to realise the need for the conscious nurturing of the tree. The authors argued that once students had examined their possible selves, they were more inclined to believe that they could do well in school and in life:

> In effect, they begin to view learning as a pathway to their hopes and expectations and as a way to prevent feared possible selves from materializing. Thus, learning becomes more relevant, and students increase their willingness to put forth effort and commit to learning. (Hock et al., 2006, p. 214)

Activating the Ideal L2 Self: Keeping the vision alive

Very little is said in the literature about activating the ideal self, but this is an area where language teachers have, perhaps unknowingly, a great deal of experience. Classroom activities such as warmers and icebreakers as well as various communicative tasks (see for example, Dörnyei and Murphey, 2003) can all be turned into effective ways of *keeping the vision alive*, and inviting role models to class, playing films and music, and engaging in cultural activities such as French cheese parties or 'Cook Your Wicked Western Burger' evenings can all serve as potent ideal self reminders. Indeed, good teachers in any subject matter seem to have the instinctive talent to provide an engaging framework that keeps the enthusiasts going and the less-than-enthusiasts thinking.

Developing an action plan: Operationalising the vision

It was argued earlier, and virtually all the researchers in the area of possible/ideal selves point out in one way or another that future self-guides are only effective if they are accompanied by a set of concrete action plans. Therefore, the ideal self needs to come as part of a 'package' consisting of an imagery component and a repertoire of appropriate plans, scripts and self-regulatory strategies. This is clearly an area where L2 motivation research and language teaching methodology overlap. An effective action plan will contain a goal-setting component, which is a motivational issue, but it will also include individualised study plans and instructional avenues, which are methodological in nature. For an Olympic athlete the coach and the training plan are just as much a part of the complete vision as the image of stepping onto the top of the podium. Thus, in many ways, several of the components underpinning the ideal self package are not strictly speaking self-specific and have in fact been addressed in detail in the past. The important lesson from our point of view is that these methodological aspects must not be overlooked because even the most galvanising vision might fall flat without any concrete pathways into which to channel the individual's energy. For this reason, in Hock et al.'s (2006, p. 214) training programme the final component involves a thorough check-up phase, in which 'task completion is reviewed, goals and action plans are modified, goal attainment is celebrated, new goals are added, and hopes, expectations, and fears are continually examined'.

Considering failure: Counterbalancing the vision

Oyserman and Markus (1990) proposed that for maximum effectiveness, the desired self should be offset by the feared self. That is, future self-guides are most potent if they utilise the cumulative impact of both approach and avoid tendencies — we do something because we want to do it but also because not doing it would lead to undesired results. Indeed, the perceived consequences of action abandonment have been known to have great energising potential (Dörnyei, 2001c), but a common human tendency is to focus on the positive goals and turn to considering the dire alternatives only when everything else fails. Oyserman and Markus's proposal intends to change this practice by making awareness of the two sides of the coin more balanced; it can be seen, therefore, as a call for the regular activation of the dreaded self. In language teaching terms this would involve regular reminders of the limitations of not knowing languages as well as recurrently priming the learners' Ought-to L2 Self by highlighting the duties and obligations the learners have committed themselves to.

CONCLUSION

This chapter discussed a major theoretical shift in L2 motivation research, describing how a new paradigm has emerged from both theoretical considerations and research results, and then presenting the main components of the newly proposed 'L2 Motivational Self System'. I would not like to draw detailed conclusions here because this will be done in the final chapter of this volume, which also outlines future research directions. Let me only make here three concluding points:

1. Reframing L2 motivation in a 'possible/ideal-self' perspective does not invalidate the results accumulated in the field of L2 motivation research in the past. On the contrary: I believe that these results will come to life and receive a new meaningfulness within the self framework.

2. Zentner and Renaud (2007) claim that stable ideal-self representations do not emerge before adolescence, and neither can younger children consider multiple perspectives on the self, most notably the ought self projected by significant others. Therefore, the self approach may not be appropriate for pre-secondary students.

3. In everyday parlance 'vision' and 'visionary' are highly loaded words, having life-changing connotations. For me this transformational potential is a real attraction of the ideal self, and therefore it has been reassuring to read Oyserman et al.'s (2006) summary:

> Our results demonstrate the real-world power of a social psychological conceptualisation of the self as a motivational resource ... we developed a process model that, when operationalized, produced lasting change on PSs [possible selves], self-regulation, academic outcomes, and depression.

(Oyserman et al., 2006, p. 201)

So, the self approach allows us to think BIG, and this is exactly what Markus (2006) did in the conclusion of her retrospective overview:

> The realm of what I might be has come under empirical and theoretical scrutiny and has yielded more than we might have imagined some twenty years ago … I hope the volume succeeds in convincing other researchers not to be faint-hearted about the imaginative capacities of the human mind and our abilities to invent ourselves and our worlds. As humans our great evolutionary advantage is our capacity for self-making and world making…In fact, our futures may rest with our shared willingness to experiment with possible selves and possible worlds, and to redesign ourselves and our worlds so that there is room for all of us. (Markus, 2006, p. xiv)

Chapter 12

Motivation and the Vision of Knowing a Second Language

In Beaven, B. (Ed.). (2009). IATEFL 2008: Exeter conference selections (pp. 16-22). Canterbury: IATEFL.

'Motivation' is one of the most important concepts in psychology as motivation theories attempt to explain nothing less than *why humans behave and think as they do*. The notion is also of great importance in language education as it is one of the most common terms teachers and students use to explain what causes success or failure in learning. Indeed, motivation provides the primary impetus to initiate second/foreign (L2) learning and later the driving force to sustain the long and often tedious learning process. Without sufficient motivation, even individuals with the most remarkable abilities cannot accomplish long-term goals, and neither are appropriate curricula and good teaching enough on their own to ensure student achievement.

In this paper I describe a new approach to conceptualising motivation that is centred around the learner's *vision*; this approach and how it has emerged in L2 motivation research is described in more detail in a recent anthology (Dörnyei and Ushioda, 2009; see especially Dörnyei, 2009b). Here I provide a brief overview, focusing mainly on the practical aspects of the theory. I start with a brief summary of the 'L2 Motivational Self System', which provides the theoretical link between motivation and vision, within a historical background.

THREE PHASES OF L2 MOTIVATION RESEARCH

L2 motivation research has been a thriving area within applied linguistics with several books and literally hundreds of articles published on the topic during the past four decades. It is useful to divide this period into three phases:

- *The social psychological period* (1959-1990), which was characterised by the work of social psychologist Robert Gardner and his students and associates in Canada (e.g. Gardner, 1985a; Gardner and Lambert, 1972; Gardner and MacIntyre, 1993). The best-known concepts stemming from this period were integrative and instrumental orientation/motivation, the former referring to the desire to learn an L2 of a valued community so that one can communicate with members of the community and sometimes even become like them, the latter to the concrete benefits that language proficiency might bring about (e.g. career opportunities, increased salary).

- *The cognitive-situated period* (during the 1990s), which was characterised by work that drew on cognitive theories imported from educational psychology, mainly conducted outside Canada. The best-known concepts associated with this period were intrinsic and extrinsic motivation, attributions, self-confidence/efficacy and situation-specific motives related to the learning environment, e.g. motives related to the L2 course, teachers, peers. (For overviews, see Dörnyei, 2001c; Williams and Burden, 1997.)

- *New approaches* (past decade), which have been characterised by an interest in motivational change and in the relationship between motivation and identity. The best-known concepts originating in this period have been the process-oriented conceptualisation of motivation (Dörnyei, 2000, 2001c), motivation as investment (Norton, 2000) and the concepts of the ideal and ought-to L2 selves, which will be described in detail below.

Motivation and the self

In 2005, I proposed a new approach to the understanding of L2 motivation (Dörnyei, 2005), conceived within an 'L2 Motivational Self System', which attempts to integrate a number of influential L2 theories (e.g. by Gardner, 2001; Noels, 2003; Norton, 2001; Ushioda, 2001) with findings of 'self research' in psychology. This initiative was rooted in an important trend in self psychology: over the past two decades self theorists have become increasingly interested in the active, dynamic nature of the self-system — the 'doing' side of personality — thus placing the self at the heart of motivation and action (Cantor, 1990). This dynamic self concept has created an intriguing interface between personality and motivational psychology.

Within the dynamic approach of linking the human self with human action, the notion of 'possible selves' offers one of the most powerful, and at the same time the most versatile, motivational self-mechanism, representing the individuals' ideas of what they *might* become, what they *would like to* become, and what they are *afraid of* becoming (Markus and Nurius, 1986). Thus, possible selves involve a person's specific image of his or her self in future states. It needs to be stressed that possible selves are more than mere long-term goals or future plans in that they involve tangible *images* and *senses*. Accordingly, imagery is a central element of possible selves theory — if we have a well-developed possible future self, we can imagine this self in vivid, realistic situations. A good example of this imagery aspect is how athletes regularly imagine themselves completing races or stepping onto the winning podium in order to increase their motivation. As Markus and Nurius (1986) emphasise, possible selves are represented in the same imaginary and semantic way as the here-and-now self, that is, they are a *reality for* the individual: people can 'see' and 'hear' a possible self. (See also Ruvolo and Markus, 1992.) Thus, in many ways possible selves are similar to *dreams* and *visions* about oneself.

Ideal selves, ought-to selves and the L2 Motivational Self System

From the point of view of education, one type of possible self, the *ideal self* appears to be a particularly useful concept, referring to the representation of the characteristics that someone would ideally like to possess — i.e. a representation of hopes, aspirations or wishes. (See Higgins, 1987, 1998.) It requires little justification that if someone has a powerful ideal self — for example a student envisions him/herself as a successful businessman or scholar — this self image can act as a potent self-guide, with considerable motivational power. This is expressed in everyday speech when we talk about someone following or living up to their dreams.

A complementary self-guide that has educational relevance is the *ought-to self*, referring to the attributes that one believes one ought to possess — i.e. representation of someone's sense of personal or social duties, obligations or responsibilities. (See Higgins, 1987, 1998.) This self-image is particularly salient in some Asian countries where students are often motivated to perform well to fulfil some family obligation or to bring honour to the family's name.

Ever since I first came across the concept of possible selves, and in particular the ideal and the ought-to selves, I have been convinced that these concepts would be highly useful for understanding the motivation to learn a foreign language. Having considered the theoretical implications of these ideas from an L2 perspective and having conducted some relevant empirical research, in 2005 I proposed (Dörnyei, 2005) a tripartite construct of L2 motivation that was made up of the following three components:

- *Ideal L2 Self* which concerns the L2-specific facet of one's *ideal self*, if the person we would like to become speaks an L2, the ideal L2 self is a powerful motivator to learn the L2 because we would like to reduce the discrepancy between our actual and ideal selves.

- *Ought-to L2 Self* which concerns the attributes that one believes one *ought to* possess to *avoid* possible negative outcomes, and which therefore may bear little resemblance to the person's own desires or wishes.

- *L2 Learning Experience*, which concerns situation-specific motives related to the immediate learning environment and experience (e.g. the positive impact of success or the enjoyable quality of a language course).

(For more details on the evolution of this model, see Dörnyei, 2009b, 2010a.) Thus, the L2 Motivational Self System covers the internal desires of the learner, the social pressures exercised by significant or authoritative people in the learner's environment and the actual experience of being engaged in the learning process.

CONDITIONS FOR THE MOTIVATING CAPACITY OF THE IDEAL AND OUGHT-TO SELVES

While future self-guides such as the ideal and the ought-to selves provide incentive, direction and impetus for action in order to reduce the discrepancy between the desired selves and the actual self, past research has shown that the motivational capacity of these future self-guides is not automatic but depends on a number of conditions. Accordingly, the Ideal L2 Self is an effective motivator only if:

- the learner *has* a desired future self-image;
- which is *elaborate* and *vivid*;
- which is perceived as *plausible* and is in harmony — or at least does not clash — with the expectations of the learner's family, peers and other elements of the social environment;
- which is *regularly activated* in his/her working self-concept;
- which is accompanied by relevant and effective *procedural strategies* that act as a *roadmap* towards the goal;
- which also contains elaborate information about the *negative consequences* of *not* achieving the desired end-state.

These conditions offer a useful framework for developing some practical implications of motivation theory: designing methods and strategies to realise these conditions in the language classroom can form the basis of an effective programme for introducing a motivational teaching practice.

Generating and enhancing a vision for language learning

Motivational strategies have received attention in applied linguistics for several decades and a comprehensive collection of practical motivating techniques has been offered by Dörnyei (2001a), covering a wide range of issues from classroom management and task presentation to student self-motivation. However, the approach discussed below opens up a whole new avenue for promoting student motivation by means of increasing the elaborateness and vividness of self-relevant imagery in the students. That is, the approach suggests that an effective way of motivating learners is to create in them an *attractive vision* of their ideal language self. This motivational programme consists of six components, which are described below.

Construction of the Ideal L2 Self: Creating the vision

The (obvious) prerequisite for the motivational capacity of future self-guides is that they *need to exist*. Therefore, the first step in a motivational intervention that follows the self approach is to help learners to construct their Ideal L2 Self — that is, to *create an L2-related vision*. The term 'constructing' the Ideal L2 Self is, in fact, not entirely accurate because it is highly unlikely that any motivational intervention will lead a student to generate an ideal self out of nothing — the realistic process is more likely to involve *awareness raising* about and *guided selection* from the multiple aspirations, dreams, desires, etc. that the student has already entertained in the past. Thus, igniting the vision involves increasing the students' mindfulness about the significance of the ideal self in general and guiding them through a number of possible selves that they have entertained in their minds in the past, while also presenting some powerful role models to illustrate potential future selves.

Imagery enhancement: Strengthening the vision

Even if a desired self image exists, it may not have a sufficient degree of elaborateness and vividness to be an effective motivator. Methods of imagery enhancement have been explored in several areas of psychological, educational and sport research in the past, and the techniques of *creative* or *guided imagery* can be utilised to promote ideal L2 self images and thus to *strengthen the students' vision*. (For reviews and resources, see for example, Berkovits, 2005; Fezler, 1989; Gould, Damarjian and Greenleaf, 2002; Hall, Hall, Stradling and Young, 2006; Horowitz, 1983; Leuner, Horn and Klessmann,1983; Singer, 2006; Taylor, Pham, Rivkin and Armor, 1998). Undoubtedly, further research is needed in applied linguistics to review the imagery enhancement techniques utilised in other fields with regard to their potential applicability to promoting L2 motivation and the vision to master a foreign language. The details of an effective 'language imagery programme' are still to be worked out, but let there be no doubt about it: "Our capacity for imagery and fantasy can indeed give us a kind of control over possible futures!" (Singer, 2006, p. 128).

Making the Ideal L2 Self plausible: Substantiating the vision

Possible selves are only effective insomuch as the learner perceives them as *possible*, that is, conceivable within the person's particular circumstances. Thus, in order for ideal self images to energise sustained behaviour, they must be anchored in a sense of realistic expectations — they need to be *substantiated*, resulting in the curious mixed aura of imagination and reality that effective images share. This process requires honest and down-to-earth reality checks as well as considering any potential obstacles and difficulties that might stand in the way of realising the ideal self. Inviting successful role models to class can send the powerful message to students that, although everybody faces certain hurdles in reaching their ideal selves, it can be, and has been, done.

Developing an action plan: Operationalising the vision

Future self-guides are only effective if they are accompanied by a set of concrete *action plans*. Therefore, the ideal self needs to come as part of a 'package' consisting of an imagery component *and* a repertoire of appropriate plans, scripts and self-regulatory strategies. Even the most galvanizing self image might fall flat without ways of *operationalising the vision*, that is, without any concrete learning pathways into which to channel the individual's energy. This is clearly an area where L2 motivation research and language teaching methodology overlap: an effective action plan will contain a goal-setting component (which is a motivational issue) as well as individualised study plans and instructional avenues (which are methodological in nature).

Activating the Ideal L2 Self: Keeping the vision alive

Very little is said in the literature about activating and re-activating the ideal self, but this is an area where language teachers have, perhaps unknowingly, a great deal of experience. Classroom activities such as warmers and icebreakers as well as various communicative tasks can all be turned into effective ways of *keeping the vision alive*, and playing films and music, or engaging in cultural activities such as French cheese parties or 'Cook your wicked western burger' evenings can all serve as potent ideal-self reminders. Indeed, good teachers in any subject matter seem to have an instinctive talent to provide an engaging framework that keeps the enthusiasts going and the less-than-enthusiasts thinking.

Considering failure: Counterbalancing the vision

For maximum effectiveness, the desired self should be *offset by the feared self*: we do something because we want to do it *and also* because not doing it would lead to undesired results. In language teaching terms this process *of counterbalancing the vision* would involve regular reminders of the limitations of not knowing foreign languages as well as regularly priming the learners' ought-to L2 self to highlight the duties and obligations they have committed themselves to.

CONCLUSION

The L2 Motivational Self System suggests that there are three primary sources of the motivation to learn a foreign/second language: (a) the learner's vision of him/herself as an effective L2 speaker, (b) the social pressure coming from the learner's environment, and (c) positive learning experiences. This paper elaborated on the first of these sources. I firmly believe that it is possible for teachers to consciously generate L2-learning vision in learners and I would like to encourage colleagues to develop a repertoire of techniques to ignite and enhance this vision. The six main areas of relevant motivational strategies presented in this talk are intended to offer a framework for future language teaching methodological developments along this line. Good luck!

Chapter 13

The Relationship between Language Aptitude and Language Learning Motivation: Individual Differences from a Dynamic Systems Perspective

In Macaro, E. (Ed.). (2010). Continuum companion to second language acquisition (pp. 247-267). London: Continuum.

Language aptitude and language learning motivation have traditionally been seen as the primary individual difference (ID) variables in the study of a second/foreign language (L2), that is, the learner characteristics that have been found to exert the greatest amount of consistent influence on the SLA process. Although other ID factors such as cognitive/learning styles or learner beliefs have also received attention in the literature (see Dörnyei, 2005), their impact on SLA has been negligible compared to that of the aptitude-motivation dyad. The magnitude of the influence exerted by aptitude and motivation depends on how these constructs are assessed and what the criterion measures are, but correlations between aptitude and L2 attainment indices are often as high as .50 and meaningful correlations with motivation have usually been reported within the range of .30 to .40. However, regarding the assessment of motivation, if (a) the criterion measure is related to learner behaviours rather than holistic proficiency measures (e.g., the extent of learners' participation in a task rather than, say, TOEFL scores); (b) the motivation measure is situated (i.e., it focuses on aspects of the learners' classroom experience); and (c) the co-construction of motivation by the participants is taken into account (i.e., by pooling the motivation of both learners in a task performed by dyads), then correlations with motivational factors can exceed .50 and multiple correlations involving all the assessed motives together can reach .70 (Dörnyei, 2002; Kormos and Dörnyei, 2004).

A common conception of aptitude and motivation has been that the former is the most important *cognitive* variable, while motivation is the primary *affective* factor shaping second language acquisition/learning (see, e.g., Gardner and MacIntyre, 1992, 1993). As a result, including both an aptitude and a motivation measure in a research paradigm has typically been seen as a fairly comprehensive characterisation of the learner's contribution to the SLA process. Thus, the current task of addressing the relationship between aptitude and motivation in this chapter goes beyond merely looking at two specific ID factors — it concerns, in effect, the broader examination of how individual difference variables in general are related to each other and how they exert their cumulative impact. As we will see below, answering these questions will lead us to the re-analysis of the overall nature of learner characteristics within the learner-environment learning complex.

In the following discussion I first provide a brief outline of the history of L2 research on aptitude and motivation, highlighting emerging problems about the traditional conceptualisation of the concepts. I then present a novel approach to understanding learner characteristics which replaces the modular view of individual differences involving multiple discrete ID factors with a tripartite system of the human mind that comprises *cognition*, *affect* and *motivation* within a dynamic systems framework. I will argue that from this perspective identifying 'pure' individual difference factors has only limited value; instead, a potentially more fruitful approach is to focus on certain higher-order combinations of different attributes — or trait complexes — that act as integrated wholes. I conclude this chapter by introducing three attribute complex candidates for the new approach, *aptitude/trait complexes*, *interests* conceptualised in a broad sense and *possible selves*.

A BRIEF HISTORY OF LANGUAGE APTITUDE RESEARCH

Following the success of intelligence research in educational psychology at the beginning of the twentieth century, language aptitude research was initiated in the USA in the 1920s (for a historical overview, see Spolsky, 1995). The main objective of the pioneering language aptitude tests was, similar to the first intelligence test developed by Binet and Simon in France in 1905, to increase the cost-effectiveness of language education in the public school system by identifying slow L2 learners. This prognosis aspect of aptitude tests also motivated the second wave of aptitude test development 30 years later, in the 1950s and 1960s, which produced the two best-known language aptitude batteries, the *Modern Language Aptitude Test* (MLAT; Carroll and Sapon, 1959), and the *Pimsleur Language Aptitude Battery* (PLAB; Pimsleur, 1966). These batteries became so widespread both in research and in various educational practices that the L2 research community developed the tacit understanding that language aptitude is simply what language aptitude tests measure. From a theoretical point of view this has been somewhat problematic given that both the MLAT and the PLAB had been developed without any well-established underlying theoretical construct, largely through a trial-and-error process that involved administering a great number of different tasks to learners and selecting those that discriminated best between good language learners and their slower peers

(Dörnyei, 2005).

So, what exactly is 'language aptitude'? Most scholars would agree that the concept covers a range of different cognitive factors making up a composite measure that can, in turn, be referred to as the learner's overall capacity to master a foreign language. In other words, foreign language aptitude is not a unitary factor but rather a complex of 'basic abilities that are essential to facilitate foreign language learning' (Carroll and Sapon, 1959, p. 14). In one of the best-known taxonomies, Carroll (1981, p. 105) proposed that the language aptitude construct comprised four constituent abilities:

1. *Phonetic coding ability*, which is considered the most important component and is defined as 'an ability to identify distinct sounds, to form associations between these sounds and symbols representing them, and to retain these associations'.

2. *Grammatical sensitivity*, which is 'the ability to recognise the grammatical functions of words (or other linguistic entities) in sentence structures'.

3. *Rote learning ability*, which is the 'ability to learn associations between sounds and meaning rapidly and efficiently, and to retain these associations'.

4. *Inductive language learning ability*, which is 'the ability to infer or induce the rules governing a set of language materials, given samples of language materials that permit such inferences'.

Carroll's (1981) taxonomy was derived from extensive *post hoc* analyses of MLAT scores and was, therefore, inevitably determined by the composition of the actual MLAT tasks — indeed, other scholars who derived their taxonomies from using other aptitude tests produced different theoretical constructs (e.g., Pimsleur, 1966). As a result, even though the composite measures yielded by language aptitude batteries consistently explained a significant amount of variance in learning achievement, simply equating these composite test scores with 'language aptitude' was seen as increasingly unsatisfactory because the notion of language aptitude defined in this way was too broad an umbrella term, referring to an unspecified mixture of cognitive variables (Dörnyei, 2009c). Therefore, scholars investigating specific cognitive abilities such as working memory (e.g., Miyake and Friedman, 1998) or word recognition (e.g., Dufva and Voeten, 1999) started to avoid using the term altogether. Indeed, the common theme in the various post-Carroll research directions has been the examination of the SLA-specific impact of specific cognitive factors and subprocesses, thus going beyond the use of the language aptitude metaphor (see Dörnyei, 2005). For recent reviews of language aptitude research, see Ranta (2008) and Robinson (in press).

A BRIEF HISTORY OF L2 LEARNING MOTIVATION RESEARCH

Many overviews exist to describe the history of L2 motivation research from its genesis at the end of the 1950s in Canada by the work of Robert Gardner and Wallace Lambert (1959) to the most contemporary process-oriented or self-based approaches (see e.g., Clément and Gardner, 2001; Dörnyei, 2005; Dörnyei and Ushioda, 2011; MacIntyre, 2002; MacIntyre, MacKinnon and Clément, 2009a; Ushioda and Dörnyei, 2009). These reviews vary somewhat in their emphases, because the scope of the various approaches of understanding what motivates language learners to initiate and sustain the lengthy process of mastering an L2 encompasses a wide range of different theoretical perspectives. Gardner and his colleagues' initial stance involved a social-psychological perspective and the motivation construct they developed was centred around language attitudinal variables. The key component of Gardner's (1985a) theory was the *integrative motive*, which concerns a positive interpersonal/affective disposition towards the L2 group and the desire to interact with and even become similar to valued members of that community. It implies an openness to and respect for other cultural groups and ways of life; in the extreme, it might involve complete identification with the community and possibly even withdrawal from one's original group.

In the 1990s there was a broadening of perspectives in L2 motivational research, exploring a number of different motivational dimensions originally introduced in educational psychology (for a review, see Dörnyei, 2001c). This 'cross-fertilisation' led to an unprecedented boom in L2 motivation studies and a variety of new models and approaches were put forward in the literature, resulting in what Gardner and Tremblay (1994b) called a 'motivational renaissance'. A common feature of these new research attempts was the move towards a more *situated approach* to the study of motivation, examining how the immediate learning context influences the learners' overall disposition and how motivation, in turn, effects concrete learning processes within a classroom context. It was argued that the classroom environment had a much stronger motivational impact than had been proposed before, highlighting the significance of motives associated with the L2 course, the L2 teacher and the learner group.

Thus, by the end of the 1990s motivation research was characterised by a colourful spectrum of diverse theoretical strands and constructs, and in the absence of a 'gravitational centre' scholars often followed a 'pick-and-mix' method in conceptualizing motivation for their particular research purposes. This eclectic background provided fertile ground for theoretical developments, giving rise to a number of salient research programmes: Kim Noels and her colleagues (e.g., Noels, 2003, 2009; Noels, Clément and Pelletier, 1999, 2001) implemented Deci and Ryan's (1985) well-known *self-determination theory* for the purpose of studying SLA, examining how the various intrinsic/extrinsic components were related to orientations developed in L2 research, and how the learners' level of self-determination (i.e., autonomous self-regulation) was affected by various classroom practices. MacIntyre and his colleagues (e.g., MacIntyre, Clément, Dörnyei and Noels, 1998, 2003) adapted

McCroskey's notion of L1 *willingness to communicate* (WTC) to the study of L2 communication. Other researchers such as Dörnyei (2000, 2001c; Dörnyei and Ottó, 1998), Ushioda (2001) and Williams and Burden (1997) adopted a *process-oriented perspective*, highlighting the fact that an individual's motivation is never stable but continuously shows a certain degree of fluctuation. Still others linked motivation with various aspects of the learner's *identity*, either by adopting a postmodern, poststructuralist approach (e.g., Norton, 2000, 2001; Pavlenko, 2002; Ushioda, 2007) or by drawing on social psychological research on the self (e.g., Higgins, 1987, 1998; Markus and Nurius, 1986) in conceptualizing *motivational self-guides* (e.g., Dörnyei, 2005, 2009b) — I will come back to this latter strand below when discussing motivation-cognition overlaps and again later when describing higher-order amalgams of learner characteristics.

PROBLEMS WITH THE MODULAR VIEW OF INDIVIDUAL DIFFERENCE VARIABLES

As the previous sections illustrated, the conceptualisations of language aptitude and motivation have been diverse over the years, and in fact, in a book-length overview of individual differences I have concluded that 'all the variables described in this book are either in the process of, or in desperate need of, theoretical "restructuring"' (Dörnyei, 2005, p. 218). Yet, at that stage I did not question the general concept of modular ID variables being the core building blocks of learner characteristics. Indeed, the notion of ID factors appeared to be solid and the ID concept had been well established in SLA research in a relatively straightforward manner: IDs were usually seen as background learner variables that modified and personalised the overall trajectory of the language acquisition processes, accounting for *why, how long and how hard* (motivation), *how well* (aptitude), *how proactively* (learning strategies) and *in what way* (learning styles) the learner engaged in the learning process.

Recently, however, I have come to a new understanding of individual differences and argued (Dörnyei, 2009c) that the seemingly comprehensive and straightforward picture of IDs being stable and monolithic learner traits that concern distinct learner characteristics is part of an idealised 'individual differences myth' that may not hold up against scientific scrutiny. As far as I can see, the basic problem is that if we take a situated and process-oriented perspective of SLA — which I think we ought to — we simply cannot fail to realise that the various learner attributes are neither stable nor context-independent, but display a considerable amount of variation from time to time and from situation to situation. Furthermore, and what is particularly relevant to the current chapter, a closer look at both language aptitude and motivation reveals that neither construct is monolithic but is, instead, made up of a number of constituent components.

Kosslyn and Smith (2000) explain that cognitive abilities in general can be divided into 'lower' and 'higher' brain functions: Lower functions such as early perception and motor control rely on a relatively small collection of processes that display straightforward interactions. In contrast, higher functions are made up of the integrated operation of a relatively large numbers of processes, which may themselves have complex internal structures. It is clear that the ID variables that SLA research has been interested in — such as language aptitude and motivation — are complex, higher-order attributes, which was already recognised in the literature by the fact that — as shown above — neither language aptitude, nor L2 motivation has been seen as uniform, heterogeneous factors but rather composite measures. This is in line with Kosslyn and Smith's (2000) argument that higher-order learner characteristics comprise a selection of hierarchically organised and dynamically interacting sub-components.

Once we take such a multicomponential view of L2 ID factors, however, we are forced to move even further in our thinking because a closer look reveals that many (if not most) learner characteristics mentioned in the literature involve at one level or another the cooperation of components whose nature is very different from that of the main attribute in question — for example, motivational factors may involve cognitive constituents — resulting in 'hybrid' attributes. This means that not only is the stable and context-independent nature of ID variables highly doubtful, but there are also serious questions about the whole theoretical foundation of the traditional view of individual differences as a modular collective of distinct ID factors. As a result, over the past two years I have come to conclude that the traditional conception of learner characteristics fuelled by the 'individual differences myth' does not do justice to the dynamic, fluid and continuously fluctuating nature of learner factors and neither does it account for the complex internal and external interactions that we can observe in higher-order intellectual functions (for specific illustrations of such interactions within SLA, see the next section below). The following description of motivation by Ellis and Larsen-Freeman (2006, p. 563) is, I believe, characteristic of ID variables in general: 'Motivation is less a trait than fluid play, an ever-changing one that emerges from the processes of interaction of many agents, internal and external, in the ever-changing complex world of the learner.'

As a result of these considerations, I have recently proposed the adoption of a new dynamic systems perspective on individual differences (Dörnyei, 2009c), according to which individual variation in performance is not so much a function of the strength of any individual determinant (e.g., aptitude or motivation) as of the way by which the complex system of all the relevant factors works together. I will describe this dynamic view in more detail below, but before doing so let us have a specific look at the interaction and overlap of the two key learner characteristics in focus in this chapter, language aptitude — or more generally, cognition — and motivation.

COGNITION-MOTIVATION INTERACTION AND OVERLAP IN SLA RESEARCH

As mentioned in the introduction, a common conception of

aptitude and motivation has been that the former is the most important *cognitive* variable, while motivation is the primary *affective* factor shaping SLA. They have traditionally been seen as distinct from each other with no interaction or overlap, and this view was formalised in Robert Gardner's socio-educational model of second language learning (Gardner, 1985a, 2005; Gardner and MacIntyre, 1992, 1993), according to which 'there are two primary individual difference variables involved in language learning, viz., ability and motivation. These two factors are expected to be relatively independent because some students high in ability may be high or low in motivation for any host of reasons, and vice versa' (Gardner, 2005, p. 5).

This traditional view has been questioned recently on a number of accounts. To start with, strictly speaking there is no such thing as 'language aptitude' or 'motivation', because we have seen above that both constructs are umbrella terms subsuming a rather diverse range of factors. Therefore, proposing that aptitude and motivation are the two lynchpins of individual differences is problematic in itself. Furthermore, there is an obvious second concern with the cognitive/affective dichotomy of aptitude and motivation, namely that almost all influential contemporary motivation theories in psychology are cognitive in nature and affective (i.e., emotional) issues hardly ever feature on motivation research agendas. As Schumann (2004, p. 3) has concluded, 'motivation is not independent of cognition (as it is frequently treated in SLA research), but instead it is part of cognition, and therefore, there can be no "cognitive" approaches to SLA that do not include motivation.' If this is so, however, in what way is motivation different from language aptitude, which — as we have seen above — is the collective term used to refer to a mixture of cognitive factors?

The aptitude-motivation distinction becomes even more untenable if we look at the details of specific motivation constructs. What we find is that at one level or another certain established cognitive constructs play a salient role in determining the motivational outcome. Let me describe three examples of this motivation-cognition interplay: 'flow' (Csikszentmihalyi, 1990; Egbert, 2003), 'motivational task processing' (Dörnyei, 2003; Dörnyei and Tseng, 2009) and the 'ideal L2 self' (Dörnyei, 2005, 2009b).

Flow

The experience of 'flow' is a theoretically intriguing and intuitively appealing phenomenon, making its chief advocate, Mihaly Csikszentmihalyi (1990), both a bestselling author and a leading international psychologist. The popularity of the concept is due to the fact that it concerns a highly valued experience that many of us have had in the past: Flow entails a state of intensive involvement in and focused concentration on a task that feels so absorbing that people often compare it to being outside everyday reality. This state is, however, not the kind of passive spiritual experience that some people can evoke through meditation; to the contrary, flow is experienced while people are at their most active or creative, being engaged in completing an absorbing task. Thus, flow can be seen as a heightened level of motivated task engagement; in many ways it is the optimal task experience. It happens when, faced with a challenging activity, people are fully aware of what needs to be done and how, and at the same time they are confident that the task is doable and their skills are sufficient to succeed. An often mentioned feature of a fully fledged flow experience is that the extent of absorption can be such that people even lose self-consciousness and a track of time. While this may sound like a science-fiction fantasy, all we need to do is observe children (and even adults) playing computer games to realise that flow is a very real phenomenon.

In a pioneering study on the role of flow in SLA, Egbert (2003) found that the task conditions under which flow occurs can be organised along four dimensions: (1) there is a perceived balance of task challenge and participant skills during the task, (2) the task offers opportunities for intense concentration and the participants' attention is focused on the pursuit of clear task goals, (3) the participants find the task intrinsically interesting or authentic and (4) the participants perceive a sense of control over the task process and outcomes. These underlying dimensions display a balanced mixture of cognitive and motivational constituents (see also Guastello, Johnson and Rieke, 1999): While flow is usually discussed under the motivation rubric as a specific type of intrinsic motivation (explained by the experience of enjoyment that is one of the key features of flow), it is fundamentally determined by cognitive factors such as the appraisal of the challenge of the activity; the self-appraisal of the level of the individual's skills and competence involved in the activity; a firm sense of control over the completion of the task; clarity about the task goals; and focused attention. The reason why flow is a particularly good example for the integrated operation of motivational and cognitive aspects is that the flow experience can only occur if all these conditions are met; that is, the cognitive factors are prerequisites rather than mere modifiers of the motivational phenomenon.

Motivational Task Processing

In a recent study, Dörnyei and Tseng (2009) examined the validity of a theoretical construct that I proposed in 2003 concerning motivational task processing (Dörnyei, 2003). As I argued then, the motivational dynamics of learning tasks are dependent on how the participating learners process the various motivational stimuli they encounter and, as a result, how they activate certain necessary motivational strategies. The construct suggests that L2 learners are engaged in an ongoing appraisal and response process, involving their continuous monitoring and evaluating how well they are doing in a task, and then making possible amendments if something seems to be going amiss. This process can be represented through a dynamic *task processing system* that consists of three interrelated mechanisms: *task execution*, *appraisal* and *action control* (see Figure 13.1).

*Figure 13.1   Schematic Representation of the Three Mechanisms Making up the
Proposed Motivational Task Processing System*

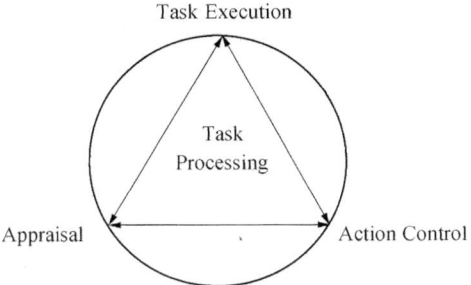

*Figure 13.2   Structural Equation Diagram of Motivational Task
Processing (Dörnyei and Tseng, 2009)*

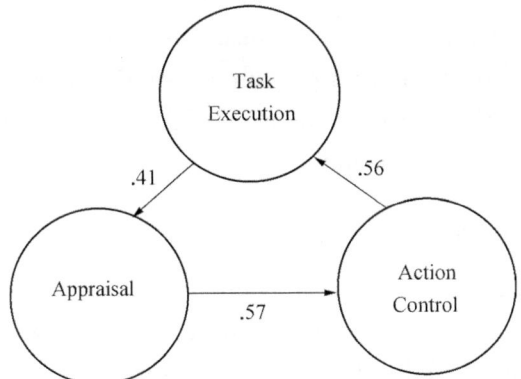

Task execution refers to the learners' engagement in task-supportive
learning behaviours in accordance with the task goals and the action
plan that were either provided by the teacher (through the task
instructions) or drawn up by the student or the task team. In other
words, this is the level of actual 'learning'. *Task appraisal* refers to the
learner's continuous processing of the multitude of stimuli coming
from the environment regarding the progress made towards the action
outcome, comparing the actual performance with the predicted or
hoped-for ones or with the likely performance that alternative action

sequences would offer. *Action control* processes denote self-regulatory mechanisms that are called into force in order to enhance, scaffold or protect learning-specific action; active use of such mechanisms may 'save' the action when ongoing monitoring reveals that progress is slowing, halting or backsliding.

Dörnyei and Tseng's (2009) validation study has involved a structural equation modelling (SEM) analysis of the proposed construct, and has confirmed the circular relationship of the three components (see Figure 13.2): Signals from the appraisal system concerning task execution trigger the need to activate relevant action control strategies, which in turn further facilitate the execution process. Thus, a process that is primarily motivational in nature relies heavily on a cognitive appraisal component. Interestingly, the inclusion of appraisal broader non-cognitive constructs is not unique to this example because, for example, most theoretical conceptualisations of emotion contain a cognitive appraisal component that is responsible for the evaluation of the situation that evokes an emotional response (Lewis, 2005).

The Ideal L2 Self

The *ideal L2 self* is the central component of a new conceptualisation of L2 motivation, the 'L2 Motivational Self System', which I proposed in 2005 (Dörnyei, 2005). The main objective of developing the new construct had been to synthesise a number of influential approaches in the field (e.g., Gardner, 1985a; Noels, 2003; Ushioda, 2001) and at the same time also to broaden the scope of L2 motivation theory to make it applicable in diverse language learning environments in the current, increasingly globalised world (for a detailed description, see Dörnyei, 2009b). The ideal L2 self is the L2-specific facet of one's *ideal self*, which refers to the representation of the attributes that someone would ideally like to possess (i.e., representation of hopes, aspirations or wishes) (see Higgins, 1987, 1998; Markus and Nurius, 1986). The theory suggests that if the person we would like to become speaks an L2, the ideal L2 self is a powerful motivator to learn the L2 because of the desire to reduce the discrepancy between our actual and ideal selves. This is expressed in everyday speech when we talk about someone following, or living up to, their dreams.

Thus, the ideal L2 self acts as a future self-guide, providing incentive, direction and impetus for action. However, past research has shown that the motivational capacity of this self-guide is not automatic but depends on a number of conditions; accordingly, the ideal L2 self is an effective motivator only if:

1. the learner *has* a desired future self-image;

2. which is elaborate and vivid;

3. which is perceived as *plausible* and is in harmony — or at least does not clash — with the expectations of the learner's family, peers and other elements of the social environment;

4. which is *regularly activated* in his/her working self-concept;

5. which is accompanied by relevant and effective *procedural strategies* that act as a *roadmap* towards the goal;

6. which also contains elaborate information about the *negative consequences* of *not* achieving the desired end-state.

What is important from our perspective is that the effective functioning of the ideal L2 self is dependent on the operation of several underlying cognitive components, most notably on the learners' self-appraisal of their capabilities and evaluation of the affordances of their personal circumstances in order to anchor their vision in a sense of realistic expectations. As Pizzolato (2006, p. 59) puts it, 'The relation between what students want to become and what students actually become may be mediated by what students feel they are able to become'. In addition, learners also need a repertoire of task-related strategies that are activated by the priming of the ideal L2 self: Effective future self-guides need to come as part of a 'package', consisting of an imagery/vision component and a repertoire of appropriate plans, scripts and self-regulatory strategies (Dörnyei, 2009c). In a study examining the relationship between motivation, cognition and action, Locke (2000) calls the knowledge of such strategies 'task knowledge' and he also argues that this knowledge illustrates the interdependence of cognition and motivation. This integrated operation of cognition and motivation is expressed clearly by Cross and Markus (1994, pp. 434–435):

> A possible self may serve as a node in an associative network of experiences, strategies and self-knowledge. In this way, the possible self may link effective steps and strategies ... with beliefs about one's ability and competence in the domain.

COGNITION-MOTIVATION OVERLAP IN COGNITIVE PSYCHOLOGY

The three examples described above offer specific illustrations of the interplay and cooperation of cognition and motivation in SLA, but this overlap is not restricted to L2 research. In the psychological literature we find many examples for motivation-cognition interfaces, and in a study specifically focusing on the integration of motivation and cognition, Bickhard (2003) argues that the common view of modelling motivation and cognition as distinct processes — 'motivation as some form of initiating and directing — pushing and pulling — behaviour, and cognition as the manipulation of encoded representations in memory' (p. 41) — is inaccurate and counterproductive because it makes it difficult to understand interrelationships between them or their interactions in behaviour and development. This claim was further substantiated in a high-profile volume edited by Dai and Sternberg (2004) on *'Motivation, Emotion, and Cognition: Integrative Perspectives on Intellectual Functioning and Development'*. As the title suggests, the contributors of this book — some of the best-known contemporary cognitive and educational psychologists — set out to present a powerful case for the need to view cognition and motivation as two interlocked facets of an integrated mental system, with emotion being a third constituent. In the Introduction, the editors summarise this objective as follows:

> In this introduction chapter, we attempt to make a case that intellectual functioning and development never occur as solely cognitive events but involve motivation and emotion, or the whole person vis-à-vis adaptive pressures and challenges. Going beyond cognitivism does not imply that motivational and emotional issues are more important than or as important as cognitive processes and mechanisms. Rather, our point is that without taking into consideration the motivational and emotional aspects of intellectual functioning and development, we cannot even properly understand cognitive processes involved. Reducing intellectual functioning and development to merely cognitive matters is simply no longer tenable both on theoretical grounds and in light of empirical evidence. (Dai and Sternberg, 2004, p. 29)

Following the Introduction, the volume contains 12 further chapters on various cognition-motivation-emotion interfaces, ranging from motivational effects on attention, cognition and performance (Dweck, Mangels and Good, 2004) to the role of interest in combining affective and cognitive functioning (Hidi, Renninger and Krapp, 2004). Thus, this volume opens up a whole range of new perspectives and research agendas, providing support for Linnenbrink and Pintrich's (2004, p. 83) conclusion that the 'relation between affect and engagement as well as cognitive processing suggests that there may be a complex interplay among affect, cognition, and motivation that needs to be further investigated'. Although looking at cognition and motivation (and affect) in such a blended manner is still a very recent research orientation, it can potentially offer substantial gains because the evidence presented in the above volume and elsewhere in the literature leaves no doubt that the availability/allocation of cognitive resources is very closely linked to the direction, intensity and persistence of action, that is, with the traditionally conceived central motivational domains.

A DYNAMIC SYSTEMS APPROACH TO UNDERSTANDING LEARNER CHARACTERISTICS IN SLA

Having illustrated the reality of the cognition/motivation interface in SLA and having shown that the separation of cognition and motivation has been increasingly seen as an outdated and inaccurate conceptualisation in cognitive and educational psychology, let us return to the question of adopting a new, dynamic systems perspective on individual differences as suggested earlier in this chapter. As I have argued (Dörnyei, 2009c), the 'individual differences myth' claims that while the main trajectory of SLA is determined by language acquisitional processes, relatively stable and monolithic learner attributes — called individual differences — cause systematic deviations from the overall trend. However, when we look at them more closely, individual learner characteristics appear to be rather different from the meaning we tend to assign to them in everyday parlance or in traditional professional discourse: They are not at all stable but show salient temporal and situational variation, and they are not monolithic either but constitute complex constellations that are made up of different parts that interact with each other and the environment synchronically and diachronically. As a result, simple cause-effect relationships are unable to do justice to these multi-level interactions and temporal changes. Instead, I would suggest, individual learner variation can be better accounted for in terms of the operation of a complex dynamic system in the sense that high-level mental attributes and functions are determined by an intricate set of interconnected components that continuously evolve over time and which also interact with the environment in an ongoing manner. The value of each constituent keeps changing depending on the overall state of the system and in response to external influences, making ID factors dynamic system variables. Therefore, the logical next step of conceptualizing individual differences is to attempt to reframe them within a dynamic systems perspective.

Although describing the nature and the operation of dynamic systems goes beyond the scope of this chapter (for L2-related overviews, see e.g., de Bot, Lowie and Verspoor, 2007; Dörnyei, 2009c; Ellis and Larsen-Freeman, 2006; Larsen-Freeman and Cameron, 2008a; van Geert, 2008), we can conclude that, broadly speaking, a system can be considered dynamic if it has two or more elements that are interlinked with each other and which also change in time. In such systems the complex interferences between the multiple system components' developmental trajectories make the system's behaviour unpredictable as it follows non-linear changes. In the social sciences, dynamic systems have been discussed by four interrelated theories: *dynamic systems theory, complexity theory, chaos theory* and *emergentism*, which can be seen as overlapping strands within the same broad theoretical family, each examining complex, dynamic, non-linear systems. While the four theories are associated with somewhat different research traditions and priorities, the labels describing them have not been used consistently across disciplines and in most cases the four theories converge in the same general non-linear systems approach.

Dynamic systems display — by definition — continuous fluctuation, yet a very important point from the perspective of this chapter is the fact that there are also times of seeming stability in most systems, when the system behaviour seems to be predictable. How can we explain these non-dynamic, settled states within a dynamic systems framework? The answer is provided by the concept of *attractors* and *attractor states*. These refer to preferred patterns to which the system is attracted (hence the name) and in which the elements are coherent and resist change. Not every system reaches such settled attractor states, but if there are strong attractors in place, a relatively wide range of starting points will eventually converge on a much smaller set of states because the process unfolds in the direction of the attractor (Nowak, Vallacher and Zochowski, 2005). In contrast, unstable phases in the development of the system are characterised by weak or changing attractors. In the light of these considerations, it is not unreasonable to suggest that higher-order ID variables can be seen as powerful attractors that act as stabilizing forces; for example, a strong goal, incentive, talent or interest can definitely bring stability to the system of learner characteristics/behaviour, and this stability, in turn, translates into consistency and predictability (see Dörnyei, 2009c).

A Tripartite Framework of Learner Characteristics

Given the dynamics of learner characteristics and the complex and interlocking nature of higher-order cognitive human functioning described above, is there any justification for proposing any macro-structuring principles to individual variation in human mental functions such as separating certain cognitive and motivational functions? In other words, if we look at the tapestry of human mental characteristics as an interwoven and fluid system, does it make any sense to keep speaking about any subsets of these characteristics (such as motivational or cognitive factors) as distinct entities? I believe that the answer is yes, because there is one perspective from which such a separation is justifiable: the *phenomenological* (i.e., experiential) perspective. Motivation and cognition can be differentiated from each other because they 'feel' different: If we want something, we have the distinct experience of 'wanting' it and we can even grade this experience in terms of its strength (e.g., *I can hardly wait ...* or *I really-really-really want it!*); and similarly, cognition/thoughts also have their distinct experiential feel, which is revealed in phrases such as 'cold intellect', capturing a key feature of cognition, namely that it has no valence (i.e., it is not gradable in terms of intensity either in the positive or negative directions).

It is important to note here that in addition to these two basic types of mental functions (i.e., cognition and motivation), we can also identify a third salient phenomenological category, *emotions* or *affect* (e.g., fear, anger, distress or joy), that is clearly distinguishable from the previous two. Thus, although this chapter does not cover affective issues (for a review, see Dörnyei, 2009c), it needs to be pointed out that emotions constitute the third main dimension of learner-based characteristics, adding up to a comprehensive, tripartite framework. Each of the three mental dimensions can be viewed as dynamic subsystems that have continuous and complex interaction with each other and which cannot exist in isolation from one another. As Buck (2005, p. 198) put it, 'In their fully articulated forms, emotions imply cognitions imply motives imply emotions, and so on'.

Interestingly, scholars have traditionally divided mental processes along this tripartite structure. Scherer (1995) explains that already Plato proposed that the human soul contained three components: *cognition* (corresponding to thought and reason and associated with the ruling class of philosophers, kings and statesmen), *emotion/passion* (corresponding to anger or spirited higher ideal emotions and associated with the warrior class) and *conation/motivation* (associated with impulses, cravings, desires and associated with the lower classes). This division into 'an appetitive part that produces various irrational desires, a spirited part that produces anger and other feelings, and a reasoning part that permits reflection and rationality' (Parrott, 2004, p. 7) has traditionally been referred to as the 'trilogy of mind', reflecting three interrelated but conceptually distinct mental systems.

In conclusion, I have been arguing above that the complex of learner characteristics can be best understood at the interface of two somewhat conflicting perspectives: On the one hand, given the integrated nature of mental functions, the modular view of individual differences — consisting of stable and monolithic personality traits — is untenable. This would suggest that there is not much point in examining factors such as language aptitude or motivation independently of each other. On the other hand, I believe that it is worth maintaining a broad, phenomenologically validated organizing framework of cognition, motivation and affect, as long as we recognise that these dimensions are best seen as interlocking complex subsystems.

HIGHER-ORDER AMALGAMS OF LEARNER CHARACTERISTICS

Where do all the above considerations leave us? What is the main advantage of introducing a dynamic systems perspective in the study of learner differences? It certainly won't make life easier for us, since thinking of the human mind in such an integrated way is admittedly rather difficult (for a discussion of this difficulty, see Dörnyei in press). Indeed, our natural tendency is to isolate the most relevant subsystem or factor and try to establish its impact on the phenomenon in focus (which is why we have so many studies on 'motivation and SLA' or 'language aptitude and SLA'). However, the problem with such a discrete treatment of dispositional attributes, as Lubinski and Webb (2003) conclude, is that examining them individually is often challenging and unfruitful, because the manner in which each operates depends on the full constellation of personal characteristics. As these authors conclude, even people with outwardly similar ID patterns can travel very different paths as a result of some difference in a personality constituent that is seemingly irrelevant or of secondary importance — this is exactly what dynamic systems theory would expect. This would imply, then, that trying to isolate discrete ID factors such as various aptitude or motivational components or cognitive styles is unlikely to take us too far. Instead, it is my belief that the best way forward is to identify higher-level amalgams or constellations of cognition, motivation and affect that are relatively stable (i.e., are governed by a strong attractor) and which act as 'wholes'. In other words, and related to the specific topic of this chapter, if we can identify optimal combinations of cognitive and motivational (and emotional) factors, these can have the potential to work as powerful attractors, which would make the system of learner characteristics/behaviour predictable and therefore researchable.

Do we know of any such ID complexes from the literature? We do, and it is in fact a strong validity argument for the theoretical considerations described above that ID complexes of this sort constitute some of the most promising cutting-edge findings in the study of learner characteristics both in educational psychology and in SLA research. In the following I describe three such constructs: *aptitude/trait complexes*, the broad notion of *interest* and *possible selves*.

Aptitude/trait complexes

A central issue in ID research over the past decade, and one that has emerged in aptitude research in particular, has been the suggestion that although isolated ID factors and personality traits are often shown to have a substantial impact on learning outcomes, certain optimal combinations of such traits are likely to have more predictive power than traits in isolation. One researcher in particular, Richard Snow, was influential in highlighting the potential importance of such ID constellations, or as he called them, *aptitude complexes* (for an overview of the legacy of Richard Snow written by his former students and associates, see Corno et al., 2002). His initiative has been taken up by several of his followers because, 'Although isolated traits often have . . . substantial impact on learning outcomes, it may be that combinations of traits have more predictive power than traits in isolation' (Ackerman, 2003, p. 92).

The best-known work to date along these lines has been Phillip Ackerman and his colleagues' conceptualisation of 'trait complexes' (e.g., Ackerman, 2003, 2005; Ackerman and Heggestad, 1997; Ackerman and Kanfer, 2004). These scholars have identified four broad trait complexes, called 'social', 'clerical/conventional', 'science/math', and 'intellectual/ cultural'. They are made up of various combinations of cognitive abilities, personality dimensions and interests, and they function as 'wholes' in affecting the direction and intensity of the investment of cognitive effort and the type of knowledge/expertise acquired during adulthood. Interestingly, Ackerman (2005) stresses that these complexes are only the beginning, because they represent 'only a small sampling of underlying cognitive, affective, and conative communalities' (p. 104). Future, more principled research might be able to extend the current conceptualisations and may add new ability trait operationalisations; Ackerman mentions 'emotional intelligence' as a likely candidate for the latter (for more information on emotional intelligence, see Dewaele, Petrides and Furnham, 2008).

In SLA, the notion of trait complexes has been addressed by Peter Robinson's (e.g., 2001a, 2002b, 2007) research programme on language aptitude-treatment interaction. He conceptualised language aptitude as the sum of lower-level abilities, grouped into cognitive factors, which differentially support learning in various learning situations/conditions. A particularly interesting feature of Robinson's proposal is his attempt to describe concrete sets of cognitive demands that can be associated with some basic learning types/tasks, and then to identify specific aptitude complexes to match these cognitive processing conditions. Robinson distinguished three conditions of exposure to input — implicit, incidental and explicit learning — and then discussed a number of *cognitive resources* (e.g., attentional or working memory capacity) and *primary abilities* (e.g., pattern recognition or processing speed) that combine to define sets of *higher-order abilities* directly involved in carrying out learning tasks (e.g., noticing the gap, or metalinguistic rule rehearsal). These second-order abilities can then be grouped into aptitude complexes that exert an optimal influence on learning in specific learning conditions, such as focus on form via recasts; incidental learning via oral or written content (by means of orally or typographically salient 'input floods'); and explicit rule learning.

Interest

The term 'interest' in the psychological literature is often used more broadly than, for example, the 'interest in foreign languages' category in Gardner's (1985a) integrative motivation construct. It refers to a broad orientational dimension that has been found to be defined by six general interest themes: 'realistic' (working with things and tools), 'investigative' (scientific pursuits), 'artistic' (aesthetic pursuits and self-expression), 'social' (contact with and helping people), 'enterprising' (buying, marketing and selling), and 'conventional' (office practices and well-structured tasks) (Lubinski and Webb, 2003). Some scholars have reduced these themes to two broad dimensions, 'people' versus 'things' and 'data' versus 'ideas', and the strength of the people/thing factor is evidenced by the fact that, as Lubinski and Webb (2003) describe, it displays some of the largest sex differences discovered by psychological science on a continuous dimension (with women towards the 'people' end of the cline, and men towards the 'things' end). Interests are heritable, are predictive of a broad spectrum of criteria in areas ranging from educational and vocational settings to activities in everyday life (hobbies and pastimes), and the concept appears to be theoretically more straightforward and temporarily more stable than several other ID factors.

Lubinski and Webb (2003) report an interesting longitudinal study in which they compared, over a period of 10 years, the developmental trajectory of three different types of profoundly gifted individuals. The three groups consisted of students who were (a) high on mathematical reasoning and relatively low on verbal reasoning; (b) high on verbal reasoning and relatively low on mathematical reasoning; and (c) high on both abilities. As could be expected, the abilities acted as strong attractors for long-term development, and differential interests were apparent in the three groups in their choice of favourite courses in high school and college, as well as in the awards and other accomplishments they achieved: high-math individuals tended to succeed in areas of science and technology, whereas high-verbal individuals tended to succeed in the humanities and arts. This study provides a clear illustration of how long-term interests are made up of a combination of cognitive and motivational factors.

Possible selves

Possible selves represent the individuals' ideas of what they *might* become, what they *would like* to become and what they are *afraid of* becoming (Markus and Nurius, 1986). The novelty of the possible self concept lies in the fact that it concerns how people conceptualise their as-yet unrealised potential and as such, it also draws on hopes, wishes and fantasies. In this sense, possible selves act as 'self-guides', reflecting a dynamic, forward-pointing conception that can explain how someone is moved from the present towards the future. From an educational perspective the most important possible self is the 'ideal self', which has already been described earlier when illustrating the cognition-motivation interaction in the L2 field. It was pointed out there that the ideal L2 self is a powerful motivator to learn the L2 because of the desire to reduce the discrepancy between our actual and ideal selves.

Although in my 'L2 Motivational Self System' (Dörnyei, 2005) I emphasised the motivational capacity of the ideal L2 self, possible selves present broad, overarching constellations that blend together motivational, cognitive and affective areas. Already the originator of the concept, Hazel Markus (2006), pointed out that the possible self-structure could be seen as a 'dynamic interpretive matrix for thought, feeling and action' (p. xi), and I have demonstrated earlier that the ideal self does indeed have a salient cognitive component. In addition to this, MacIntyre et al. (2009a) also highlight the emotional aspect of possible selves, because without a strong tie to the learner's emotional system, possible selves exist as 'cold cognition, and therefore lack motivational potency' (p. 47). As the authors explain, 'When emotion is a prominent feature of a possible self, including a strong sense of fear, hope, or even obligation, a clear path exists by which to influence motivation and action' (p. 47).

Finally, this cognition-emotion-motivation amalgam features a further significant dimension, a salient *imagery* component: Markus and Nurius (1986) emphasise that possible selves involve tangible *images* and *senses*, as they are represented in the same imaginary and semantic way as the here-and-now self; that is, they are a *reality* for the individual: people can 'see' and 'hear' a possible self. In this sense, possible selves are not unlike visions — an Olympic athlete's ideal self is not merely an intellectual goal but a vision of him/herself walking into the Olympic Stadium, completing the race and then stepping onto the top of the podium. As Markus and Ruvolo (1989, p. 213) summarise, 'imaging one's own actions through the construction of elaborated possible selves achieving the desired goal may thus directly facilitate the translation of goals into intentions and instrumental actions', and a similar idea has been expressed by Wenger (1998, p. 176) when he described the concept of 'imagination':

> My use of the concept of imagination refers to a process of expanding our self by transcending our time and space and creating new images of the world and ourselves. Imagination in this sense is looking at an apple seed and seeing a tree. It is playing scales on a piano, and envisioning a concert hall.

Thus, in many ways it is the integration of fantasy with the self-concept construct that marks Markus and Nurius's (1986) work as truly innovative (Segal, 2006). This is certainly the aspect that grasped my own attention when I first encountered this work, and this is, I believe, what makes the concept of possible selves a particularly powerful ID constellation that encompasses the whole spectrum of the human mind, from our thoughts and feelings to our senses.

CONCLUSION

I pointed out in the introduction of this chapter that the task of addressing the relationship between aptitude and motivation goes beyond merely looking at two specific ID factors, as it concerns, in effect, the broader examination of how individual difference variables in general are related to each other and how they exert their cumulative impact. I further argued that the traditional notion of individual difference factors conceived as stable and monolithic learner characteristics that act as modifying filters in the SLA process (i.e., the 'individual differences myth'), is untenable because it ignores the multicomponential nature of these higher-order attributes and because the constituent components continuously interact with each other and the environment, thereby changing and causing change, and subsequently displaying highly complex developmental patterns. The study of such complex constellations of factors requires a dynamic systems approach, and this perspective would suggest that identifying 'pure' individual difference factors has only limited value both from a theoretical and a practical point of view; instead, a potentially more fruitful approach is to focus on certain higher-order combinations of different attributes that act as integrated wholes.

In the light of this theoretical backdrop, specifying the relationship between language aptitude and motivation — which has been the specific theme of this chapter — requires a new, integrated approach whereby we focus on the blended operation of cognition and motivation rather than the discrete treatment of the two ID variables. Thus, I do not believe that it is a particularly worthwhile scientific endeavour to examine the impact of isolated areas of L2 aptitude or motivation; instead, we should try and identify viable constellations whereby the cognitive and the motivational (and also the emotional) subsystems of the human mind cooperate in a constructive manner. This chapter presented several concrete illustrations of the reality and validity of such an integrated approach and I do hope that these have convinced the readers that this admittedly difficult agenda is worth pursuing.

Chapter 14

Motivation from a Complex Dynamic Systems Perspective

In Dörnyei, Z. and Ushioda, E. (2011). Teaching and researching motivation (2nd ed.) (pp. 88-99). Harlow: Longman.

When we talk about 'complex dynamic systems' within the socio-dynamic phase of L2 motivation research, we use the terms 'complex' and 'dynamic' in a specific sense, referring to *complexity theory* and especially one key strand within this theory, *dynamic systems theory*. These approaches have been specifically developed to describe development in complex, dynamic systems (see Concept below) that consist of multiple interconnected parts and in which the multiple interferences between the components' own trajectories result in non-linear, emergent changes in the overall system behaviour (for overviews, see e.g. de Bot, Lowie and Verspoor, 2007; Dörnyei, 2009c; Ellis and Larsen-Freeman, 2006; Larsen-Freeman and Cameron, 2008a; van Geert, 2008).

Concept: Complex dynamic systems and the double pendulum

A system can be considered dynamic if it has two or more elements that are (a) interlinked with each other and (b) which also change in time. These two simple conditions can result in highly complex system behaviour — this is well illustrated by the bizarre movement of the 'double pendulum', which can be seen as the simplest dynamic system, consisting of only two components (the two arms of the pendulum): As we move the upper arm of the pendulum, the lower arm will soon go 'wild', moving all over the place, which in turn upsets the initially regular movement of the upper arm, which causes further havoc in the whole system. Thus, in dynamic systems the ongoing interferences between the multiple system components' developmental trajectories make the system's behaviour highly complex and unpredictable.

We have already mentioned briefly in the previous chapters that a situated and process-oriented account of motivation inevitably leads us to a dynamic conception of the notion of motivation that integrates the various factors related to the learner, the learning task and the learning environment into one complex system whose ultimate outcome can be seen as the regulator of learning behaviour. How do we conceptualise motivation within this paradigm? Traditionally, motivation was discussed within the framework of *individual differences* (IDs), which are conceived to be traitlike attributes that mark a person as a distinct and unique human being. Of course, people differ from each other in respect of a vast number of traits, of which ID research has traditionally focused only on those personal characteristics that are enduring, that are assumed to apply to everybody, and on which people differ by degree. In other words, ID factors concern stable and systematic deviations from a normative blueprint (Dörnyei, 2005).

IDs have been well established in SLA research as a relatively straightforward concept: They have usually been seen as background learner variables that modify and personalise the overall trajectory of the language acquisition processes; thus, in many ways, IDs have been typically thought of as the systematic part of the background 'noise' in SLA. However, in a recent overview of the psychology of SLA, Dörnyei (2009c) has proposed that the seemingly comprehensive and straightforward picture of IDs being stable and monolithic learner traits that concern distinct learner characteristics is part of an idealised narrative that may not hold up against scientific scrutiny. The core of the problem is that if we take a situated and process-oriented perspective of SLA, we cannot fail to realise that the various learner attributes display a considerable amount of variation from time to time and from situation to situation — in the way as we have argued in previous chapters motivation also does.

The fact that IDs are not independent of contextual and temporal variation considerably undermines the traditional view of IDs as being robust attributes that can be generalised across situations and time, but we also face a further complication: most human attributes are higher-order mental characteristics and are as such multicomponential, made up of the dynamic interaction of several lower layers of constituents (Kosslyn and Smith, 2000). Accordingly, many (if not most) learner characteristics mentioned in the literature involve at one level or another the cooperation of some components that are of a different nature from the general character of the attribute in question. For example, motivational factors may involve some important cognitive or emotional elements, thus creating 'hybrid' attributes. We have already mentioned the existence of such blended, 'cross-attributional' cooperation briefly in several places in this book, and in the following sections we will elaborate on this and give detailed illustrations.

Quote: MacIntyre, Burns and Jessome on the need to extend the ID paradigm

Much of the previous literature on WTC has presented the concept as an internal attribute, an individual difference variable affecting the communication process and an outcome of language learning. Although we believe that an individual differences approach retains its value, perhaps it is time to widen the scope of the WTC concept to more explicitly take into account moment-to-moment dynamics within the social situation and the key role played by the communication partner(s). (MacIntyre, Burns & Jessome, 2011, p. 93)

A TRIPARTITE FRAMEWORK OF LEARNER CHARACTERISTICS

Given the dynamics of learner characteristics and the complex and interlocking nature of higher-order cognitive human functioning described above, is there any justification for talking about distinct 'motivational' processes? That is, if we look at the tapestry of human mental characteristics as an interwoven and fluid system, does it make any sense to distinguish subsets of these characteristics and talk about, say, motivational or cognitive factors? In Dörnyei's (2009c) view, the answer is affirmative, because from the phenomenological (i.e. experiential) perspective at least three broad distinctions can be made, between motivation, cognition and affect (i.e. emotions). They can be differentiated from each other because they 'feel' different: If we want something, we have the distinct experience of 'wanting' it and we can even grade this experience in terms of its strength (e.g. *I can hardly wait…* or *I really-really-really want it!*). People typically have no problem with distinguishing such a motivational experience from emotional experiences such as feeling happy or sad or angry, which are also gradable. Finally, cognition/thoughts also have their distinct experiential feel, which is revealed in phrases such as 'cold intellect', capturing a key feature of cognition, namely that it has no valence (i.e. it is not gradable in terms of intensity either in the positive or negative directions).

Thus, according to Dörnyei (2009c), the phenomenological

distinctness of motivation, cognition and affect warrant their use as primary organising principles of learner-based characteristics, but in line with a complex dynamic systems approach, each should be viewed as dynamic subsystems that have continuous and complex interaction with each other and which cannot exist in isolation from one another (see also Dörnyei, 2010b). As Buck (2005, p. 198) has succinctly put it, 'In their fully articulated forms, emotions imply cognitions imply motives imply emotions, and so on'. Interestingly, scholars have traditionally divided mental processes along this tripartite structure. Scherer (1995) explains that already Plato proposed that the human soul contained three components: *cognition* (corresponding to thought and reason and associated with the ruling class of philosophers, kings and statesmen), *emotion/passion* (corresponding to anger or spirited higher ideal emotions and associated with the warrior class), and *conation/motivation* (associated with impulses, cravings, desires and associated with the lower classes). This division into 'an appetitive part that produces various irrational desires, a spirited part that produces anger and other feelings, and a reasoning part that permits reflection and rationality' (Parrott, 2004, p.7) has traditionally been referred to as the 'trilogy of mind'.

Quote: Scherer on the significance of the 'trilogy of the mind'

Since people seem to like to think in threes, so the tripartite soul stayed with us till today. It seems to be the single most important classification principle in the field of psychology, judging from subdivisions in textbooks and professional associations, from journal titles, and from perceived affiliations. This is true despite the fact that the distinction may sometimes get overshadowed by a dominant ideology — as during the heyday of behaviorism, or in periods of cognitive imperialism. (Scherer, 1995, p. 3)

MOTIVATIONAL CONGLOMERATES

In the light of the above, we have come to believe that rather than following the traditional practice of trying to isolate distinct motives and examine their operation in isolation, a more fruitful way forward would involve taking a *systemic* approach by identifying higher-order 'motivation conglomerates' that also include cognitive and affective factors and which act as 'wholes'. We agree with Lubinski and Webb (2003), who conclude that examining learner attributes individually is often challenging and unfruitful, because the manner in which each operates depends on the full constellation of personal characteristics (for an illustration, see MacIntyre, Burns and Jessome's quote below). In the following, therefore, we are going to describe four constellations that might serve as templates when looking for situated motivational conglomerates in specific studies: *interest, motivational flow, motivational task processing* and *future self-guides.*

Quote: MacIntyre, Burns and Jessome on the dynamic cooperation of learner and learning situation

Arguably, the key implication drawn from the diaries is that the situations in which learners are most willing to communicate are not radically different from those in which they are least willing. Subtle features of the learner or the context can lead a student to speak up or remain quiet, and the psychological situation can change rapidly. It might be helpful for teachers to approach students as if they lived in a state of ambivalence toward learning — experiencing both reasons to approach and reasons to avoid speaking the L2. (MacIntyre, Burns & Jessome, 2011, p. 93)

Interest

The term 'interest' in the psychological literature is used in a variety of contexts and meanings, usually referring to a broader concept than, for example, the 'interest in foreign languages' category in Gardner's (1985a) integrative motivation construct. In many ways, interest is a prime example of a motivational conglomerate: On the one hand, it has impeccable motivational credentials, as it features in expectancy-value theories under the rubric of 'intrinsic/interest value' denoting the anticipated enjoyment of engaging in the activity (Eccles, 2009), and intrinsic interest is also a central component of self-determination theory, referring to the inherent satisfaction and enjoyment of a behaviour (for a recent discussion, see La Guardia, 2009). On the other hand, besides its obvious motivational connotations, the notion of interest also involves a salient cognitive aspect — the curiosity in and engagement with a specific domain — as well as a prominent affective dimension concerning the joy associated with this engagement.

Quote: Renninger, Bachrach and Posey on interest

Interest ... describes both a state of heightened affect and a developing predisposition to reengage work with particular domain content (e.g. music, science). Interest is identified based on learner's feelings, principled knowledge, and value for particular domain content, and evolves over time through interactions with the others and objects/activities in the environment. (Renninger, Bachrach and Posey, 2008, p. 463)

In an influential analysis of interest, Hidi and Renninger (2006) specifically state that 'interest includes both affective and cognitive components as separate but interacting systems, a position supported by neuroscientific research' (p. 112). As they explain, 'Typically, the affective component of interest describes positive emotions accompanying engagement, whereas the cognitive component refers to perceptual and representational activities related to engagement' (ibid.). According to the authors, the dynamic nature of the concept is particularly salient in its development:

> [I]nterest is the outcome of an interaction between a person and a particular content. The potential for interest is in the person but the content and the environment define the direction of interest and contribute to its development. Thus, other individuals, the organisation of the environment, and a person's own efforts, such as self-regulation, can support interest development. (p. 112)

Recently, Renninger (2009) has further analysed the change in a person's phase of interest for content over time and concluded that this development was dependent on feelings as well as stored knowledge and stored values. Thus, interest in this sense 'is both a cognitive and affective motivational variable that develops, is experienced-based, and is not necessarily age-related' (p. 206). Lubinski and Webb (2003) have painted a similarly complex picture when they described interest as a broad orientational dimension that has been found to be defined by six general interest themes: 'realistic' (working with things and tools), 'investigative' (scientific pursuits), 'artistic' (aesthetic pursuits and self-expression), 'social' (contact with and helping people), 'enterprising' (buying, marketing, and selling), and 'conventional' (office practices and well-structured tasks).

Motivational flow

The experience of 'flow' (Csikszentmihalyi, 1990) is a theoretically intriguing and intuitively appealing phenomenon, entailing a state of intensive involvement in and focused concentration on a task that feels so absorbing that people often compare it to being outside everyday reality. This state is, however, not the kind of passive spiritual experience that some people can evoke through meditation; to the contrary, flow is experienced while people are at their most active or creative, being engaged in performing an absorbing task. Thus, flow can be seen as a heightened level of motivated task engagement; in many ways it is the optimal task experience. It happens when, faced with a challenging activity, people are fully aware of what needs to be done and how, and at the same time they are confident that the task is doable and their skills are sufficient to succeed. An often mentioned feature of a fully-fledged flow experience is that the extent of absorption can be such that people even lose self-consciousness and track of time. While this may sound like science fiction fantasy, all we need to do is observe children (and even adults) playing computer games to realise that flow is a very real phenomenon.

Quote: Csikszentmihalyi on flow

Artists, athletes, composers, dancers, scientists, and people from all walks of life, when they describe how it feels when they are doing something that is worth doing for its own sake, use terms that are interchangeable in their minutest details. This unanimity suggests that order in consciousness produces a very specific experiential state, so desirable that one wishes to replicate it as often as possible. To this state we have given the name of 'flow,' using a term that many respondents used in their interviews to explain what the optimal experience felt like. (Csikszentmihalyi, 1988, p. 29)

In a pioneering study on the role of flow in SLA, Egbert (2003) found that the task conditions under which flow occurs can be organised along four dimensions: (1) there is a perceived balance of task challenge and participant skills during the task, (2) the task offers opportunities for intense concentration and the participants' attention is focused on the pursuit of clear task goals, (3) the participants find the task intrinsically interesting or authentic, and (4) the participants perceive a sense of control over the task process and outcomes. These underlying dimensions display a balanced mixture of motivational, cognitive and affective constituents (see also Guastello, Johnson and Rieke,

1999): While flow is usually discussed under the motivation rubric as a specific type of intrinsic motivation (explained by the experience of enjoyment that is one key feature of flow), it is fundamentally determined by cognitive factors such as the appraisal of the challenge of the activity; the self-appraisal of the level of the individual's skills and competence involved in the activity; a firm sense of control over the completion of the task; clarity about the task goals; and focussed attention.

Motivational task processing

Looking at the motivational basis of student performance on learning tasks is probably the most situated lens we can adopt to study the motivational dimension of learning behaviours. In order to account for the state motivation that energises the learners' moment-to-moment task participation, we need to examine how the participating learners process the various motivational stimuli they encounter and, as a result, how they activate certain necessary motivational strategies. Dörnyei (2003a) has proposed a simple model to describe the dynamics of this ongoing appraisal and response process that involves the learners' continuous monitoring and evaluating how well they are doing in a task, and then making possible amendments if something seems to be going amiss. Thus, this *task processing system* consists of three interrelated mechanisms: *task execution, appraisal,* and *action control* (see Figure 14.1). *Task appraisal* refers to the learner's continuous processing of the multitude of stimuli coming from the environment regarding the progress made toward the action outcome, comparing the actual performance with the predicted or hoped-for ones or with the likely performance that alternative action sequences would offer. *Action control* processes denote self-regulatory mechanisms that are called into force in order to enhance, scaffold or protect learning-specific action; active use of such mechanisms may 'save' the action when ongoing monitoring reveals that progress is slowing, halting or backsliding.

*Figure 14.1   Schematic Representation of the Three Mechanisms Making up
the Motivational Task Processing System*

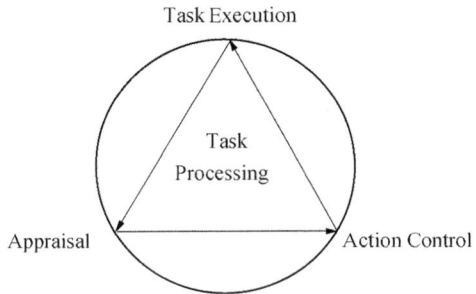

In a recent study, Dörnyei and Tseng's (2009) used structural equation modelling to validate the proposed construct, and confirmed the circular relationship of the three components: signals from the appraisal system concerning task execution trigger the need to activate relevant action control strategies, which in turn further facilitate the execution process. Thus, a process that is primarily motivational in nature relies heavily on a cognitive appraisal component. Interestingly, the inclusion of appraisal in broader non-cognitive constructs is not unique to this example because, for example, most theoretical conceptualisations of emotion contain a cognitive appraisal component that is responsible for the evaluation of the situation that evokes an emotional response (Lewis, 2005).

Future self-guides

Although earlier in this chapter we discussed primarily the motivational capacity of future self-guides, let us highlight here the fact that possible selves present broad, overarching constellations that blend together motivational, cognitive and affective areas. Already the originator of the concept, Hazel Markus (2006), pointed out that the possible self-structure could be seen as a 'dynamic interpretive matrix for thought, feeling and action' (p. xi), and MacIntyre, MacKinnon and Clément (2009a) also highlight the emotional aspect of possible selves, because without a strong tie to the learner's emotional system, possible selves exist as 'cold cognition, and therefore lack motivational potency' (p. 47). As they further explain, 'When emotion is a prominent feature of a possible self, including a strong sense of fear, hope, or even obligation, a clear path exists by which to influence motivation and action' (ibid.).

Then, in a previous section we discussed the prerequisites for the motivational capacity of future self-guides, and a closer look at the list of necessary conditions reveals that the effective functioning of these self-guides is dependent on the operation of several underlying cognitive components, most notably the learners' self-appraisal of their capabilities and evaluation of the affordances of their personal circumstances in order to anchor their vision in a sense of realistic expectations. As Pizzolato (2006, p. 59) puts it, 'The relation between what students want to become and what students actually become may be mediated by what students feel they are able to become'. In addition, learners also need a repertoire of task-related strategies that are activated by the priming of the ideal L2 self. Thus, effective future self-guides need to come as part of a 'package', consisting of an imagery/vision component that activates appropriate emotions and is cued to a variety of appropriate plans, scripts and self-regulatory strategies. Because of the integrated functioning of such diverse components, we would suggest that this motivation-cognition-emotion amalgam can be seen as the ultimate motivational conglomerate.

CONCLUDING REMARKS ON THE COMPLEX DYNAMIC SYSTEMS VIEW OF MOTIVATION

How can we summarise the essence of a complex dynamic systems view of motivation? Perhaps the most important aspect of this approach is to find the right level of abstraction for looking at motivation in any given situation. Traditionally, we have tried to break down motivation to the smallest possible constituents, hoping that these motives would be 'pure' components that can then serve as common denominators for all

motivational phenomena. We have argued above that this approach —
which was at the heart of the 'individual differences paradigm' — has
by and large failed, because the dynamic complexity and interference
of mental processes and attributes do not allow us to meaningfully
distinguish more than three main dimensions: motivation, cognition and
affect. We believe that all the learner attributes discussed in the literature
form different conglomerates made up of these three constituents of
the 'trilogy of the mind'. The task, then, is to find the level of analysis
that captures the right combination of these three ingredients in a given
situation — what might be true of emigrant women learning English
in Canada is not likely to hold in the same form amongst, say, Japanese
learners of English studying in a junior high school in Osaka.

Thus, the key issue is the level of abstraction of the examination, that
is, how wide we open our investigative lenses in a particular study. How
can we identify the 'right' level? This will be a central topic to address
in a later section of this book , which focuses on researching motivation.
Let us conclude here with one important observation. It seems to us
that effective combination patterns of motivation, cognition and affect
have a great deal of intuitive salience for non-specialists; folk wisdom
on motivation often correctly identifies the right level of cooperation of
these components, which is why concepts such as 'interest' and 'vision'
are intuitively appealing not just to researchers but also to laypeople. Even
a relatively newly identified conglomerate such as 'flow' has immediately
caught the imagination of the public, making Mihaly Csikszentmihalyi
not only a world-famous psychologist but also a bestselling author of
popular non-fiction.

If it is indeed the case that effective motivation-cognition-affect
combinations are perceivable by non-specialists, this is promising news
for researchers. It suggests that qualitative exploratory investigations
of language learners' self-reports might contain sufficient clues about
the right angle to motivation and motivated behaviour to adopt. The
dynamic systems approach predicts that no behavioural phenomenon has

a single explanation — writing a book like this, for example, may have been energised by a number of diverse factors such as our interest in the topic, our expectation of success, our perceived competence in writing and enjoying it, the dynamics of our collaboration, the academic pressure to maintain our reputation, a sabbatical leave on offer that needed to be meaningfully filled, our personal needs to produce neatly bound final products, the desire to help our students, financial considerations, an invitation from the publisher, and so on. All these and many other potential motives might have contributed to producing the final outcome, but only a carefully executed deep interview study would have the chance to get to the bottom of this. Thus, all we need to do is ask the right questions!

Chapter 15

Conclusion: The Way Forward

The papers in this collection span almost two decades and offer an illustration of the evolution of research on language learning motivation. This process of development has been cumulative: Gardner's original ideas have never been discarded, but subsequent generations of scholars have added new perspectives and priorities to the overall motivation construct. As the last two chapters described, the current phase of our thinking on L2 motivation can be characterised by a concern with the situated complexity of the L2 motivation process and its organic development in dynamic interaction with a multiplicity of internal, social and contextual factors. This move towards more socially grounded, dynamic and complex interacting systems in the analysis of L2 motivation is also in keeping with wider contemporary trends within the field of applied linguistics that have highlighted emergentist and dynamic systems approaches to understanding SLA (e.g. de Bot, Lowie & Verspoor, 2007; Dörnyei, 2009c; Ellis & Larsen-Freeman, 2006; Larsen-Freeman & Cameron, 2008a; van Geert, 2008; Verspoor, de Bot & Lowie, 2011).

I described briefly in the Introduction how my earlier process model of L2 motivation fell somewhat short of the mark in that although it reframed motivation as a dynamically changing cumulative arousal in a person, it was still conceptualised within a process-oriented paradigm characterised by a network of linear cause-effect relations. Unfortunately, the multiple parallel and interacting cause-effect links accompanied by several circular feedback loops within the model made the validity of the overall linear nature of the construct highly questionable. Thus, it was only a matter of time before I had to accept that a radical reformulation was needed. This reformulation involved eventually adopting a complex dynamic systems perspective, and I believe that this perspective will gain increasing significance in the field over the next decade. In an inherently social process such as language acquisition, the learner cannot be meaningfully separated from the social environment within which he/she operates, and therefore the challenge for future motivation research is to adopt a dynamic perspective that allows us to consider simultaneously the ongoing multiple influences between environmental and learner factors in all their componential complexity.

However, we must also acknowledge that these new developments are not without challenges: while approaching second language acquisition from a complex dynamic systems perspective makes a lot of intuitive sense, it cannot be denied that it is difficult to operationalise such a dynamic approach in research terms for a number of reasons. For example, the most common research paradigms in the social sciences tend to examine variables in relative isolation rather than as part of a system or network, and most established quantitative data analytical procedures (e.g. correlation analysis or structural equation modelling) are based on linear rather than nonlinear relationships. A serious concern, therefore, is the absence of sufficient research templates for the research community to approach second language acquisition from a dynamic systems perspective. Some initiative have already been taken in this respect (see e.g. Dörnyei, in press; Dörnyei & Ushioda, 2011; Larsen-Freeman & Cameron, 2008b; Verspoor et al., 2011) but the jury is admittedly still out as to how widespread this perspective will become.

With regard to practical developments concerning strategies of increasing learner motivation, I believe that the concepts of 'vision' and 'future self-guides' will play a key role in the next decades. Techniques are currently being developed to utilize activities aimed at enhancing the self as well as promoting visualisation and guided imagery in the language classroom (see e.g., Arnold, Puchta & Rinvolucri, 2007; Hadfield & Dörnyei, in press), and the initial positive perception of the self-based approach by teachers all over the world suggests that this is a direction that might activate considerable creative energy at the classroom level. This would be very welcome, because most readers would probably agree that the way we currently tend to approach classroom processes and events — and more generally, the psychological reality of the language classroom — has been due for a major overhaul for some time now. I believe that it is no exaggeration to state that motivational issues still do not receive their due importance in language teacher education and teachers are expected to meet the challenging demands of managing complex classrooms without sufficient awareness and training to tackle the psychological level. Yet, hopefully there is a growing awareness in the profession of the wealth of strategies and approaches language teachers have at their disposal to motivate their learners and create motivational classroom environments. This may be more difficult in some contexts than in others, but as the saying goes, 'Where there is a will, there is a way!'

References

NOTE: *Most of my own work can be found on my personal website in a downloadable form:* http://www.nottingham.ac.uk/~aezweb/research/cral/doku.php? id=people:zoltan

Ackerman, P. L. (2003). Aptitude complexes and trait complexes. *Educational Psychologist, 38*, 85–93.

Ackerman, P. L., and Heggestad, E. D. (1997). Intelligence, personality, and interests: Evidence for overlapping traits. *Psychological Bulletin, 121*, 219–245.

Ackerman, P. L., and Kanfer, R. (2004). Cognitive, affective, and conative aspects of adult intellect within a typical and maximal performance framework. In D. Y. Dai and R. J. Sternberg (Eds.), *Motivation, emotion, and cognition: Integrative perspectives on intellectual functioning and development* (pp. 119–141). Mahwah, NJ: Lawrence Erlbaum.

Ackerman, P. L., Beier, M. E., and Boyle, M. O. (2005). Working memory and intelligence: The same or different constructs? *Psychological Bulletin, 131*, 30–60.

Ajzen, I. (1988). *Attitudes, personality and behaviour.* Chicago: Dorsey Press.

Al-Shehri, A. S. (2009). Motivation and vision: The relation between the Ideal L2 Self, imagination and visual style. In Z. Dörnyei and E. Ushioda (Eds.), *Motivation, language identity and the L2 self* (pp. 164–171). Clevedon: Multilingual Matters.

Alison, J. (1993). *Not bothered? Motivating reluctant language learners in Key Stage 4.* London: Centre for Information on Language Teaching and Research (CILT).

Ames, C. (1992). Classrooms, goals, structures, and student motivation. *Journal of Educational Psychology, 84*, 267–271.

Ames, C., and Ames, R. (1984). Systems of student and teacher motivation: Toward a qualitative definition. *Journal of Educational Psychology, 76*, 535–556.

Arnett, J. J. (2002). The psychology of globalization. *American Psychologist, 57*, 774–783.

Arnold, J., Puchta, H., and Rinvolucri, M. (2007). *Imagine that! Mental imagery in the EFL classroom.* Cambridge: Cambridge University Press.

Atkinson, J. W., and Birch, D. (1974). The dynamics of achievement-oriented activity. In J. W. Atkinson and J. O. Raynor (Eds.), *Motivation and achievement* (pp. 271–325). Washington, DC: Winston and Sons.

Au, S. Y. (1988). A critical appraisal of Gardner's social-psychological theory of second-language (L2) learning. *Language Learning, 38*, 75–100.

Ausubel, D., Novak, J. D., and Hanesian, H. (1978). *Educational psychology: A cognitive view* (2nd ed.). New York: Holt and Rinehart.

Baddeley, A. D. (2003). Working memory and language: An overview. *Journal of Communication Disorders, 36*, 189–208.

Bandura, A., and Schunk, D. (1981). Cultivating competence, self-efficacy and intrinsic interest through proximal self-motivation. *Journal of Personality and Social Psychology, 41*, 586–598.

Bar-Tal, Y., and Bar-Tal, D. (1986). Social psychological analysis of classroom interaction. In R. S. Feldman (Ed.), *The social psychology of education: Current research and theory* (pp. 132–149). Cambridge: Cambridge University Press.

Bargh, J. A. (1990). Auto-motives: Preconscious determinants of social interaction. In E. T. Higgins and R. M. Sorrentino (Eds.), *Handbook of motivation and cognition: Foundations of social behaviour* (Vol. 2, pp. 93–130). New York: Guilford Press.

Baumeister, R. F. (1996). Self-regulation and ego threat: Motivated cognition, self-deception, and destructive goal setting. In P.M. Gollwitzer and J. A. Bargh (Eds.), *The psychology of action: Linking cognition and motivation to behaviour* (pp. 27–47). New York: Guilford Press.

Bejarano, Y. (1987). A cooperative small-group methodology in the language classroom. *TESOL Quarterly, 21*, 483–504.

Berkovits, S. (2005). *Guided imagery: Successful techniques to improve school performance and self-esteem.* Duluth, MN: Whole Person Associates.

Berliner, D. C. (1989). Furthering our understanding of motivation and environments. In C. Ames and R. Ames (Eds.), *Research on motivation in education, Vol. 3: Goals and cognitions* (pp. 317–343). New York: Academic Press.

Bickhard, M. H. (2003). An integration of motivation and cognition. In L. Smith, C. Rogers and P. Tomlinson (Eds.), *Development and motivation: Joint perspectives* (pp. 41–56). Leicester: British Psychological Society.

Bigelow, M. and Tarone, E. (2004). The role of literacy level in SLA: Doesn't *who* we study determine *what* we know? *TESOL Quarterly, 38*, 689–700.

Blumenfeld, P. C. (1992). Classroom learning and motivation: Clarifying and expanding goal theory. *Journal of Educational Psychology, 84*, 272–281.

Boekaerts, M. (1988). Motivated learning: Bias in appraisals. *International Journal of Educational Research, 12*, 267–280.

Boekaerts, M. (1994). Action control: How relevant is it for classroom learning? In J. Kuhl and J. Beckmann (Eds.), *Volition and personality: Action versus state orientation* (pp. 427–435). Seattle, WA: Hogrefe and Huber.

Boekaerts, M. (1995). Self-regulated learning: Bridging the gap between metacognitive and metamotivation theories. *Educational Psychologist, 30*, 195–200.

Boekaerts, M. (1998). Boosting students' capacity to promote their own learning: A goal theory perspective. *Research Dialogue in Learning and Instruction, 1*, 13–22.

Boekaerts, M., Pintrich, P. R., and Zeidner, M. (2000). *Handbook on self-regulation.* San Diego: Academic Press.

Boyatzis, R. E., and Akrivou, K. (2006). The ideal self as the driver of intentional change. *Journal of Management Development, 25*, 624–642.

Brophy, J. E. (1987). Synthesis of research on strategies for motivating students to learn. *Educational Leadership, 45*, 40–48.

Brophy, J. E. (1998). *Motivating students to learn.* Boston, MA: McGraw-Hill.

Brophy, J. E., and Good, T. L. (1986). Teacher behaviour and student achievement. In M. C. Wittrock (Ed.), *Handbook of research on teaching* (3rd ed., pp. 328–375). New York: Macmillan.

Brophy, J. E., and Kher, N. (1986). Teacher socialization as a mechanism for developing student motivation to learn. In R. S. Feldman (Ed.), *The social psychology of education: current research and theory* (pp. 257–288). Cambridge: Cambridge University Press.

Brown, H. D. (1981). Affective factors in second language learning. In J. E. Alatis, H. B. Altman and P. M. Alatis (Eds.), *The second language classroom: Directions for the eighties* (pp. 111–129). New York: Oxford University Press.

Brown, H. D. (1990). M&Ms for language classrooms? Another look at motivation. In J. E. Alatis (Ed.), *Georgetown University round table on language and linguistics* (pp. 383–393). Washington, DC: Georgetown University Press.

Brown, H. D. (1994). *Teaching by principles.* Englewood Cliffs, NJ: Prentice Hall.

Brown, J. D., Cunha, M. I. A., Frota, S. F. N., and Ferreira, A. B. F. (2001). The development and validation of a Portuguese version of the Motivated Strategies for Learning Questionnaire. In Z. Dörnyei and R. Schmidt (Eds.), *Motivation and second language acquisition* (pp. 259–272). Honolulu, HI: University of Hawaii Second Language Teaching and Curriculum Center.

Buck, R. (2005). Adding ingredients to the self-organizing dynamic system stew: Motivation, communication, and higher-level emotions — and don't forget the genes! *Behavioral and Brain Science, 28*, 197–198.

Bygate, M. (1999). Task as context for the framing, reframing and unframing of language. *System, 27*, 33–48.

Bygate, M., Skehan, P., and Swain, M. (Eds.). (2001). *Researching pedagogic tasks: Second language learning, teaching and testing.* Harlow, England: Longman.

Cantor, N. (1990). From thought to behaviour: 'Having' and 'doing' in the study of personality and cognition. *American Psychologist, 45*, 735–750.

Carroll, J. B. (1962). The prediction of success in intensive foreign language training. In R. Glaser (Ed.), *Training, Research, and Education* (pp. 87–136). Pittsburgh, PA: University of Pittsburgh Press.

Carroll, J. B. (1981). Twenty-five years of research in foreign language aptitude. In K. C. Diller (Ed.), *Individual differences and universals in language learning aptitude* (pp. 83–118). Rowley, MA: Newbury House.

Carroll, J. B. (1990). Cognitive abilities in foreign language aptitude: Then and now. In T. Parry and C. Stansfield (Eds.), *Language Aptitude Reconsidered* (pp. 11–29). Englewood Cliffs, NJ: Prentice-Hall Regents.

Carroll, J. B., and Sapon, S. (1959). *The Modern Language Aptitude Test.* San Antonio, TX: Psychological Corporation.

Carver, C. S., Reynolds, S. L., and Scheier, M. F. (1994). The possible selves of optimists and pessimists. *Journal of Research in Personality, 28*, 133–141.

Case, D., & Wilson, K. (1979). *Off stage.* London: Heinemann.

Celce-Murcia, M., Dörnyei, Z., and Thurrell, S. (1995). Communicative competence: A pedagogically motivated model with content specifications. *Issues in Applied Linguistics, 6*, 5–35.

Celce-Murcia, M., Dörnyei, Z., & Thurrell, S. (1997). Direct approaches in L2 instruction: A turning point in communicative language teaching? *TESOL Quarterly, 31*, 141–152.

Celce-Murcia, M., Dörnyei, Z., & Thurrell, S. (1998). On directness in communicative language teaching. *TESOL Quarterly, 32*, 116–119.

Chambers, G. N. (1993). Talking the de out of demotivation. *Language*

Learning Journal, 7, 13–16.

Chambers, G. N. (1999). *Motivating language learners.* Clevedon: Multilingual Matters.

Chamot, A. U. (2001). The role of learning strategies in second language acquisition. In M. P. Breen (Ed.), *Learner contributions to language learning: New directions in research* (pp. 25–43). Harlow: Longman.

Chamot, A. U., Barnhardt, S., El-Dinary, P. B., and Robbins, J. (1999). *The learning strategies handbook.* New York: Longman.

Chang, K-Y. R., and Smith, W. F. (1991). Cooperative learning and CALL/IVD in beginning Spanish: An experiment. *Modern Language Journal, 75*, 205–211.

Chen, J. F., Warden, C. A., and Chang, H-T. (2005). Motivators that do not motivate: The case of Chinese EFL learners and the influence of culture on motivation. *TESOL Quarterly, 39*, 609–633.

Clément, R. (1980). Ethnicity, contact and communicative competence in a second language. In H. Giles, W. P. Robinson and P. M. Smith (Eds.), *Language: Social psychological perspectives* (pp. 147–154). Oxford: Pergamon.

Clément, R., Dörnyei, Z., & Noels, K. (1994). Motivation, self-confidence and group cohesion in the foreign language classroom. *Language Learning, 44*, 417–448.

Clément, R., and Gardner, R. C. (2001). Second language mastery. In H. Giles and W. P. Robinson (Eds.), *The new handbook of language and social psychology* (2nd ed., pp. 489–504). London: John Wiley and Sons.

Clément, R., and Kruidenier, B. G. (1983). Orientations in second language acquisition: The effects of ethnicity, milieu and their target language on their emergence. *Language Learning, 33*, 273–291.

Clément, R., and Kruidenier, B. G. (1985). Aptitude, attitude and motivation in second language proficiency: A test of Clément's model. *Journal of Language and Social Psychology, 4*, 21–37.

Clément, R., and Noels, K. A. (1992). Toward a situated approach to ethnolinguistic identity: The effects of status on individuals and groups. *Journal of Language and Social Psychology, 11*, 203–232.

Clément, R., Dörnyei, Z., and Noels, K. (1994). Motivation, self-confidence and group cohesion in the foreign language classroom. *Language Learning, 44*, 417–448.

Coelho, E. (1992). Cooperative learning: Foundation for a communicative curriculum. In C. Kessler (Ed.), *Cooperative language learning: A teacher's resource book* (pp. 31–49). Englewood Cliffs, NJ: Prentice Hall Regents.

Coelho, E., Winer, L., and Olsen, J. W-B. (1989). *All sides of the issue: Activities for cooperative Jigsaw Groups*. Englewood Cliffs, NJ: Alemany Press.

Coetzee-Van Rooy, S. (2006). Integrativeness: Untenable for world Englishes learners? *World Englishes, 25*, 437–450.

Coffield, F., Moseley, D., Hall, E., and Ecclestone, K. (2004). *Learning styles and pedagogy in post-16 learning: A systematic and critical review*. London: Learning and Skills Research Centre.

Cohen, A. D. (1998). *Strategies in learning and using a second language*. Harlow: Longman.

Cohen, A. D. (2002). Preparing teachers for styles- and strategies-based instruction. In V. Crew, C. Davison and B. Mak (Eds.), *Reflecting on language in education* (pp. 49–69). Hong Kong: The Hong Kong Institute of Education.

Cohen, A. D., and Weaver, S. J. (2004). *A teachers' guide to styles- and strategies-based instruction. Revised version of CARLA (Working Paper Series #7)*. Minneapolis, MN: Center for Advanced Research on Language Acquisition.

Cohen, A. D., Oxford, R. L., and Chi, J. C. (2001). *Learning style survey*, from http://carla.acad.umn.edu/profiles/Cohen-profile.html

Cohen, E. (1994). *Designing groupwork* (2nd ed.). New York: Teachers College Press.

Cooper, C. (2002). *Individual differences* (2nd ed.). London: Arnold.

Corno, L. (1993). The best-laid plans: Modern conceptions of volition and educational research. *Educational Researcher, 22*, 14–22.

Corno, L. (1994). Student volition and education: Outcomes, influences, and practices. In D. H. Schunk and B. J. Zimmerman (Eds.), *Self-regulation of learning and performance: Issues and educational applications* (pp. 229–251). Hillsdale, NJ: Lawrence Erlbaum.

Corno, L., and Kanfer, R. (1993). The role of volition in learning and performance. *Review of Research in Education, 19*, 301–341.

Corno, L., Cronbach, L. J., Kupermintz, H., Lohman, D. F., Mandinach, E. B., Porteus, A. W., et al. (2002). *Remaking the concept of aptitude: Extending the legacy of Richard E. Snow*. Mahwah, NJ: Lawrence Erlbaum.

Covington, M. (1999). Caring about learning: The nature and nurturing of subject-matter appreciation. *Educational Psychologist, 34*, 127–136.

Covington, M. V., and Roberts, B. W. (1994). Self-worth and college achievement: Motivational and personality correlates. In P. R. Pintrich, D. R. Brown and C. E. Weinstein (Eds.), *Student motivation, cognition, and learning* (pp. 157–187). Hillsdale, NJ: Lawrence Erlbaum.

Covington, M., and Teel, K. (1996). *Overcoming student failure: Changing motives and incentives for learning*. Washington, DC: American Psychological Association.

Crookes, G., and Gass, S. M. (1993a). *Tasks in a pedagogical context: Integrating theory and practice*. Clevedon: Multilingual Matters.

Crookes, G., and Gass, S. M. (1993b). *Tasks and language learning: Integrating theory and practice*. Clevedon: Multilingual Matters.

Crookes, G., and Schmidt, R. (1991). Motivation: Reopening the research agenda. *Language Learning, 41*, 469–512.

Cross, S. E., and Markus, H. R. (1994). Self-schemas, possible selves, and competent performance. *Journal of Educational Psychology, 86*, 423–438.

Csikszentmihalyi, M. (1988). The flow experience and its significance for human psychology. In M. Csikszentmihalyi and I. S. Csikszentmihalyi (Eds.), *Optimal experience: Psychological studies of flow in consciousness* (pp. 15–35). Cambridge: Cambridge University Press.

Csikszentmihalyi, M. (1990). *Flow: The psychology of optimal experience.* New York: Harper and Row.

Csizér, K., and Dörnyei, Z. (2005). The internal structure of language learning motivation: Results of structural equation modelling. *Modern Language Journal, 89*, 19–36.

Csizér, K., and Kormos, J. (2009). Learning experiences, selves and motivated learning behaviour: A comparative analysis of structural models for Hungarian secondary and university learners of English. In Z. Dörnyei and E. Ushioda (Eds.), *Motivation, language identity and the L2 self* (pp. 98–119). Bristol: Multilingual Matters.

Cumming, J. L., and Ste-Marie, D. M. (2001). The cognitive and motivational effects of imagery training: A matter of perspective. *The Sport Psychologist, 15*, 276–288.

Dai, D. Y., and Sternberg, R. J. (2004). Beyond cognitivism: Toward an integrated understanding of intellectual functioning and development. In D. Y. Dai and R. J. Sternberg (Eds.), *Motivation, emotion, and cognition: Integrative perspectives on intellectual functioning and development* (pp. 3–38). Mahwah, NJ: Lawrence Erlbaum.

Damen, L. (1987). *Culture learning: The fifth dimension in the language classroom.* Reading, MA: Addison-Wesley.

Daniels, R. (1994). Motivational mediators of cooperative learning. *Psychological Reports, 74*, 1011–1022.

Davies, P., and Rinvolucri, M. (1990). *The confidence book.* London: Longman.

de Bot, K., Lowie, W., and Verspoor, M. (2007). A Dynamic Systems Theory approach to second language acquisition. *Bilingualism: Language and Cognition, 10*, 7–21.

De Raad, B. (2000). Differential psychology. In A. E. Kazdin (Ed.), *Encyclopedia of psychology* (Vol. 3, pp. 41–44). Oxford: American Psychological Association and Oxford University Press.

Deci, E. L. (1992). The relation of interest to the motivation of behaviour: A self-determination theory perspective. In K. A. Renninger, S. Hidi and A. Krapp (Eds.), *The role of interest in learning and development* (pp. 43–70). Hillsdale, NJ: Lawrence Erlbaum.

Deci, E. L., and Ryan, R. M. (1985). *Intrinsic motivation and self-determination in human behaviour*. New York: Plenum.

Deci, E. L., Vallerand, R. J., Pelletier, L. G., and Ryan, R. M. (1991). Motivation and education: The self-determination perspective. *Educational Psychologist, 26*, 325–346.

Dembo, M. H. (2000). *Motivation and learning strategies for college success: A self-management approach*. Mahwah, NJ: Lawrence Erlbaum.

Deutsch, M. (1962). An experimental study of the effects of cooperation and competition upon group process. *Human Relations, 2*, 199–231.

Dewaele, J-M. (2002). Psychological and sociodemographic correlates of communicative anxiety in L2 and L3 production. *International Journal of Bilingualism, 6*, 23–39.

Dewaele, J-M. (2004). Individual differences in the use of colloquial vocabulary: The effects of sociobiological and psychological factors. In P. Bogaards and B. Laufer (Eds.), *Vocabulary in a second language: Selection, acquisition, and testing* (pp. 127–153). Amsterdam: John Benjamins.

Dewaele, J-M., and Furnham, A. (1999). Extraversion: The unloved variable in applied linguistic research. *Language Learning, 43*, 509–544.

Dewaele, J-M., and Furnham, A. (2000). Personality and speech production: A pilot study of second language learners. *Personality and Individual Differences, 28*, 355–365.

Dewaele, J-M., Petrides, K. V., and Furnham, A. (2008). The effects of trait emotional intelligence and sociobiographical variables on communicative anxiety and foreign language anxiety among adult multilinguals: A review and empirical investigation. *Language Learning, 58*, 911–960.

Dickinson, L. (1995). Autonomy and motivation: A literature review. *System, 23*, 165-174.

Dörnyei, Z. (1990a, April). *Analysis of motivation components in foreign language learning.* Paper presented at the 9th World Congress of Applied Linguistics, Thessaloniki-Halkidiki, Greece. [ERIC DOC ED 323 810].

Dörnyei, Z. (1990b). Conceptualizing motivation in foreign language learning. *Language Learning, 40,* 46–78.

Dörnyei, Z. (1994a). Motivation and motivating in the foreign language classroom. *Modern Language Journal, 78,* 273–284.

Dörnyei, Z. (1994b). Understanding second language motivation: On with the challenge! *Modern Language Journal, 78,* 515–523.

Dörnyei, Z. (1995). On the teachability of communication strategies. *TESOL Quarterly, 29,* 55–85.

Dörnyei, Z. (1996). Moving language learning motivation to a larger platform for theory and practice. In R. L. Oxford (Ed.), *Language Learning Motivation: Pathways to the New Century* (pp. 89–101). Honolulu, HI: The University of Hawaii Press.

Dörnyei, Z. (1997). Psychological processes in cooperative language learning: Group dynamics and motivation. *Modern Language Journal, 81,* 482–493.

Dörnyei, Z. (1998a). *Demotivation in foreign language learning.* Paper presented at TESOL 98 Conference, Seattle, WA.

Dörnyei, Z. (1998b). Motivation in second and foreign language learning. *Language Teaching, 31,* 117–135.

Dörnyei, Z. (1999). Motivation. In J. Verschueren, J.-O. Östmann, J. Blommaert and C. Bulcaen (Eds.), *Handbook of pragmatics 1999* (pp. 1–22). Amsterdam: John Benjamins.

Dörnyei, Z. (2000). Motivation in action: Toward a process-oriented conceptualisation of student motivation. *British Journal of Educational Psychology, 70,* 519–538.

Dörnyei, Z. (2001a). *Motivational strategies in the language classroom.* Cambridge: Cambridge University Press.

Dörnyei, Z. (2001b). New themes and approaches in second language motivation research. *Annual Review of Applied Linguistics, 21,* 43–59.

Dörnyei, Z. (2001c). *Teaching and researching motivation*. Harlow: Longman.

Dörnyei, Z. (2002). The motivational basis of language learning tasks. In P. Robinson (Ed.), *Individual differences in second language acquisition* (pp. 137–158). Amsterdam: John Benjamins.

Dörnyei, Z. (2003a). Attitudes, orientations, and motivations in language learning: Advances in theory, research, and applications. In Z. Dörnyei (Ed.), *Attitudes, orientations, and motivations in language learning* (pp. 3–32). Oxford: Blackwell.

Dörnyei, Z. (2003b). *Questionnaires in second language research: Construction, administration, and processing*. Mahwah, NJ: Lawrence Erlbaum.

Dörnyei, Z. (2005). *The psychology of the language learner: Individual differences in second language acquisition*. Mahwah, NJ: Lawrence Erlbaum.

Dörnyei, Z. (2007a). Creating a motivating classroom environment. In J. Cummins and C. Davison (Eds.), *International handbook of English language teaching* (Vol. 2, pp. 719–731). New York: Springer.

Dörnyei, Z. (2007b). *Research methods in applied linguistics: Quantitative, qualitative and mixed methodologies*. Oxford: Oxford University Press.

Dörnyei, Z. (2009a). Motivation and the vision of knowing a second language. In B. Beaven (Ed.), *IATEFL 2008: Exeter conference selections* (pp. 16–22). Canterbury: IATEFL.

Dörnyei, Z. (2009b). The L2 Motivational Self System. In Z. Dörnyei and E. Ushioda (Eds.), *Motivation, language identity and the L2 self* (pp. 9–42). Bristol: Multilingual Matters.

Dörnyei, Z. (2009c). *The psychology of second language acquisition*. Oxford: Oxford University Press.

Dörnyei, Z. (2010a). Researching motivation: From integrativeness to the ideal L2 self. In S. Hunston and D. Oakey (Eds.), *Introducing applied linguistics: Concepts and skills* (pp. 74–83). London: Routledge.

Dörnyei, Z. (2010b). The relationship between language aptitude and language learning motivation: Individual differences from a dynamic systems perspective. In E. Macaro (Ed.), *Continuum companion to second language acquisition* (pp. 247–267). London: Continuum.

Dörnyei, Z., (2010). *Questionnaires in second language research: Construction, administration, and processing* (2nd ed.). London: Routledge.

Dörnyei, Z. (in press). Researching complex dynamic systems: 'Retrodictive qualitative modelling' in the language classroom. *Language Teaching.*

Dörnyei, Z., and Clément, R. (2001). Motivational characteristics of learning different target languages: Results of a nationwide survey. In Z. Dörnyei and R. Schmidt (Eds.), *Motivation and second language acquisition* (pp. 399–432). Honolulu, HI: University of Hawaii Press.

Dörnyei, Z., and Csizér, K. (1998). Ten commandments for motivating language learners: Results of an empirical study. *Language Teaching Research, 2,* 203–229.

Dörnyei, Z., and Csizér, K. (2002). Some dynamics of language attitudes and motivation: Results of a longitudinal nationwide survey. *Applied Linguistics, 23,* 421–462.

Dörnyei, Z., & Kormos, J. (1998). Problem-solving mechanisms in L2 communication: A psycholinguistic perspective. *Studies in Second Language Acquisition, 20,* 349–385.

Dörnyei, Z., and Kormos, J. (2000). The role of individual and social variables in oral task performance. *Language Teaching Research, 4,* 275–300.

Dörnyei, Z., and Malderez, A. (1997). Group dynamics and foreign language teaching. *System, 25,* 65–81.

Dörnyei, Z., and Malderez, A. (1999). Group dynamics in foreign language learning and teaching. In J. Arnold (Ed.), *Affective language learning* (pp. 155–169). Cambridge: Cambridge University Press.

Dörnyei, Z., and Murphey, T. (2003). *Group dynamics in the language classroom.* Cambridge: Cambridge University Press.

Dörnyei, Z., and Ottó, I. (1998). Motivation in action: A process model of L2 motivation. *Working Papers in Applied Linguistics (Thames Valley University, London), 4,* 43–69.

Dörnyei, Z., Salamon, G., & Szesztay, M. (1986). *Words on your own.* Budapest: International House.

Dörnyei, Z., and Schmidt, R. (Eds.) (2001). *Motivation and second language acquisition* (Technical report #23). Honolulu, HI: University of Hawaii Second Language Teaching and Curriculum Center.

Dörnyei, Z., & Scott, M. L. (1997). Communication strategies in a second language: Definitions and taxonomies. *Language Learning*, 47, 173–210.

Dörnyei, Z., and Skehan, P. (2003). Individual differences in second language learning. In C. J. Doughty and M. H. Long (Eds.), *The handbook of second language acquisition* (pp. 589–630). Oxford: Blackwell.

Dörnyei, Z., & Thurrell, S. (1991). Strategic competence and how to teach it. *ELT Journal*, 45, 16–23.

Dörnyei, Z., and Thurrell, S. (1992). *Conversation and dialogues in action.* Hemel Hempstead: Prentice Hall.

Dörnyei, Z., and Thurrell, S. (1994). Teaching conversational skills intensively: Course content and rationale. *ELT Journal*, 48, 40–49.

Dörnyei, Z., and Tseng, W-T. (2009). Motivational processing in interactional tasks. In A. Mackey and C. Polio (Eds.), *Multiple perspectives on interaction: Second language research in honor of Susan M. Gass* (pp. 117–134). Mahwah, NJ: Lawrence Erlbaum.

Dörnyei, Z., and Ushioda, E. (2011). *Teaching and researching motivation* (2nd ed.). Harlow: Longman.

Dörnyei, Z., and Ushioda, E. (Eds.). (2009). *Motivation, language identity and the L2 self.* Bristol: Multilingual Matters.

Dörnyei, Z., Csizér, K., and Németh, N. (2006). *Motivation, language attitudes and globalisation: A Hungarian perspective.* Clevedon, England: Multilingual Matters.

Dörnyei, Z., Nyilasi, E., and Clément, R. (1996). Hungarian school children's motivation to learn foreign languages: A comparison of five target languages. *Novelty*, 3, 6–16.

Douglas, T. (1983). *Groups: Understanding people gathered together.* London: Tavistock Press.

Doyle, T., and Kim, Y. M. (1999). Teacher motivation and satisfaction in the United States and Korea. *MEXTESOL Journal*, 23, 35–48.

Dufva, M., and Voeten, M. J. M. (1999). Native language literacy and phonological memory as prerequisites for learning English as a foreign language. *Applied Psycholinguistics, 20*, 329–348.

Dunkel, C., Kelts, D., and Coon, B. (2006). Possible selves as mechanisms of change in therapy. In C. Dunkel and J. Kerpelman (Eds.), *Possible selves: Theory, research and applications* (pp. 187–204). New York: Nova Science.

Dweck, C. S., Mangels, J. A., and Good, C. (2004). Motivational effects on attention, cognition, and performance. In D. Y. Dai and R. J. Sternberg (Eds.), *Motivation, emotion, and cognition: Integrative perspectives on intellectual functioning and development* (pp. 41–55). Mahwah, NJ: Lawrence Erlbaum.

Eccles, J. S. (2009). Who am I and what am I going to do with my life? Personal and collective identities as motivators of action. *Educational Psychologist, 44*, 78–89.

Eccles, J. S., Wigfield, A. and Schiefele, A. (1998). Motivation to succeed. In W. Damon and N. Eisenberg (Eds.), *Handbook of child psychology* (5th ed.), *Vol. 3: Social, emotional, and personality development* (pp.1017–1095). New York: John Wiley and Sons.

Egbert, J. (2003). A study of flow theory in the foreign language classroom. *Modern Language Journal, 87*, 499–518.

Ehrman, M. E. (1996). *Understanding second language difficulties*. Thousand Oaks, CA: Sage.

Ehrman, M. E., and Dörnyei, Z. (1998). *Interpersonal and group dynamics in the second language classroom*. Thousand Oaks, CA: Sage.

Ehrman, M. E., and Leaver, B. L. (2003). Cognitive styles in the service of language learning. *System, 31*, 391–415.

Ellis, G., and Sinclair, B. (1989). *Learning to learn English: A course in learner training*. Cambridge: Cambridge University Press.

Ellis, N. C. (2001). Memory for language. In P. Robinson (Ed.), *Cognition and second language acquisition* (pp. 33–68). New York: Cambridge University Press.

Ellis, N. C., and Larsen-Freeman, D. (2006). Language emergence: Implications for applied linguistics — Introduction to the special issue. *Applied Linguistics*, *27*, 558–589.

Ellis, R. (1985). *Understanding second language acquisition*. Oxford: Oxford University Press.

Ellis, R. (2000). Task-based research and language pedagogy. *Language Teaching Research*, *4*, 193–220.

Ellis, R. (2004). Individual differences in second language learning. In A. Davies and C. Elder (Eds.), *The handbook of applied linguistics* (pp. 525–551). Oxford: Blackwell.

Evans, C. R., and Dion, K. L. (1991). Group cohesion and performance: A meta-analysis. *Small Group Research*, *22*, 175–186.

Eysenck, H. J., and Eysenck, M. W. (1985). *Personality and individual differences*. New York: Plenum.

Eysenck, M. W. (1994). *Individual differences: Normal and abnormal*. Hove: Lawrence Erlbaum.

Farsides, T., and Woodfield, R. (2003). Individual differences and undergraduate academic success: The roles of personality, intelligence, and application. *Personality and Individual Differences*, *34*, 1225–1243.

Fezler, W. (1989). *Creative imagery: How to visualize in all five senses*. New York: Simon and Schuster.

Ford, M. (1992). *Motivating humans*. Newbury Park, CA: Sage.

Forsyth, D. R. (1990). *Group dynamics* (2nd ed.). Pacific Grove, CA: Brooks/Cole.

Forsyth, D. R. (1999). *Group dynamics* (3rd ed.). Pacific Grove, CA: Brooks/Cole.

Foster, P. (1998). A classroom perspective on the negotiation of meaning. *Applied Linguistics*, *19*, 1–23.

Foster, P., and Skehan, P. (1996). The influence of planning on performance in task-based learning. *Studies in Second Language Acquisition*, *18*, 299–324.

Frank, C., & Rinvolucri, M. (1983). *Grammar in action again: Awareness activities for language learning.* Oxford: Pergamon.

Fraser, B., and Walberg, H. (Eds.). (1991). *Educational environments: Evaluation, antecedents and consequences.* Oxford: Pergamon.

Freud, S. (1966). *The complete introductory lectures on psychoanalysis.* New York: Norton.

Furnham, A. (1990). Language and personality. In H. Giles and W. P. Robinson (Eds.), *Handbook of Language and Social Psychology* (pp. 73–95). London: John Wiley.

Galloway, D., Rogers, C., Armstrong, D., and Leo, E. (1998). *Motivating the difficult to teach.* Harlow: Longman.

Garcia, T., and Pintrich, P. R. (1994). Regulating motivation and cognition in the classroom: The role of self-schemas and self-regulatory strategies. In D. Schunk and B. J. Zimmerman (Eds.), *Self-regulation of learning and performance: Issues and educational applications* (pp. 127–153). Hillsdale, NJ: Lawrence Erlbaum.

Gardner, R. C. (1985a). *Social psychology and second language learning: The role of attitudes and motivation.* London: Edward Arnold.

Gardner, R. C. (1985b). *The attitude/motivation test battery: Technical report.* London, ON: University of Western Ontario.

Gardner, R. C. (2001). Integrative motivation and second language acquisition. In Z. Dörnyei and R. Schmidt (Eds.), *Motivation and second language acquisition* (pp. 1–20). Honolulu, HI: University of Hawaii Press.

Gardner, R. C. (2005 May). Integrative motivation and second language acquisition, *Joint Convention of the Canadian Association of Applied Linguistics and the Canadian Linguistics Association.* London, Canada.

Gardner, R. C., and Clément, R. (1990). Social psychological perspectives on second language acquisition. In H. Giles and W. P. Robinson (Eds.), *Handbook of Language and Social Psychology* (pp. 495–517). London: John Wiley.

Gardner, R. C., and Lambert, W. E. (1959). Motivational variables in second language acquisition. *Canadian Journal of Psychology, 13,* 266–

272.

Gardner, R. C., and Lambert, W. E. (1972). *Attitudes and motivation in second language learning.* Rowley, MA: Newbury House.

Gardner, R. C., and MacIntyre, P. (1992). A student's contributions to second language learning. Part I: Cognitive variables. *Language Teaching, 25,* 211–220.

Gardner, R. C., and MacIntyre, P. D. (1993). A student's contributions to second-language learning. Part II: Affective variables. *Language Teaching, 26,* 1–11.

Gardner, R. C., & Tremblay, P. F. (1994a). On motivation, research agendas and theoretical frameworks. *Modern Language Journal, 78,* 359–368.

Gardner, R. C., and Tremblay, P. F. (1994b). On motivation: Measurement and conceptual considerations. *Modern Language Journal, 78,* 524–527.

Gardner, R. C., Masgoret, A-M., and Tremblay, P. F. (1999). Home background characteristics and second language learning. *Journal of Language and Social Psychology, 18,* 419–37.

Gardner, R. C., Masgoret, A.-M., Tennant, J., and Mihic, L. (2004). Integrative motivation: Changes during a year-long intermediate-level language course. *Language Learning, 54,* 1–34.

Gardner, R. C., Tremblay, P. F., and Masgoret, A-M. (1997). Toward a full model of second language learning: An empirical investigation. *Modern Language Journal, 81,* 344–62.

Giles, H., and Byrne, J. L. (1982). An intergroup approach to second language acquisition. *Journal of Multilingual and Multicultural Development, 3,* 17–40.

Goldberg, L. R. (1992). The development of markers for the Big-Five factor structure. *Psychological Assessment, 4,* 26–42.

Goldberg, L. R. (1993). The structure of phenotypic personality traits. *American Psychologist, 48,* 26–34.

Gollwitzer, P. M. (1990). Action phases and mind-sets. In E. T. Higgins and R. M. Sorrentino (Eds.), *Handbook of motivation and cognition: Foundations of social behaviour* (Vol. 2, pp. 53–92). New York: Guilford

Press.

Good, T. L., and Brophy, J. E. (1994). *Looking in classrooms* (6th ed.). New York: Harper Collins.

Good, T. L., and Brophy, J. E. (2002). *Looking in classrooms* (9th ed.). Needham Heights, MA: Allyn and Bacon.

Goodenow, C. (1992). Strengthening the links between educational psychology and the study of social contexts. *Educational Psychologist*, *27*, 177–196.

Gould, D., Damarjian, N., and Greenleaf, C. (2002). Imagery training for peak performance. In J. L. Van Raalte and B. W. Brewer (Eds.), *Exploring sport and exercise psychology* (2nd ed., pp. 49–74). Washington, DC: American Psychological Association.

Graham, C. (1978). *Jazz chants*. Oxford: Oxford University Press.

Graham, S. (1994). Classroom motivation from an attributional perspective. In H. F. O'Neil, Jr. and M. Drillings (Eds.), *Motivation: Theory and research* (pp. 31–48). Hillsdale, NJ: Lawrence Erlbaum.

Greene, C. N. (1989). Cohesion and productivity in small groups. *Small Group Behaviour*, *20*, 70–86.

Gregg, M., and Hall, C. (2006). Measurement of motivational imagery abilities in sport. *Journal of Sports Sciences*, *24*, 961–971.

Grenfell, M., and Harris, V. (1999). *Modern languages and learning strategies: In theory and practice*. London: Routledge.

Grigorenko, E., Sternberg, R., and Ehrman, M. E. (2000). A theory based approach to the measurement of foreign language learning ability: The Canal-F theory and test. *Modern Language Journal*, *84*, 390–405.

Guastello, S. J., Johnson, E. A., and Rieke, M. L. (1999). Nonlinear dynamics of motivational flow. *Nonlinear Dynamics, Psychology, and Life Sciences*, *3*, 259–273.

Gunderson, B., and Johnson, D. W. (1980). Building positive attitudes by using cooperative learning groups. *Foreign Language Annals*, *13*, 39–43.

Hadfield, J. (1992). *Classroom dynamics*. Oxford: Oxford University Press.

Hadfield, J., & Dörnyei, Z. (in press). *Theory into practice: Motivation and the*

Ideal Self. London: Longman.

Hall, E., Hall, C., Stradling, P., and Young, D. (2006). *Guided imagery: Creative interventions in Counselling and psychotherapy.* London: Sage.

Harris, V. (2003). Adapting classroom-based strategy instruction to a distance learning context. *TESL-EJ, 7*(2), 1–19.

Heckhausen, H. (1991). *Motivation and action.* New York: Springer.

Heckhausen, H., and Kuhl, J. (1985). From wishes to action: The dead ends and short cuts on the long way to action. In M. Frese and J. Sabini (Eds.), *Goal-directed behaviour: The concept of action in psychology* (pp. 134–160). Hillsdale, NJ: Lawrence Erlbaum.

Herbst, K. C., Gaertner, L., and Insko, C. A. (2003). My head says yes but my heart says no: Cognitive and affective attraction as a function of similarity to the ideal self. *Journal of Personality and Social Psychology, 84,* 1206–1219.

Heron, J. (1999). *The complete facilitator's handbook.* London: Kogan Page.

Hickey, D. T. (1997). Motivation and contemporary socio-constructivist instructional perspectives. *Educational Psychologist, 32,* 175–193.

Hidi, S., and Renninger, K. A. (2006). The four-phase model of interest development. *Educational Psychologist, 41,* 111–127.

Hidi, S., Renninger, K. A., and Krapp, A. (2004). Interest, a motivational variable that combines affective and cognitive functioning. In D. Y. Dai and R. J. Sternberg (Eds.), *Motivation, emotion, and cognition: Integrative perspectives on intellectual functioning and development* (pp. 89–115). Mahwah, NJ:

Higgins, E. T. (1987). Self-discrepancy: A theory relating self and affect. *Psychological Review, 94,* 319–340.

Higgins, E. T. (1996). The 'self-digest': Self-knowledge serving self-regulatory functions. *Journal of Personality and Social Psychology, 71,* 1062–1083.

Higgins, E. T. (1998). Promotion and prevention: Regulatory focus as a motivational principle. *Advances in Experimental Social Psychology, 30,* 1–46.

Higgins, E. T., Klein, R., and Strauman, T. (1985). Self-concept discrepancy theory: A psychological model for distinguishing among different aspects of depression and anxiety. *Social Cognition, 3,* 51–76.

Higgins, E. T., Roney, C. J. R., Crowe, E., and Hymes, C. (1994). Ideal versus ought predilections for approach and avoidance: Distinct self-regulatory systems. *Journal of Personality and Social Psychology, 66,* 276–286.

Hock, M. F., Deshler, D. D., and Schumaker, J. B. (2006). Enhancing student motivation through the pursuit of possible selves. In C. Dunkel and J. Kerpelman (Eds.), *Possible selves: Theory, research and application* (pp. 205–221). New York: Nova Science.

Holt, D. D. (Ed.). (1992). *Cooperative learning.* Washington, DC: Center for Applied Linguistics and ERIC Clearinghouse on Languages and Linguistics.

Hook, P., and Vass, A. (2000). *Confident classroom leadership.* London: David Fulton.

Horowitz, M. J. (1983). *Image formation and psychotherapy.* Northvale, NJ: Jason Aronson.

Hoyle, R. H., and Sherrill, M. R. (2006). Future orientation in the self-system: Possible selves, self-regulation, and behaviour. *Journal of Personality, 74,* 1673–1696.

Husman, J., and Lens, W. (1999). The role of the future in student motivation. *Educational Psychologist, 34,* 113–125.

Inbar, O., Donitsa-Schmidt, S., and Shohamy, E. (2001). Students motivation as a function of language learning: The teaching of Arabic in Israel. In Z. Dörnyei and R. Schmidt (Eds.), *Motivation and second language acquisition* (pp. 292–308). Honolulu, HI: University of Hawaii Second Language Teaching and Curriculum Center.

Inbar, O., Shohamy, E., and Donitsa-Schmidt, S. (1999, March). The effect of teaching spoken Arabic on students attitudes and motivation. Paper presented at the American Association for Applied Linguistics Conference, Stamford, CT.

Irie, K. (2003). What do we know about the language learning motivation of university students in Japan? Some patterns in survey studies. *JALT Journal, 25,* 86–100.

Jacob, E., Rottenberg, L., Patrick, S., and Wheeler, E. (1996). Cooperative learning: Context and opportunities for acquiring academic English. *TESOL Quarterly, 30,* 253–280.

Jacques, S. R. (2001). Preferences for instructional activities and motivation: A comparison of student and teacher perspectives. In Z. Dörnyei and R. Schmidt (Eds.), *Motivation and second language acquisition* (pp. 187–214). Honolulu, HI: University of Hawaii Second Language Teaching and Curriculum Center.

Johnson, D. W., and Johnson, R. T. (1995). Cooperative learning and nonacademic outcomes of schooling. In J. E. Pedersen and A. D. Digby (Eds.), *Secondary schools and cooperative learning* (pp. 81–150). New York: Garland.

Johnson, D. W., Johnson, R. T., and Smith, K. A. (1995). Cooperative learning and individual student achievement in secondary schools. In J. E. Pedersen and A. D. Digby (Eds.), *Secondary schools and cooperative learning* (pp. 3–54). New York: Garland.

Johnson, D., W., and Johnson, R. T. (1991). Cooperative learning and classroom and school climate. In J. F. Barry and H. J. Walberg (Eds.), *Educational environments* (pp. 55–74). Oxford: Pergamon.

Jones, F., and Jones, L. (2000). *Comprehensive classroom management: Creating communities of support and solving problems* (6th ed.). Needham Heights, MA: Allyn and Bacon.

Julkunen, K. (1989). *Situation- and task-specific motivation in foreign language learning and teaching.* Joensuu: University of Joensuu.

Julkunen, K. (1991). Situation- and task-specific motivation in foreign language learning and teaching. *University of Joensuu Dissertation Abstracts, 52,* 716C.

Julkunen, K., and Borzova, H. (1996). *English language learning motivation in Joensuu and Petrozavodsk.* Joensuu, Finland: University of Joensuu.

Julkunen, K., (2001). Situation- and task-specific motivation in foreign language learning. In Z. Dörnyei and R. Schmidt (Eds.), *Motivation and second language acquisition* (pp. 29–42). Honolulu, HI: University of Hawaii Second Language Teaching and Curriculum Center.

Juvonen, J., and Nishina, A. (1997). Social motivation in the classroom: Attributional accounts and developmental analysis. *Advances in Motivation and Achievement, 10,* 181–211.

Kagan, S., and McGroarty, M. (1993). Principles of cooperative learning for language and content gains. In D. D. Holt (Ed.), *Cooperative learning* (pp. 47–66). Washington, DC: Center for Applied Linguistics and ERIC Clearinghouse on Languages and Linguistics.

Kanfer, R. (1996). Self-regulatory and other non-ability determinants of skill acquisition. In P. M. Gollwitzer and J. A. Bargh (Eds.), *The psychology of action: Linking cognition and motivation to behaviour* (pp. 404–423). New York: Guilford Press.

Karniol, R., and Ross, M. (1996). The motivational impact of temporal focus: Thinking about the future and the past. *Annual Review of Psychology, 47,* 593–620.

Kassabgy, O., Boraie, D., and Schmidt, R. (2001). Values, rewards, and job satisfaction in ESL/EFL. In Z. Dörnyei and R. Schmidt (Eds.), *Motivation and second language acquisition* (pp. 215–240). Honolulu, HI: University of Hawaii Second Language Teaching and Curriculum Center.

Keller, J. M. (1983). Motivational design of instruction. In C. M. Reigelruth (Ed.), *Instructional design theories and models: An overview of their current status* (pp. 383–434). Hillsdale, NJ: Lawrence Erlbaum.

Kellerman, H. (1981). The deep structures of group cohesion. In H. Kellerman (Ed.), *Group cohesion: Theoretical and clinical perspectives* (pp. 3–21). New York: Grune and Stratton.

Kessler, C. (Ed.) (1992). *Cooperative language learning: A teacher's resource book.* Englewood Cliffs, NJ: Prentice Hall Regents.

Klein, J. D., Erchul, J. A., and Pridemore, D. R. (1994). Effects of individual versus cooperative learning and type of reward on performance and continuing motivation. *Contemporary Educational Psychology, 19*, 24–32.

Kolb, D. A., Boyatzis, R. E., and Mainemelis, C. (2001). Experiential learning theory: Previous research and new directions. In R. J. Sternberg and L.-F. Zhang (Eds.), *Perspectives on thinking, learning, and cognitive styles.* (pp. 227–247). Mahwah, NJ: Lawrence Erlbaum.

Kormos, J., and Dörnyei, Z. (2004). The interaction of linguistic and motivational variables in second language task performance. *Zeitschrift für Interkulturellen Fremdsprachenunterricht [Online]* , *9*, pp. 19. (Available online at: http://zif.spz.tu-darmstadt.de/jg-09-2/beitrag/kormos2.htm).

Kosslyn, S. M., and Smith, E. E. (2000). Introduction to Part VIII: Higher cognitive functions. In M. S. Gazzaniga (Ed.), *The new cognitive neurosciences* (2nd ed., pp. 961–963). Cambridge, MA: MIT Press.

Kosslyn, S. M., Cacioppo, J. T., Davidson, R. J., Hugdahl, K., Lovallo, W. R., Spiegel, D., et al. (2002). Bridging psychology and biology: The analysis of individuals in groups. *American Psychologist, 57*, 341–351.

Kosslyn, S. M., Thompson, W. L., and Ganis, G. (2006). *The case for mental imagery.* New York: Oxford University Press.

Kuhl, J. (1985). Volitional mediators of cognition-behaviour consistency: Self-regulatory processes and action versus state orientation. In J. Kuhl and J. Beckmann (Eds.), *Action control: From cognition to behaviour* (pp. 101–128). New York: Springer.

Kuhl, J. (1986). Motivation and information processing: A new look at decision making, dynamic change, and action control. In R. M. Sorrentino and E. T. Higgins (Eds.), *Handbook of motivation and cognition: Foundations of social behaviour* (pp. 404–434). New York: Guilford Press.

Kuhl, J. (1987). Action control: The maintenance of motivational states. In F. Halish and J. Kuhl (Eds.), *Motivation, intention and volition* (pp. 279–291). Berlin: Springer.

Kuhl, J. (1992). A theory of self-regulation: Action versus state orientation, self-discrimination, and some applications. *Applied Psychology: An*

International Review, 41, 97–129.

Kuhl, J., and Beckmann, J. (Eds.). (1994). *Volition and personality: Action versus state orientation.* Seattle, WA: Hogrefe and Huber.

Kyriacou, C., and Benmansour, N. (1997). Motivation and learning preferences of high school students learning English as a foreign language in Morocco. *Mediterranean Journal of Educational Studies, 2,* 79–86.

Labrie, N., and Clément, R. (1986). Ethnolinguistic vitality, self-confidence and second language proficiency: An investigation. *Journal of Multilingual and Multicultural Development, 7,* 269–282.

La Guardia, J. G. (2009). Developing who I am: A self-determination theory approach to the establishment of healthy identities. *Educational Psychologist, 44,* 90–104.

Laine, E. J. (1981). *Foreign language learning motivation: Old and new variables.* Paper presented at the 5th Congress of l'Association internationale de linguistique appliquée. Ed. Jean-Guy Savard and Lorne Laforge. Québec: Les Presses de l'Université Laval, 1981: 302–312.

Laine, E. J. (1995) *Learning second national languages: A research report.* Frankfurt: Peter Lang.

Lamb, M. (2002). Explaining successful language learning in difficult circumstances. *Prospect, 17,* 35–52.

Lamb, M. (2004). Integrative motivation in a globalizing world. *System, 32,* 3–19.

Larsen-Freeman, D., and Cameron, L. (2008a). *Complex systems and applied linguistics.* Oxford: Oxford University Press.

Larsen-Freeman, D., & Cameron, L. (2008b). Research methodology on language development from a complex systems perspective. *Modern Language Journal, 92*(2), 200–213.

Leary, M. R. (2007). Motivational and emotional aspects of the self. *Annual Review of Psychology, 58,* 317–344.

Leaver, B. L., Ehrman, M. E., and Shekhtman, B. (2005). *Achieving success in second language acquisition.* Cambridge: Cambridge University Press.

Leuner, H., Horn, G., and Klessmann, E. (1983). *Guided affective imagery with children and adolescents*. New York: Plenum.

Levine, J. M., and Moreland, R. L. (1990). Progress in small group research. *Annual Review of Psychology, 41*, 585–634.

Lewin, K., Lippitt, R., and White, R. (1939). Patterns of aggressive behaviour in experimentally created 'social climate.' *Journal of Psychology, 10*, 271–299.

Lewis, M. D. (2005). Bridging emotion theory and neurobiology through dynamic systems modeling. *Behavioral and Brain Science, 28*, 169–245.

Lim, H. Y. (2002). The interaction of motivation, perception, and environment: One EFL learner's experience. *Hong Kong Journal of Applied Linguistics, 7*, 91–106.

Linnenbrink, E. A., and Pintrich, P. R. (2004). Role of affect in cognitive processing in academic contexts. In D. Y. Dai and R. J. Sternberg (Eds.), *Motivation, emotion, and cognition: Integrative perspectives on intellectual functioning and development* (pp. 57–87). Mahwah, NJ: Lawrence Erlbaum.

Locke, E. A. (2000). Motivation, cognition, and action: An analysis of studies of task goals and knowledge. *Applied Psychology: An International Review, 49*, 408–429.

Locke, E. A., and Latham, G. P. (1990). *A theory of goal setting and task performance*. Englewood Cliffs, NJ: Prentice Hall.

Long, M. H., and Porter, P. A. (1985). Group work, interlanguage talk, and second language acquisition. *TESOL Quarterly, 19*, 207–228.

Long, M., and Crookes, G. (1992). Three approaches to task-based syllabus design. *TESOL Quarterly, 26*, 27–55.

Lubinski, D., and Webb, R. M. (2003). Individual differences. In L. Nadel (Ed.), *Encyclopedia of cognitive science* (Vol. 2, pp. 503–510). London: Nature Publishing.

Macaro, E. (2001). *Learning strategies in foreign and second language classrooms*. London: Continuum.

MacFarlane, A., and Wesche, M. B. (1995). Immersion outcomes: Beyond language proficiency. *Canadian Modern Language Review*, *51*, 250–274.

MacIntyre, P. D. (1999). Language anxiety: A review of the research for language teachers. In D. J. Young (Ed.), *Affect in foreign language and second language learning* (pp. 24–45). Boston, MA: McGraw-Hill.

MacIntyre, P. D. (2002). Motivation, anxiety and emotion in second language acquisition. In P. Robinson (Ed.), *Individual differences in second language acquisition* (pp. 45–68). Amsterdam: John Benjamins.

MacIntyre, P. D., and Noels, K. A. (1996). Using social-psychological variables to predict the use of language learning strategies. *Foreign Language Annals*, *29*, 373–386.

MacIntyre, P. D., Babin, P. A., and Clément, R. (1999). Willingness to communicate: Antecedents and consequences. *Communication Quarterly*, *47*, 215–229.

MacIntyre, P. D., Baker, S. C., Clément, R., and Donovan, L. A. (2003). Talking in order to learn: Willingness to communicate and intensive language programs. *Canadian Modern Language Review*, *59*, 589–607.

MacIntyre, P. D., Burns, C., and Jessome, A. (2011). Ambivalence about communicating in a second language: A qualitative study of French immersion students' willingness to communicate. *Modern Language Journal*, *95*, 81–96.

MacIntyre, P. D., Clément, R., Dörnyei, Z., and Noels, K. A. (1998). Conceptualizing willingness to communicate in a L2: A situated model of confidence and affiliation. *Modern Language Journal*, *82*, 545–562.

MacIntyre, P. D., MacKinnon, S. P., and Clément, R. (2009a). The baby, the bathwater, and the future of language learning motivation research. In Z. Dörnyei and E. Ushioda (Eds.), *Motivation, language identity and the L2 self* (pp. 43–65). Bristol: Multilingual Matters.

MacIntyre, P. D., MacKinnon, S. P., and Clément, R. (2009b). Toward the development of a scale to assess possible selves as a source of language learning motivation. In Z. Dörnyei and E. Ushioda (Eds.), *Motivation, language identity and the L2 self* (pp. 193–214). Bristol: Multilingual

Matters.

MacIntyre, P. D., MacMaster, K., and Baker, S. C. (2001). The convergence of multiple models of motivation for second language learning: Gardner, Pintrich, Kuhl, and McCroskey. In Z. Dörnyei and R. Schmidt (Eds.), *Motivation and second language acquisition* (pp. 461–492). Honolulu, HI: University of Hawaii Press.

Maley, A., and Duff, A. (1982). *Drama techniques in language learning* (2nd ed.). Cambridge: Cambridge University Press.

Manolopoulou-Sergi, E. (2004). Motivation within the information processing model of foreign language learning. *System, 32*, 427–441.

Markus, H. R. (2006). Foreword. In C. Dunkel and J. Kerpelman (Eds.), *Possible selves: Theory, research and applications* (pp. xi–xiv). New York: Nova Science.

Markus, H. R., and Nurius, P. (1986). Possible selves. *American Psychologist, 41*, 954–969.

Markus, H. R., and Ruvolo, A. (1989). Possible selves: Personalized representations of goals. In L. A. Pervin (Ed.), *Goal concepts in personality and social psychology* (pp. 211–241). Hillsdale, NJ: Lawrence Erlbaum.

Masgoret, A-M., and Gardner R. C., (1999). A causal model of Spanish immigrant adaptation in Canada. *Journal of Multilingual and Multicultural Development, 20*, 216–36.

Masgoret, A-M., and Gardner, R. C. (2003). Attitudes, motivation, and second language learning: A meta-analysis of studies conducted by Gardner and associates. *Language Learning, 53*, 123–163.

Masgoret, A-M., Bernaus, M., and Gardner, R. C. (2000, July). *The influence of instructor variables in foreign language acquisition*. Paper presented at the 7th International Conference on Language and Social Psychology, Cardiff.

Matthews, G., Davies, D. R., Westerman, S. J., and Stammers, R. B. (2000). *Human performance: Cognition, stress and individual differences*. Hove, England: Psychology Press.

McClelland, N. (2000). Goal orientations in Japanese college students learning EFL. In S. D. Cornwell and P. Robinson (Eds.), *Individual differences in foreign language learning: Effects of aptitude, intelligence, and motivation* (pp. 99–115). Tokyo: Japanese Association for Language Teaching.

McCombs, B., and Whisler, J. (1997). *The learner-centred classroom and school: Strategies for increasing student motivation and achievement.* San Francisco, CA: Jossey-Bass.

McCrae, R. R., and Costa, P. T. (2003). *Personality in adulthood: A five-factor theory perspective* (2nd ed.). New York: Guilford Press.

McCroskey, J. C., and Richmond, V. P. (1987). Willingness to communicate. In J. C. McCroskey and J. A. Daly (Eds.), *Personality and interpersonal communication* (pp. 129–156). Newbury Park, CA: Sage.

McCroskey, J. C., and Richmond, V. P. (1991). Willingness to communicate: A cognitive view. In M. Booth-Butterfield (Ed.), *Communication, cognition and anxiety* (pp. 19–37). Newbury Park, CA: Sage.

McDonell, W. (1992). The role of the teacher in the cooperative learning classroom. In C. Kessler (Ed.), *Cooperative language learning: A teacher's resource book* (pp. 163–174). Englewood Cliffs, NJ: Prentice Hall Regents.

McDonough, S. (1999). Learner strategies. *Language Teaching Research, 32,* 1–18.

McGroarty, M. (1993). Cooperative learning and second language acquisition. In D. D. Holt (Ed.), *Cooperative learning* (pp. 19–46). Washington, DC: Center for Applied Linguistics and ERIC Clearinghouse on Languages and Linguistics.

McGroarty, M. (1998). Constructive and constructivist challenges for applied linguistics. *Language Learning, 48,* 591–622.

McGroarty, M. (2001). Situating second language motivation. In Z. Dörnyei and R. Schmidt (Eds.), *Motivation and second language acquisition* (pp. 69–90). Honolulu: University of Hawaii Second Language Teaching and Curriculum Center.

McMahon, C. E. (1973). Images as motives and motivators: A historical perspective. *American Journal of Psychology, 86,* 465–490.

Miller, R. B., and Brickman, S. J. (2004). A model of future-oriented motivation and self-regulation. *Educational Psychology Review, 16,* 9–33.

Milleret, M. (1992). Cooperative learning in the Portuguese for Spanish speakers classroom. *Foreign Language Annals, 25,* 435–440.

Miyake, A., and Friedman, D. (1998). Individual differences in second language proficiency: Working memory as language aptitude. In A. F. Healy and L. E. Bourne (Eds.), *Foreign Language Learning: Psycholinguistic studies on training and retention* (pp. 339–364). Mahwah, N.J.: Lawrence Erlbaum.

Modell, A. H. (2003). *Imagination and the meaningful brain.* Cambridge, MA: MIT Press.

Morgan, C. (1993). Attitude change and foreign language culture learning. *Language Teaching, 26,* 63–75.

Mullen, B., and Copper, C. (1994). The relationship between group cohesiveness and performance: An integration. *Psychological Bulletin, 115,* 210–227.

Nichols, J. D., and Miller, R. B. (1994). Cooperative learning and student motivation. *Contemporary Educational Psychology, 19,* 167–178.

Nikolov, M. (1999). Why do you learn English? Because the teacher is short. A study of Hungarian children's foreign language learning motivation. *Language Teaching Research, 3,* 33–56.

Nikolov, M. (2001). A study of unsuccessful language learners. In Z. Dörnyei and R. Schmidt (Eds.), *Motivation and second language acquisition* (pp. 147–172). Honolulu, HI: University of Hawaii Second Language Teaching and Curriculum Center.

Noels, K. A. (2001). New orientations in language learning motivation: Toward a contextual model of intrinsic, extrinsic, and integrative orientations and motivation. In Z. Dörnyei and R. Schmidt (Eds.),

Motivation and second language acquisition (pp. 43–68). Honolulu, HI: University of Hawaii Second Language Teaching and Curriculum Center.

Noels, K. A. (2003). Learning Spanish as a second language: Learners' orientations and perceptions of their teachers' communication style. In Z. Dörnyei (Ed.), *Attitudes, orientations, and motivations in language learning* (pp. 97–136). Oxford: Blackwell.

Noels, K. A. (2009). The internalisation of language learning into the self and social identity. In Z. Dörnyei and E. Ushioda (Eds.), *Motivation, language identity and the L2 self.* Bristol: Multilingual Matters.

Noels, K. A., and Clément, R. (1996). Communication across cultures: Social determinants and acculturative consequences. *Canadian Journal of Behavioural Science, 28,* 214–228.

Noels, K. A., Clément, R., and Pelletier, L. G. (1999). Perceptions of teachers' communicative style and students' intrinsic and extrinsic motivation. *Modern Language Journal, 83,* 23–34.

Noels, K. A., Clément, R., and Pelletier, L. G. (2001). Intrinsic, extrinsic, and integrative orientations of French Canadian learners of English. *Canadian Modern Language Review, 57,* 424–444.

Noels, K. A., Pelletier, L G., Clément, R., and Vallerand, R. J. (2000). Why are you learning a second language? Motivational orientations and self-determination theory. *Language Learning, 50,* 57–85.

Norton, B. (2000). *Identity and language learning: Social processes and educational practice.* Harlow: Pearson.

Norton, B. (2001). Non-participation, imagined communities and the language classroom. In M. P. Breen (Ed.), *Learner contributions to language learning: New directions in research* (pp. 159–171). Harlow, England: Longman.

Nowak, A., Vallacher, R. R., and Zochowski, M. (2005). The emergence of personality: Dynamic foundations of individual variation. *Developmental Review, 25,* 351–385.

Oller Jr, J. W. (1981). Can affect be measured? *IRAL, 19,* 227–235.

Olsen, R. E. W-B., and Kagan, S. (1992). About cooperative learning. In C. Kessler (Ed.), *Cooperative language learning: A teacher's resource book* (pp. 1–30). Englewood Cliffs, NJ: Prentice Hall Regents.

Oxford, R. L. (1990). *Language learning strategies: What every teacher should know*. New York: Newbury House.

Oxford, R. L. (1994). Where are we with language learning motivation? *Modern Language Journal, 78*, 512–514.

Oxford, R. L. (Ed.). (1996). *Language learning strategies around the world: Cross-cultural perspectives*. Honolulu, HI: University of Hawaii Press.

Oxford, R. L. (1998, March). *The unravelling tapestry: Teacher and course characteristics associated with demotivation in the language classroom.* Paper presented at TESOL-98 Conference, Seattle, WA.

Oxford, R. L. (1999). Learning strategies. In B. Spolsky (Ed.), *Concise encyclopedia of educational linguistics* (pp. 518–522). Oxford: Elsevier.

Oxford, R. L., and Shearin, J. (1994). Language learning motivation: Expanding the theoretical framework. *Modern Language Journal, 78*, 12–28.

Oyserman, D., and Markus, H. R. (1990). Possible selves and delinquency. *Journal of Personality and Social Psychology, 59*, 112–125.

Oyserman, D., Bybee, D., and Terry, K. (2006). Possible selves and academic outcomes: How and when possible selves impel action. *Journal of Personality and Social Psychology, 91*, 188–204.

Oyserman, D., Terry, K., and Bybee, D. (2002). A possible selves intervention to enhance school involvement. *Journal of Adolescence, 25*, 313–326.

O'Malley, J. M. and Chamot, A. U. (1990). *Learning strategies in second language acquisition*. New York: Cambridge.

Paivio, A. (1985). Cognitive and motivational functions of imagery in human performance. *Canadian Journal of Applied Sport Sciences, 10*, 228–288.

Paris, S. G., and Turner, J. C. (1994). Situated motivation. In P. R. Pintrich, D. R. Brown and C. E. Weinstein (Eds.), *Student motivation, cognition, and learning* (pp. 213–237). Hillsdale, NJ: Lawrence Erlbaum.

Parrott, W. G. (2004). The nature of emotion. In M. B. Brewer and M. Hewstone (Eds.), *Emotion and motivation* (pp. 5–20). Oxford: Blackwell.

Parry, T. S., and Stansfield, C. (Eds.). (1990). *Language aptitude reconsidered.* Englewood Cliffs, NJ: Prentice-Hall Regents.

Pavlenko, A. (2002). Poststructuralist approaches to the study of social factors in second language learning and use. In V. Cook (Ed.), *Portraits of the L2 user* (pp. 277–302). Clevedon: Multilingual Matters.

Pennington, M. C. (1995). *Work satisfaction, motivation and commitment in teaching English as a second language.* (ERIC Document Reproduction Service No. ED 404850).

Pimsleur, P. (1966). *The Pimsleur Language Aptitude Battery.* New York: Harcourt, Brace, Jovanovic.

Pintrich, P. R., and Schunk, D. H. (1996). *Motivation in education: Theory, research and applications.* Englewood Cliffs, NJ: Prentice Hall.

Pintrich, P. R., Smith, D. A. F., and McKeachie, W. J. (1989). *Motivated Strategies for Learning Questionnaire (MSLQ).* Ann Arbor: National Center for Research to Improve Postsecondary Teaching and Learning, University of Michigan.

Pittaway, D. S. (2004). Investment and second language acquisition. *Critical Inquiry in Language Studies: An International Journal, 1,* 203–218.

Pizzolato, J. E. (2006). Achieving college student possible selves: Navigating the space between commitment and achievement of long-term identity goals. *Cultural Diversity and Ethnic Minority Psychology, 12,* 57–69.

Plough, I., and Gass, S. M. (1993). Interlocutor and task familiarity: Effects on interactional structures. In G. Crookes and S. M. Gass (Eds.), *Tasks and language learning.* Clevedon: Multilingual Matters.

Ramage, K. (1990). Motivational factors and persistence in foreign language study. *Language Learning, 40,* 189–219.

Ranta, L. (2008). Aptitude and good language learners. In C. Griffiths

(Ed.), *Lessons from good language learners* (pp. 142–155). Cambridge: Cambridge University Press.

Raynor, J. O., and Roeder, G. P. (1987). Motivation and future orientation: Task and time effects for achievement motivation. In F. Halish and J. Kuhl (Eds.), *Motivation, intention and volition* (pp. 61–71). Berlin: Springer.

Reid, J. M. (Ed.). (1995a). *Learning styles in the ESL/EFL classroom*. Boston, MA: Heinle and Heinle.

Reid, J. M. (1995b). Preface. In J. M. Reid (Ed.), *Learning styles in the ESL/ EFL classroom* (pp. viii–xvii). Boston, MA: Heinle and Heinle.

Reid, J. M. (Ed.). (1998). *Understanding learning styles in the second language classroom*. Upper Saddle River, NJ: Prentice-Hall Regents.

Renninger, K. A., Bachrach, J. E., and Posey, S. K. E. (2008). Learner interest and achievement motivation. In M. L. Maehr, S. A. Karabenick and T. C. Urdan (Eds.), *Advances in motivation and achievement 15: Social psychological perspectives* (pp. 461–491). Bingley: Emerald.

Richardson, A. (1994). *Individual differences in imaging: Their measurement, origins, and consequences*. Amityville, NY: Baywood.

Riding, R. (2000). Cognitive style: A review. In R. J. Riding and S. G. Rayner (Eds.), *Interpersonal perspectives on individual differences* (Vol. 1: Cognitive styles, pp. 315–344). Stamford, CI: Ablex.

Riding, R., and Rayner, S. G. (1998). *Cognitive styles and learning strategies: Understanding style differences in learning and behaviour*. London: David Fulton.

Robinson, G. L. (1988). *Crosscultural understanding*. Hemel Hempstead: Prentice Hall.

Robinson, P. (1995). Task complexity and second language narrative discourse. *Language Learning, 45*, 99–140.

Robinson, P. (2001a). Individual differences, cognitive abilities, aptitude complexes and learning conditions in second language acquisition. *Second Language Research, 17*, 368–392.

Robinson, P. (2001b). Task complexity, task difficulty, and task production:

Exploring interactions in a componential framework. *Applied Linguistics*, *22*, 27–57.

Robinson, P. (2002a). Effects of individual differences in intelligence, aptitude and working memory on adult incidental SLA: A replication and extension of Reber, Walkenfield and Hernstadt (1991). In P. Robinson (Ed.), *Individual differences and instructed language learning* (pp. 211–266). Amsterdam: John Benjamins.

Robinson, P. (2002b). Learning conditions, aptitude complexes and SLA: A framework for research and pedagogy. In P. Robinson (Ed.), *Individual differences and instructed language learning* (pp. 113–133). Amsterdam: John Benjamins.

Robinson, P. (2003). Attention and memory during SLA. In C. J. Doughty and M. H. Long (Eds.), *The handbook of second language acquisition* (pp. 631–678). Oxford: Blackwell.

Robinson, P. (2007). Aptitudes, abilities, contexts, and practice. In R. M. DeKeyser (Ed.), *Practice in second language learning: Perspectives from linguistics and cognitive psychology* (pp. 256–286). Cambridge: Cambridge University Press.

Robinson, P. (in press). *Aptitude in second language learning*. Oxford: Oxford University Press.

Roffe, L., Schmidt, K., and Ernst, E. (2005). A systematic review of guided imagery as an adjuvant cancer therapy. *Psycho-Oncology*, *14*, 607–617.

Rogers, C. (1983). *Freedom to learn for the 80's*. Columbus, OH: Merrill.

Rubin, J. (2001). Language learner self-management. *Journal of Asian Pacific Communication*, *11*, 25–37.

Rubin, J. (2005). The expert language learner: A review of good language learner studies and learner strategies. In K. Johnson (Ed.), *Expertise in Second Language Learning and Teaching* (pp. 37–63). Basingstoke: Palgrave Macmillan.

Ruvolo, A. P., and Markus, H. R. (1992). Possible selves and performance: The power of self-relevant imagery. *Social Cognition*, *10*, 95–124.

Ryan, S. (2006). Language learning motivation within the context of globalization: An L2 self within an imagined global community. *Critical Inquiry in Language Studies: An International Journal, 4,* 23–45.

Ryan, S. (2009). Self and identity in L2 motivation in Japan: The ideal L2 self and Japanese learners of English. In Z. Dörnyei and E. Ushioda (Eds.), *Motivation, language identity and the L2 self* (pp. 120–143). Clevedon: Multilingual Matters.

Sawyer, M., and Ranta, L. (2001). Aptitude, individual differences, and instructional design. In P. Robinson (Ed.), *Cognition and second language acquisition* (pp. 319–353). New York: Cambridge University Press.

Scherer, K. R., (1995). Plato's legacy: Relationships between cognition, emotion, and motivation. *Geneva Studies in Emotion and Communication, 9,* 1–7 (Available online at: http://citeseerx.ist.psu/viewdoc/download? doi=10.1.1.118.6522andrep=rep1andtype=pdf).

Schmidt, R., and Watanabe, Y. (2001). Motivation, strategy use, and pedagogical preferences in foreign language learning. In Z. Dörnyei and R. Schmidt (Eds.), *Motivation and second language acquisition* (pp. 309–356). Honolulu, HI: University of Hawaii Second Language Teaching and Curriculum Center.

Schmidt, R., Boraie, D., and Kassabgy, O. (1996). Foreign language motivation: Internal structure and external connections. In R. Oxford (Ed.), *Language learning motivation: Pathways to the new century* (pp. 9–70). Honolulu, HI: University of Hawaii Press.

Schmuck, R., and Schmuck, P. (2001). *Group processes in the classroom* (8th ed.). Boston, MA: McGraw Hill.

Schumann, J. H. (1978). The acculturation model for second language acquisition. In R. Gingras (Ed.), *Second language acquisition and foreign language teaching* (pp. 27–107). Arlington, VA: Center for Applied Linguistics.

Schumann, J. H. (1998). *The neurobiology of affect in language.* Oxford: Blackwell.

Schumann, J. H. (1999). A neurobiological perspective on affect and methodology in second language learning. In J. Arnold (Ed.), *Affect in language learning* (pp. 28–42). Cambridge: Cambridge University Press.

Schumann, J. H. (2001a). Appraisal psychology, neurobiology, and language. *Annual Review of Applied Linguistics, 21*, 23–42.

Schumann, J. H. (2001b). Learning as foraging. In Z. Dörnyei and R. Schmidt (Eds.), *Motivation and second language acquisition* (pp. 21–28). Honolulu, HI: University of Hawaii Second Language Teaching and Curriculum Center.

Schumann, J. H. (2004). Introduction. In J. H. Schumann, S. E. Crowell, N. E. Jones, N. Lee, S. A. Schuchert and L. A. Wood (Eds.), *The neurobiology of learning: Perspectives from second language acquisition* (pp. 1–6). Mahwah, NJ: Lawrence Erlbaum.

Schunk, D. H. (1991). Self-efficacy and academic motivation. *Educational Psychologist, 26*, 207–231.

Schwarz, N., and Bohner, G. (1996). Feelings and their motivational implications: Moods and the action sequence. In P. M. Gollwitzer and J. A. Bargh (Eds.), *The psychology of action: Linking cognition and motivation to behaviour* (pp. 119–145). New York: Guilford Press.

Segal, H. G. (2006). Possible selves, fantasy distortion, and the anticipated life history: Exploring the role of imagination in social cognition. In C. Dunkel and J. Kerpelman (Eds.), *Possible selves: Theory, research and applications* (pp. 79–96). New York.

Senior, R. (1997). Transforming language classes into bonded groups. *ELT Journal, 51*, 3–11.

Senior, R. (2002). A class-centred approach to language teaching. *ELT Journal, 56*, 397–403.

Sharan, S. (1995). Group investigation: Theoretical foundations. In J. E. Pedersen and A. D. Digby (Eds.), *Secondary schools and cooperative learning* (pp. 251–277). New York: Garland.

Sharan, S., and Shaulov, A. (1990). Cooperative learning, motivation to learn, and academic achievement. In S. Sharan (Ed.), *Cooperative learning: Theory and research* (pp. 173–202). New York: Praeger.

Shaw, M. E. (1981). *Group dynamics: The psychology of small group behaviour* (3rd ed.). New York: McGraw-Hill.

Shedivy, S. L. (2004). Factors that lead some students to continue the study of foreign language past the usual 2 years in high school. *System, 32*, 103–119.

Sheldon, K. M., and Lyubomirsky, S. (2006). How to increase and sustain positive emotion: The effects of expressing gratitude and visualizing best possible selves. *Journal of Positive Psychology, 1*, 73–82

Shoaib, A., and Dörnyei, Z. (2005). Affect in life-long learning: Exploring L2 motivation as a dynamic process. In P. Benson and D. Nunan (Eds.), *Learners' stories: Difference and diversity in language learning* (pp. 22–41). Cambridge: Cambridge University Press.

Singer, J. L. (2006). *Imagery in psychotherapy*. Washington, DC: American Psychological Association.

Skehan, P. (1989). *Individual differences in second language learning*. London: Edward Arnold.

Skehan, P. (1991). Individual differences in second language learning. *Studies in Second Language Acquisition, 13*, 275–298.

Skehan, P. (1998a). *A cognitive approach to language learning*. Oxford: Oxford University Press.

Skehan, P. (1998b). Task-based instruction. *Annual Review of Applied Linguistics, 18*, 268–289.

Skehan, P. (2002). Theorising and updating aptitude. In P. Robinson (Ed.), *Individual differences and instructed language learning* (pp. 69–93). Amsterdam: John Benjamins.

Skehan, P., and Foster, P. (1999). The influence of task structure and processing conditions on narrative retellings. *Language Learning, 49*, 93–120.

Slavin, R. E. (1996). Research on cooperative learning and achievement: What we know, what we need to know. *Contemporary Educational Psychology, 21*, 43-69.

Snow, R. E., and Jackson, D. N. (1994). Individual differences in conation: Selected constructs and measures. In H. F. O'Neil, Jr. and M. Drillings (Eds.), *Motivation: Theory and research* (pp. 71–99). Hillsdale, NJ: Lawrence Erlbaum.

Snow, R. E., Corno, L., and Jackson, D. (1996). Individual differences in affective and conative functions. In D. C. Berliner and R. C. Calfee (Eds.), *Handbook of educational psychology* (pp. 243–310). New York: Macmillan.

Sorrentino, R. M. (1996). The role of conscious thought in a theory of motivation and cognition: The uncertainty orientation paradigm. In P. M. Gollwitzer and J. A. Bargh (Eds.), *The psychology of action: Linking cognition and motivation to behaviour* (pp. 619–644). New York: Guilford Press.

Sparks, R. L., and Ganschow, L. (1991). Foreign language learning differences: Affective or native language aptitude differences? *Modern Language Journal, 75*, 3–16.

Sparks, R. L., and Ganschow, L. (2001). Aptitude for learning a foreign language. *Annual Review of Applied Linguistics, 21*, 90–111.

Sparks, R. L., Javorsky, J., Patton, J., and Ganschow, L. (1998). Factors in the prediction of achievement and proficiency in a foreign language. *Applied Language Learning, 9*, 71–105.

Spolsky, B. (1995). Prognostication and language aptitude testing, 1925–1962. *Language Testing, 12*, 321–340.

Sternberg, R. J. (2002). The theory of successful intelligence and its implications for language-aptitude testing. In P. Robinson (Ed.), *Individual differences and instructed language learning* (pp. 13–43). Amsterdam: John Benjamins.

Stipek, D. J. (1996). Motivation and instruction. In D. C. Berliner and R. C. Calfee (Eds.), *Handbook of educational psychology* (pp. 85–113). New York: Macmillan.

Swain, M., and Lapkin, S. (2000). Task-based second language learning: The uses of the first language. *Language Teaching Research, 4*, 251–274.

Swezey, R. W., Meltzer, A. L., and Salas, E. (1994). Some issues involved in motivating teams. In H. F. O'Neil and M. Drillings (Eds.), *Motivation: Theory and research* (pp. 141–169). Hillsdale, NJ: Lawrence Erlbaum.

Syed, Z. (2001). Notions of self in foreign language learning: A qualitative analysis. In Z. Dörnyei and R. Schmidt (Eds.), *Motivation and second language acquisition* (pp. 125–146). Honolulu, HI: University of Hawaii Second Language Teaching and Curriculum Center.

Szostek, C. (1994). Assessing the effects of cooperative learning in an honors foreign language classroom. *Foreign Language Annals, 27*, 252–261.

Taguchi, T., Magid, M., and Papi, M. (2009). The L2 motivational self system amongst Chinese and Japanese learners of English: A comparative study. In Z. Dörnyei and E. Ushioda (Eds.), *Motivation, language identity and the L2 self* (pp. 66–97). Bristol: Multilingual Matters.

Tarone, E. and Bigelow, M. (2005). Impact of literacy on oral language processing: Implications for SLA research. *Annual Review of Applied Linguistics, 25*, 77–97.

Taylor, S. E., Pham, L. B., Rivkin, I. D., and Armor, D. A. (1998). Harnessing the imagination: Mental simulation, self-regulation, and coping. *American Psychologist, 53*, 429–439.

Tremblay, P. F. (2001). Research in second language learning motivation: Psychometric and research design considerations. In Z. Dörnyei and R. Schmidt (Eds.), *Motivation and second language acquisition* (pp. 241–258). Honolulu, HI: University of Hawaii Second Language Teaching and Curriculum Center.

Tremblay, P. F., and Gardner, R. C. (1995). Expanding the motivation construct in language learning. *Modern Language Journal, 79*, 505–520.

Tremblay, P. F., Goldberg, M. P., and Gardner, R. C. (1995). Trait and state motivation and the acquisition of Hebrew vocabulary. *Canadian Journal of Behavioural Science, 27*, 356–370.

Tseng, W-T., Dörnyei, Z., and Schmitt, N. (2006). A new approach to assessing strategic learning: The case of self-regulation in vocabulary acquisition. *Applied Linguistics, 27*, 78–102.

Turner, J. C. (1984). Social identification and psychological group formation. In H. Tajfel (Ed.), *The social dimension: European studies in social psychology* (pp. 518–538). Cambridge: Cambridge University Press and Paris: Editions de la Maison des Sciences de l'Homme.

Ushioda, E. (1996a). Developing a dynamic concept of motivation. In T. Hickey and J. Williams (Eds.), *Language, education and society in a changing world* (pp. 239–245). Clevedon: Multilingual Matters.

Ushioda, E. (1996b). *Learner autonomy 5: The role of motivation.* Dublin: Authentik.

Ushioda, E. (1997). The role of motivational thinking in autonomous language learning. In D. Little and B. Voss (Eds.), *Language centres: Planning for the new millennium* (pp. 39–50). Plymouth, England: University of Plymouth, Centre for Modern Languages.

Ushioda, E. (1998). Effective motivational thinking: A cognitive theoretical approach to the study of language learning motivation. In E. A. Soler and V. C. Espurz (Eds.), *Current issues in English language methodology* (pp. 77–89). Castelló de la Plana, Spain: Universitat Jaume I.

Ushioda, E. (2001). Language learning at university: Exploring the role of motivational thinking. In Z. Dörnyei and R. Schmidt (Eds.), *Motivation and second language acquisition* (pp. 91–124). Honolulu, HI: University of Hawaii Press.

Ushioda, E. (2003). Motivation as a socially mediated process. In D. Little, J. Ridley and E. Ushioda (Eds.), *Learner autonomy in the foreign language classroom: Teacher, learner, curriculum, assessment* (pp. 90–102). Dublin: Authentik.

Ushioda, E. (2006). Language motivation in a reconfigured Europe: Access, identity, autonomy. *Journal of Multilingual and Multicultural Development, 27*, 148–161.

Ushioda, E. (2007). Motivation, autonomy and sociocultural theory. In P. Benson (Ed.), *Learner autonomy 8: Teacher and learner perspectives* (pp. 5–

24). Dublin: Authentik.

Ushioda, E., and Dörnyei, Z. (2009). Motivation, language identities and the L2 self: A theoretical overview. In Z. Dörnyei and E. Ushioda (Eds.), *Motivation, language identity and the L2 self* (pp. 1–8). Bristol: Multilingual Matters.

Valdes, J. M. (Ed.) (1986). *Culture bound*. Cambridge: Cambridge University Press.

Vallerand, R. J. (1997). Toward a hierarchical model of intrinsic and extrinsic motivation. *Advances in Experimental Social Psychology, 29*, 271–360.

van Geert, P. (2008). The Dynamic Systems approach in the study of L1 and L2 acquisition: An introduction. *Modern Language Journal, 92*, 179–199.

van Oostrum, J., and Rabbie, J. M. (1995). Intergroup competition and cooperation within autocratic and democratic management regimes. *Small Group Research, 26*, 269–295.

VanderStoep, S. W., and Pintrich, P. R. (2003). *Learning to learn: The skill and will of college success*. Upper Saddle River, NJ: Prentice Hall.

Verhoeven, L., and Vermeer, A. (2002). Communicative competence and personality dimensions in first and second language learners. *Applied Psycholinguistics, 23*, 361–374.

Warden, C., and Lin, H. J. (2000). Existence of integrative motivation in Asian EFL setting. *Foreign Language Annals, 33*, 535–547.

Weiner, B. (1979). A theory of motivation for some classroom experiences. *Journal of Educational Psychology, 71*, 3–25.

Weiner, B. (1984). Principles for a theory of student motivation and their application within an attributional framework. In R. Ames and C. Ames (Eds.), *Research on motivation in education: Student motivation* (Vol. 1, pp. 15–38). San Diego, CA: Academic Press.

Weiner, B. (1990). History of motivational research in education. *Journal of Educational Psychology, 82*, 616–622.

Weiner, B. (1992). *Human motivation: Metaphors, theories and research.*

Newbury Park, CA: Sage.

Weiner. B. (1994). Integrating social and personal theories of achievement motivation. *Review of Educational Research, 64*, 557–573.

Weinstein, C. E., Husman, J., and Dierking, D. R. (2000). Self-regulation interventions with a focus on learning strategies. In M. Boekaerts, P. R. Pintrich and M. Zeidner (Eds.), *Handbook of self-regulation* (pp. 727–747). San Diego: Academic Press.

Wenger, E. (1998). *Communities of practice: Learning, meaning, and identity.* Cambridge: Cambridge University Press.

Wentzel, K. R. (1999). Social-motivational processes and interpersonal relationships: Implications for understanding motivation at school. *Journal of Educational Psychology, 91*, 76–97.

Wigfield, A., Eccles, J. S., and Rodriguez, D. (1998). The development of children's motivation in school contexts. *Review of Research in Education, 23*, 73–118.

Williams, M., and Burden, R. L. (1997). *Psychology for language teachers: A social constructivist approach.* Cambridge: Cambridge University Press.

Williams, M., and Burden, R. L. (1999). Students' developing conceptions of themselves as language learners. *Modern Language Journal, 83*, 193–201.

Williams, M., Burden, R. L., and Al-Baharna, S. (2001). Making sense of success and failure: The role of the individual in motivation theory. In Z. Dörnyei and R. Schmidt (Eds.), *Motivation and second language acquisition* (pp. 173–186). Honolulu, HI: University of Hawaii Second Language Teaching and Curriculum Center.

Williams, M., Burden, R. L., and Lanvers, U. (2002). 'French is the language of love and stuff': Student perceptions of issues related to motivation in learning a foreign language. *British Educational Research Journal, 28*, 503–528.

Willis, J. (1996). *A framework for task-based learning.* Harlow: Longman.

Winne, P. H. (2001). Self-regulated learning viewed from models of information processing. In B. J. Zimmerman and D. H. Schunk (Eds.), *Self-regulated learning and academic achievement: Theoretical perspectives* (2nd ed., pp. 153–189). Mahwah, NJ: Lawrence Erlbaum.

Winne, P. H., and Marx, R. W. (1989). A cognitive-processing analysis of motivation within classroom tasks. In C. Ames and R. Ames (Eds.), *Research on motivation in education. Vol. 3: Goals and cognitions* (pp. 223–257). New York: Academic Press.

Wlodkowski, R. (1986). *Enhancing adult motivation to learn.* San Francisco, CA: Jossey-Bass.

Wolters, C. A. (1998). Self-regulated learning and college students' regulation of motivation. *Journal of Educational Psychology, 90,* 224–235.

Yamashiro, A. D., and McLaughlin, J. (2000). Relationships among attitudes, motivation, anxiety, and English language proficiency in Japanese college students. In S. Cornwell and P. Robinson (Eds.), *Individual differences in foreign language learning: Effects of aptitude, intelligence, and motivation* (pp. 9–26). Tokyo: Aoyama Gakuin University.

Yashima, T. (2000). Orientations and motivations in foreign language learning: A study of Japanese college students. *JACET Bulletin, 31,* 121–133.

Young, D. J. (1991). Creating a low-anxiety classroom environment: What does language anxiety research suggest? *Modern Language Journal, 75,* 426–439.

Yowell, C. M. (2002). Dreams of the future: The pursuit of education and career possible selves among ninth grade Latino youth. *Applied Developmental Science, 6,* 62–72.

Yule, G., and Powers, M. (1994). Investigating the communicative outcomes of task-based interaction. *System, 22,* 81–91.

Zeidner, M., Boekaerts, M., and Pintrich, P. R. (2000). Self-regulation: Directions and challenges for future research. In M. Boekaerts, P. R. Pintrich and M. Zeidner (Eds.), *Handbook of self-regulation* (pp. 749–768). San Diego: Academic Press.

Zentner, M., and Renaud, O. (2007). Origins of adolescents' ideal self: An intergenerational perspective. *Journal of Personality and Social Psychology, 92,* 557–574.